In the Footsteps of Elisha

Discovering the Prophetic Gift
in all its Fullness

By Robert I Holmes

Unless otherwise identified, all Scriptures quoted are New American Standard Bible. Copyright 1960, 1962, 1963, 1968, 1971, 1972, 1973, 1975, 1977 by the Lockerman Foundation. Used by permission. All other references are identified by their shortened version: NIV, NRSV, KJV, ASB, MSG, NKJV.

Where the original language is quoted, it will be placed in parentheses and placed in italics. Assume that Old Testament (OT) references are Hebrew and New Testament (NT) references are Greek unless otherwise specified.

References to the universal Church shall be capitalized, references to any specific local church will be lower case. We choose to include para church and meta church outreaches as part of "church". In each case we choose not to capitalise the name demon, devil or satan, as is the author's prerogative. We choose to capitalise Word of God for Jesus, but leave it lower case for the Bible.

Storm Harvest Inc.
P.O. Box 600
Cootamundra NSW 2590
Australia
Visit us at www.storm-harvest.asn.au

ISBN – 1 86263 061 5

Copyright 2006 – Robert I Holmes

Printed in Thailand by Logos Communications Int.

Cover artwork design by Lawton Ho, Animal Arc. Melbourne.

DEDICATION

To the prophets of God, throughout history, admired by some, ignored by others; approved by God, scorned by the rebellious.

To those who have died in the search for truth, longing for a city made without human hands; who have dedicated their lives to serving Jesus Christ, speaking the oracles of God to humanity.

To the prophets of the Old Testament, our thanks. Your example to us of uncompromising faithfulness inspires us to carry on. You pursued speaking truth to the death. Though you spoke at various times and in various ways, you brought us to see our Saviour.

To the prophets of the New Testament, our thanks. Your example to us of servanthood, humility and teamwork with the apostles is truly inspiring. You were filled with the Holy Spirit, and you changed the face of history. Your words remain with us to this day.

To the prophets of ancient times, our thanks. You confronted dark powers with the word of light and woke the sleeping Church in times of her deepest slumber. The path you cut for us through the jungle remains to this day, for those who would search it out.

To the prophets of the modern era, our thanks. You stood unmoved in times of shifting sand; you could be relied upon, unmoving in times of fluid morality; you modelled character in times when character became a by-word. George Warnock, T Austin Sparkes, Leonard Ravenhill, C. S Lewis, John L Sandford, Paul Cain and others, we salute you.

Lastly, to the prophets of my own nation, destined to harbour the last great revival in earth's history, my thanks. You fathered and pioneered, when the prophetic was unpopular, and few are left standing after it fell into disrepute. Shine a light, brightly. Come out from your holes and houses, and join the last great move of God. We need you!

In The Footsteps Of Elisha

THANK YOU

My sincere thanks go to John and Paula Sandford, David Ravenhill, Winkey Pratney, David White, Michael Sullivant, James Ryle and Alison Papenfus for untold hours of reading and correcting the first draft.

Also to Terry Appel, Kerry Denten, Peter Christensen, John & Hazel Alley, Martyn Webb, David Orton and John McElroy for reading over the second draft.

To the faithful staff and volunteers at Storm Harvest, who assisted with proofing, editing, re-reading and final text editing. To Bronywn Kubank, Gail Douglas, Jennifer Elmes, Phil & Jeanette Beale, Renee New, Sharon Douglas and Mario & Linda Liu, thank you.

To my faithful wife Kellie and my six beautiful children: Kia, Ariah, Mitchell, Jarrad, Elijah and Iliana. For allowing me the hundreds of hours required to complete this task.

Thank you.

ENDORSEMENTS

"In his book The Footsteps of Elisha Robert has written a comprehensive purview of the prophetic history and office. His exposition of Biblical words and phrases is extremely valuable. This is the most scholarly and comprehensive book that I have read on the subject of the prophetic. It is actually a good resource manual. One thinks of a physician referring to his manual to check to see if his remembrance of symptoms and cures is accurate. Just so, readers ought not merely read this book, and leave it dusty on the shelf. They ought to keep it at their fingertips, and refer to it when issues come up. May God bless your reading, and therefore your service in Him."

John Loren Sandford.
Co-founder, Elijah House Inc. Spokane, Wa.

"Robert Holmes is no stranger to prophetic ministry. His Biblical yet insightful look into this vital area of teaching will provide a much needed balance for those desiring to know more concerning the prophetic office/gift. This indepth study is an encyclopedia of information providing the reader with answers to virtually every question on the subject of the prophetic. I highly recommend it to you."

David Ravenhill.
Author & Itinerant Teacher. Lindale, Texas.

"By examining the life and ministry of one of the greatest prophets in the Old Testament, this book reveals a deeper understanding of God's heart and intent for the prophetic ministry under the New Covenant. Robert's work is Scripturally sound and contains an in-depth exploration into a wide range of subjects that relate to the prophetic ministry. In lovingly confronting many of the issues of the modern-day prophetic movement, this book challenges both the Church in general, and all of those called to walk with this prophetic mantle in our day. They must do so with a higher level of integrity, sacrifice and devotion to Biblical truth. This book is practically written, can be used as a teaching tool and is based on the Bible and the author's experiences. I highly recommend this book to anyone regardless of their level of maturity in the prophetic ministry."

David White
Senior Minister, Harvest Now Ministries, Moravian Falls, NC.

"Robert has provided a detailed manual on prophetic things speaking from his own journey alongside of many who have been raised fatherless in the Church. This book is timely for a few reasons but mainly as a cry of freedom of the Sons of the house (God's house), who have grown up refusing to be held down by slave thinking and the sins of their fathers. Rob is a sharp thinker and a wealth of knowledge on all things prophetic. Anyone who has a desire to learn from his wisdom will grow spiritually and live healthy as we face the challenges of the 21st century Church. Absorb this great book and receive Elisha's double portion!"

Martyn Webb
Senior Pastor, Cafe Church, Nelson Bay, NSW.

CONTENTS

Introduction		Page 9
Preface	The Secret Place	Page 13

PART I: THE PROPHETIC GIFT
Chapter

One	Character vs. Charisma	Page 19
Two	The Gift, Ministry and Mantle	Page 31
Three	The Making of a Prophet	Page 37
Four	Basic Prophecy	Page 43
Five	Hearing God's Voice	Page 49
Six	Weighing and Testing Prophecy	Page 79
Seven	Prophetic Etiquette	Page 87
Eight	The Key of Knowledge	Page 93
Nine	The Sword of the Lord	Page 99
Ten	The Prophetic Control Panel	Page 105
Eleven	Prophesying the Will of God	Page 111

PART II: PROPHECY AND THE CHURCH
Chapter

Twelve	Pitfalls of the Prophetic	Page 119
Thirteen	Levels of Prophetic in the Church	Page 125
Fourteen	Developing a Local Prophetic Policy	Page 135
Fifteen	Prayer, Praise and Prophecy	Page 143
Sixteen	The Ezekiel Fourteen Trap!	Page 149
Seventeen	Balanced Leadership	Page 161
Eighteen	Discerning of Spirits	Page 169
Nineteen	Mentoring in the Prophetic	Page 179
Twenty	Making Friends with Rejection	Page 187
Twenty-One	The Error of Balaam	Page 195
Twenty-Two	Error in Prophecy	Page 201

PART III: PROPHETS IN THE REAL WORLD
Chapter

Twenty-Three	Prophecy in Business	Page 209
Twenty-Four	Prophecy in the Marketplace	Page 215
Twenty-Five	Dream Interpretation for the Lost	Page 221
Twenty-Six	The Kingdom of God	Page 231
Twenty-Seven	The Planning Chamber	Page 239
Twenty-Eight	The Gift of Seer	Page 249
Twenty-Nine	The Offspring of Issachar	Page 259
Thirty	Prophets Serving an Apostolic Church	Page 269
Thirty-One	Apostolic – Prophetic Partnerships	Page 275
Thirty-Two	The Sons of the Prophets	Page 283
Thirty-Three	Looking Toward the Future	Page 291

APPENDICES

Appendix One:	An Example Prophetic Policy	Page 300

INTRODUCTION

When thinking of the prophetic, who comes to mind? Perhaps modern "prophets" flicker across the mind? Bob Jones, "reading people's mail" (having a word of knowledge); John G Lake, healing sickness and disease; the stern words of Art Katz calling for consecration unto the Lord. Perhaps Biblical figures such as Moses parting the Red Sea, Abraham journeying across the wilderness, Elijah calling fire from heaven or Jeremiah confronting the king at the gates.

If we run a comparison between each Biblical prophet's life and the life of Jesus Christ, Elisha stands out. He prefigured all of the significant works of the Son of God. He healed a sick general, fed the crowds, raised the dead, and held schools for his disciples. As such, he provides an excellent guide to the New Testament gift of prophecy, as practised and exhibited by Jesus.

So we have chosen the life of Elisha as an index to this book – a complete guide to the gift of prophecy, the mantle of prophet and the humanity of the prophet. Elisha will bring out the significant components of prophetic ministry in three spheres: the gift in general; the gift as it relates to the Church; and finally the gift as it relates to the world.

A BRIEF HISTORY OF THE MODERN PROPHETIC MOVEMENT

During the Welsh Revival, and the ensuing 1904 Azusa Street Revival, prophetic utterance came into vogue. In 1936, Smith Wigglesworth prophetically heralded a new, apostolic leadership when he prophesied over David du Plessis. Dennis Bennett, and Derek Prince in the US championed the gifts of the Spirit through the 1960's.

In England leaders like David Pytches, Bryn Jones, Terry Virgo, Michael Green and others lead the way in the Charismatic renewal. In the 1980's in Africa (particularly Nigeria and Kenya) there were certain expressions of the prophetic. I was saved in the late 1988 just as John Wimber, founder of the Vineyard Movement, was promoting the prophets, strong prophetic words were being given at a national level and schools were starting to be held around Australia. I recall going to one of Steve Penny's first, "Look out the prophets are coming!" conferences in Sydney.

Books started to be written about the subject, such as, "Some Said it Thundered," by David Pytches and, "The Elijah Task," by John & Paula Sandford. Since then, a plethora of books has been written on the prophetic. Most of them were excellent; none of them were complete.

In the mid 1990's, attitudes to prophetic ministry began to shift. Immorality, pride, ambition and greed began to take their toll on ministers. Those who survived the first wave of disaster, succumbed to an over-focus on signs, wonders, miracles and personal prophetic words. Some stooped to charging money for prophecy! There were "Dog and Pony Shows", celebrating the skill of the better prophets. The prophetic gift was rewarded, and character was assumed (as a by-product). There were closed room conferences, closed circuit TV, Circuit preaching, Big Tent meetings and sideshow alleys! Others got caught up in the hyper-positive, keep-it-sweet phenomenon, and conveniently adapted their theology.

Roaming unchecked through the Australian wilderness, there was also an "alternative" prophetic movement. A multitude of hurt, disillusioned and self-appointed prophets attacked the Church with harsh, derogatory, judgemental criticism. A lack of integrity, accountability and character ran amok in the Church.

INTRODUCTION

Many alternatives to prophetic ministry entered the vacuum. Worship leaders, counsellors, psychologists, preachers and coming apostolic ministries all became pseudo-prophetic.

Intercessors became the pastor's best friend. They moved from the closet to the front room of the manse; and from the prayer room to the pulpit across the Church. A new program became the flavour of the month – "prophetic intercession". In places, intercessors provided "prophetic counsel" to leaders, despite the generally taught view that prayer is directed to God! Not surprisingly, all of this generated the opportunity for Jezebelic control to influence the Church.

Those with the "gift" of criticism had a day in the sun, but within a short time they were identified (as wolves in woolly coats). Shepherds wisely closed the doors to prophets (who can blame them?). To this day, many respected church leaders are suspicious of anything calling itself prophetic.

Where, O where did the **prophets** go? They were not all wiped out in the ecclesiastical blood-letting. They went underground – and agonised before God, to see Him establish a true, balanced, safe, wholesome prophetic ministry. How many of these good people I have met! For this reason, I have given myself to work with emerging apostles; to stand alongside fathers in the Church and to mentor prophetic ministers. We **can** have a trustworthy prophetic ministry, accepted by pastors; partnered with apostles; teaming with intercessors and worship leaders.

There is an old saying, "If we do what we always did, we will get what we always got." The teaching of the 20th Century brought us to where we are today. To face the 21st Century, a new breed of prophet is needed. To raise a new paradigm in prophetic ministry, we need a new approach to teaching prophetic truths.

It needs to be new, and totally different from the scorched earth we have left behind. Yet the new approach must be built into foundations, as immutable as the word of God, and every bit as trustworthy and reliable.

A new breed of prophet must arise. These new prophets will ease us from our addiction to saccharine coated prophetic words. They will substitute a crystal clear word from heaven, slicing through the insidious pabulum of prophetic pampering going on today. Men and women who have stood the test of time; who have stood in the counsel of the Almighty. Prophets genuinely **sent** by God.

I learned from Paul Cain and Rick Joyner, that three chords balance a man or woman of God. True prophets need:

1. A love for history, for without it, they are doomed to repeat the mistakes of the fathers;
2. A love for the word of God, for without it they will stray; and
3. An unquenchable love for God – for without this, they will be blown off course by every fad, popular message, the needs of men and will not speak the truth.

Ministers who seek to be acknowledged as mature and wholesome prophets must have the basics in order. They must:

- Value character over giftedness;
- Live life knowing that gift is separate from personal identity;
- Actively acknowledge that any prophecy may be rejected;
- Be committed to long-term relationships.

This book is all about raising up such a generation, for such a time as we live in.

Preface
THE SECRET PLACE

Three millennia ago, Hilkiah was the High Priest in Israel. He had re-discovered the ancient scriptures, and was bringing reformation. The king he served was Josiah, known in history among the kings of Israel as a man who brought revival. The elders were apparently godly, seeking the counsel of Huldah, the prophetess, who lived in the old quarter of Jerusalem.[1] Huldah had announced a time of devastation because of Judah's sins, and Josiah had repented. God relented and the people enjoyed a time of free and prosperous living. Quite a turn around.

Jeremiah was Hilkiah's son. Yet here is part of his commissioning, *"Root out, pull down, destroy and throw down."* (Jeremiah 1:10). Evidently, God was not as impressed as we might be with the success of his father's generation. After lamenting the poor shepherding in the nation, Jeremiah turns in chapter 23 to lament the state of his compatriots in Samaria. He also notes the terrible things being done by the prophets of Israel. Among the most remarkable adjurations is the insistence that these prophets needed to seek God's counsel.

Jeremiah chapter 23 was written at the height of Hilkiah's reforms. To hammer home the necessity of seeking God's counsel in such a spiritual atmosphere, is like saying a supplier needs to seek his manufacturer, or a businessman needs to go to the bank! Of course, prophets need to seek God's counsel! It should go without saying – a prophet's job is defined by taking messages from the King to His subjects. Yet here we find God asking His servants, *"Who has stood in my counsel?"* and saying, *"if they had stood in my counsel..."* (Jeremiah 23:18,22).

---

1. 2 Kings 22:14

THE URGENT NEED

It is possible that this statement describes some prophetic ministry in our day. The Hebrew word for counsel here is *"sod"* (pronounced chawd), which means "secret counsel" or "secret place." Amos said that God does nothing without revealing his secrets to His servants the prophets.[2] David said that the secret counsel of God belongs to those who fear Him.[3] If we are not privy to the counsel of God today, what is the logical explanation?

In God's opinion, the prophets of Israel and Samaria had either forgotten God's address, or they had lost the key to the secret place, where they might receive His counsel. Yet these prophets were not daunted at all, they still had plenty to say! The revelations flowed thick and fast: dreams, visions, revelations, interpretations, words and prophecy; but none of it was born of the secret place. Their Internet list was pumping out loads of stuff, but none of it bore the stamp of heaven. They were not **sent**. They were, therefore, not **authorised**. The message sounded authentic but it carried no glory, no substance. In fact it made the people **worthless**.

THE SECRET PLACE

The Bible has much to say about the secret place. It is a place of hiding, a secret pavilion.[4] It is a dwelling place where God hides us in His shadow.[5] It may be found in the tabernacle of praise, or in the place of refuge.[6] Those who wait on the Lord renew their strength, those who entwine their lives in His will find His life infusing theirs.[7]

---

2. Amos 3:7   3. Psalm 25:14
4. Psalm 31:20   5. Psalm 91:1
6. Psalm 27:5   7. Isaiah 40:31

Preface

The secret place is a place of intimacy with God. Your life has become at One with His. You are dwelling in His presence, and you are seeking His face.

In this fast paced, twenty-first century life – the microchip set, micro-fibre suit wearing, micro-time management age – we struggle to find the counsel of God. O Saints! We know how to find the twenty-third enzyme on the human chromosome, but we can't walk in the twenty-third Psalm!

Isaiah entreated us, *"You who have no money, come buy and eat... without money and without price."* (Isaiah 55:1). How on earth do you buy without money, and obtain what is priceless? A friend of mine says it well: "**Spend** time and **pay** attention!" It takes time to pray, but if our prayer is all talking and no listening, we still might miss Him. It takes listening and time to dwell in the secret place.

Dwelling in the secret place may include suffering or persecution. We must find Him in the difficult times, in the dark hours, in the worst of circumstances. Perhaps that's why the Psalmist said, *"Clouds and darkness surround Him."* (Psalm 97:2). After all, the Lord did say He would dwell in a dark cloud [8] and come to us in a firestorm, consuming the mountainous high places of our lives.[9]

David uncovered the secret place during his darkest hours. When running from Saul, and hiding in a cave, David penned the following words, *"He made darkness His secret place, His canopy dark waters."* (Psalm 18:11).

---

8. 1 Kings 8:11   9. Exodus 19:9

The psalmist Asaph called it the secret place of thunder![10] The secret place isn't that hard to find. Job, with all his woes, found it. He lost his family, his house, his business, and his cattle, but not the key to the secret place. He could say, *"The counsel of the Lord was over my tent."* (Job 29:4).

Why do the majority of Christians miss it? One only needs to walk the aisles of a Christian bookstore to see why. There's plenty to keep a happy Christian busy: twelve steps to a power-prayer time, sixty seconds that will change the world and forty days of purpose. We find the seven secrets to success; the twenty-one immutable laws of corporate life, but find no mention of finding the secret place! The top ten titles overflow with positive posturing and power paradigms, but there is no mention of pain, suffering, darkness or trouble.

David found God in the back of the cave, running away from his spiritual mentor, General Saul. Frightened, alone and a castaway, David found the secret place. If David, if Job, if Asaph found God under those circumstances, perhaps we can too. If ever there was a crying need for the prophetic today, it would be to **find** the secret place.

"If they had stood in my counsel"...

---

10. Psalm 81:7

PART ONE

THE PROPHETIC GIFT

This first section of this book covers eleven subjects that relate to the prophetic gift itself, and the person in whom it is operating. We will look at character and giftedness, and how they interplay.

We will distinguish between the various kinds (levels) of prophetic gift – 1 Corinthians 12; Romans 12 and Ephesians 4. Then we will examine the making and moulding of the prophet coming into usefulness.

We look at the "core technologies" in the revelatory ministry – basic prophecy, hearing God's voice and how to weigh and test prophecy.

Prophetic etiquette could rightly be covered in the next section (on the gift and the church), but we have included it here, because etiquette is only useful if the gift bearer follows it!

The last part of this section will cover some broader issues such as the keys of knowledge, the sword of the Spirit and prophesying God's will for people.

Chapter One
CHARACTER VS CHARISMA

"[Elijah] found Elisha son of Shaphat, while he was plowing with twelve pairs of oxen before him, and he with the twelfth. And Elijah passed over to him and threw his mantle on him." (1 Kings 19:19).

Here is the son, working faithfully in the father's field. No false illusions of grandeur, just the simplicity of obedience. A young man, committed to his father's house, ready to serve and see the family prosper. This family owned twelve pair of oxen. That was like owning a million dollar John Deere Combine Harvester in those days. The son was trusted with the expensive tractor.

Elisha also had a calling. God looked down from heaven into the soul of the individual he had created in Mrs. Shaphat's womb, and saw a prophet. Before Elisha could ever be a man of God, he had to be a man of the earth. Before he could raise the dead, he had to raise corn or wheat. Before he could part the waters of the Jordan and address foreign Generals, he had to serve in the house of his spiritual father. That takes character.

What Gifts Are Not

No doctor, no test, no scan can determine how God is going to allocate talents before we are born. Genetic experts may tell us that genes play a part, psychologists may tell us that upbringing plays a part, but God's choice is **the** major determinant of how "talented" we are.

Those gifts and talents may increase or decrease in the course of time, but the shift in giftedness has nothing to do with our level of holiness, spirituality, consecration or wisdom! Gifts are not an indication of the level of God's love for us; nor of His approval of our lifestyle. They are not a reward for good performance, nor do they offer any measurement of our theological accuracy, our spiritual maturity or our Christlikeness. They are gifts; unearned, undeserved. In exactly the same way that we may abuse or destroy a Christmas gift and offend the one who gave it, we may abuse and destroy the gifts of God in us. Treat your gifts with care. Honour the giver.

THE CHARACTER CONNECTION

A highly talented runner, may be completely obnoxious. A very prophetic person – having lots of communication from the Lord – may have significant hang-ups and sins, but God commits to character, not giftedness. Paul told Timothy, *"Commit these [teachings] to faithful men who will be able to teach others also."* (2 Timothy 2:2 emphasis mine). This equation is commonly misunderstood to mean, "Commit to able men who will try to be faithful."

The critical difference is that God commits to faithfulness (character) NOT to ability (giftedness). That perversion is the key to much error in ministry, business, marriage and relationships. We think God is interested in committing His kingdom to able men, not necessarily to faithful ones.

Character is not reputation, success, achievement, what we have done or how far we have come. It is who we are. Bill Hybels provides a good working definition of character: "Character is what we do when no one is looking."[1]

---

1. "Who You Are When No One's Looking." Pg 7

Hybels identifies six essential characteristics:

- Love
- Faith (fulness)
- Vision (hope)
- Courage
- Discipline and
- Endurance

Love is clearly the most critical of these, for without love we are nothing at all.[2] The second most important aspect is faithfulness. Our character is to reflect God's character. God is faithful to His promises,[3] and Christ was faithful to the One who appointed Him.[4] We must understand that faithfulness – honesty, integrity is the foundation for character.

"Whoever is faithful in a very little is faithful also in much; and whoever is dishonest in a very little is dishonest also in much. If then you have not been faithful with the dishonest wealth, who will entrust to you the true riches? And if you have not been faithful with what belongs to another, who will give you what is your own?" (Luke 16:10-12).

We will not progress in spiritual gifts until we master earthly gifts. We will be given advancement in the Kingdom of God once we have yielded our hearts to mundane tasks. Elisha found this out, as the prophet laid his mantle on the farmer's son. The man of God visits the dusty field, has a BBQ with the ploughman and pulls him up to the heavenly call on his life.

---

2. 1 Corinthians 13:13 3. Deuteronomy 7:9
4. Hebrews 3:2

Christlikeness, obedience, brokenness, humility, fear of God, repentance and holiness are also fundamental characteristics needed for prophetic ministry. Christlikeness includes all of the aspects noted by Hybels and more!

PROPHETIC PEOPLE WITH CHARACTER

To walk in the revelatory gifts safely and appropriately, we need strong character. To stand before men on behalf of God, and speak the mind of God, requires our character to be refined and strengthened. Ambitious, proud or confused prophetic people often "kick against the goads" in their lives, not understanding this principle. It is very often a character issue, a matter of the heart, or conduct which locks the way forward for them. It is a character lock inside them, which must be turned, to open the door in front of them!

As prophetic people, we are often preoccupied with being heard, and take offense when people do not respond positively to our advice. We focus on the results (response to our word), instead of the process (growing in relationship, unity, wisdom, maturity), which God is seeking to perform in us.

God is more interested in our growth in character than He is in our giftedness or achievements in the prophetic. Why then do we persist in being so achievement oriented? Many prophetic people strive for place and position, when such ambition actually disqualifies us from the effective operation of grace in our lives.

Foundational character issues for those who wish to be "world class" prophetic ministers are:

1. Christ-likeness

John was told that, *"The spirit of prophecy is the testimony of Jesus."* (Revelation 19:10). The only foundation for prophetic utterance is a display, a witness of Christ. We are not to preach Christ, so much as be Christ. We are not so much called to tell of the gospel, but rather be the gospel. Our highest example of prophetic ministry was Christ Himself. Only when we have an insatiable appetite to be like Him, will the rest will fall into place.

2. Obedience

Saul was told why he had been passed over in God's plans. His disobedience and his pre-occupation with the "legal minimum" disqualified him. Out of Samuel's fury with Saul we obtain an eternal principle. He said, *"Obedience is better than sacrifice."* (1 Samuel 15:22). How does anyone learn obedience? From suffering.[5] We should be submitting to the challenges God places before us, and running to do as He says. Sadly the prophetic in our day has television's portrayal of God as a "blessing" God who only wants to give "good" gifts. Who defines "good"? Surely it must include the discipline of a Father, which embraces all the most unpopular aspects of character development.

3. A broken and contrite spirit

John the Baptist gave us a changeless principle of ministry: *"He [Christ] must increase, and I must decrease."* (John 3:30). The more transparent we become, the more the light of Christ will be made visible. We are clay vessels – willing to be broken, to get the treasure within.[6] Christ taught us that in the Kingdom we must expect to be crushed – just as a seed for its oil, or a grape for its juice.[7]

---

5. Hebrews 5:8　　　　　　　　6. 2 Corinthians 4:7
7. Mathew 21:44

4. Humility, repentance and fear of God

"This is the one to whom I will look, to the humble and contrite in spirit, who trembles at my word." (Isaiah 66:2). God esteems the humble person. Humility basically means not thinking of ourselves more highly than we should. We know our place and we are content. We do not big note ourselves when we are actually marginal to God's overall plans. Contrition means, one who is repentant – constantly aware of his utter failure and inadequacy before the Lord. God esteems the one who trembles at His words – who fears the Lord and reveres Him as King. How rare this is in today's society. We marginalise obedience, neglect to honour those who do not promote themselves, are embarrassed by any call to repentance and are disinclined to love God during difficult times.

5. Freedom from fear of people

The fear of people is one of the greatest character traps for prophetic people. We are told that, *"The fear of man is a trap, to ensnare the godly."* (Proverbs 29:25). Prophetic people need God's perspective, not man's. We should actively discount people's subjective approval of our ministry. There is no question that seeking people's approval clouds our discernment, and colours our motives for ministry.

6. Holiness

Prophets are the closest confidantes of a holy God; His friends, His companions. Is it any surprise that prophets are set apart, consecrated to God; dependent on the Lord? How could any holy prophet, who stands in the counsel of God, consider flirting with the world?[8]

---

8. James 4:4

The mature prophetic person seeks to walk in holiness and wholeness in every aspect of life. Our conduct ought to portray a depth of life in Christ: our resilience under stress; our calm in the midst of turmoil; our strength in times of trouble. God is especially interested in our standard of speech. How can God's word be spoken by unclean lips? How can a blessing be spoken by a mouth that has just cursed God's children? The New Testament writer, James warns us against slander, gossip, envy and back biting.[9] This is fundamental, watch what you say! The power of life and death lies in the tongue.[10]

STRIVING FOR THE GIFTS

All too often I have watched people try desperately to win God's approval, and climb the ladder to a "higher" gifting. A sad deception is at work when an intercessor (for example), is waiting for promotion to the prophetic office. The harder they work to please God (in the hope that He will bestow more giftedness on them), the more dissatisfied they become with what they already have. Soon, like an unused muscle, our real gift atrophies.

The corollary is that some highly gifted people think that God is always pleased with them. They secretly believe that God will "wink" at their hidden flaws and sins. But this is far from the truth. The higher the calling, the deeper and more severe the judgements we will face. Each one of us will be called to account for every "talent" given to us. The person who is given more will be expected to invest still more in the Kingdom of God.[11]

---

9. James 3:9-11   10. Proverbs 18:21
11. Luke 12:48

Strength of character is desperately needed in those who are walking in the anointing. Anointing can be likened to weight, or pressure. The greater the pressure, the more likely it becomes that flaws will appear and the whole façade will crumble! The more intense the anointing, the deeper is the need for solid character.

SIMON THE SORCERER

Acts 8:18-24 tells the story of Simon, a man who had a completely erroneous view of God. He misunderstood the dynamic of God's bestowing power upon men and thought that gifting could be bought. Sadly, Simon's logic was not far from that found in ministry today. The effect of working for gifts, or striving for the prophetic to function in our lives, is the same as payment for power – but instead of finance, we seek to pay in another way. If we think that by any merit or effort whatsoever we can earn gifts, we are guilty of the same error as Simon.

Too often we assume that those "on stage or behind the pulpit", have it all figured out, but this is simply not the case. Since the 1980s the moral, financial and spiritual bankruptcy of many international ministries has been demonstrated over and over again. What does their failure tell us? The anointing of God requires ongoing character development, a never-ending cycle of brokenness and humility. Too many ministries come to a point beyond which they are not willing to pay the personal price.

The danger, when caught up in the heady excitement of powerful manifestation and ecstasy of God's presence, is to take our focus off character development and place it on manifestations. We may declare, "This minister set us free," or "That minister gave us deliverance," without examining the state of the man's marriage, finances or conduct in other spheres of life.

We may become trapped in this self-fulfilling, co-dependent cycle, resulting in an ignoble and dramatic crash. Nebuchadnezzar may once have been the Lord's hand-servant to bring judgement on Jerusalem, but a few short years later he was eating grass! [12]

SAUL AND DAVID

Two old kings of Israel, Saul and David illustrate the dynamic tension between expressing the gifts in us and developing the character to support them. The Lord chose Saul in the beginning. In fact Saul was the only person in the Bible who was told, *"Do whatever your hand finds to do and the Lord will bless you in it."* (1 Samuel 10:7). Regretfully, a few short years later, because of his fear of David and his disobedience, Saul was utterly rejected by God. He acted totally against God's will. As a result, he was struck down, and finally killed in battle.

David, however, was trained for years in the wilderness; he knew much suffering at the hands of Saul and others. He developed a humble, contrite and repentant heart. In the day of his indiscretion with Bathsheba, his repentance was so complete that he cried out for mercy. [13] Though he was forgiven, a sword would never leave his house, as a constant reminder to him. David's psalms reveal a heart pleasing to the Lord.

SYMPTOMS OF WEAK CHARACTER

We must prepare for the day of our visitation, the day of anointing, when the pressure mounts. It takes time to build against the following seven symptoms of weak character:

---

12. Daniel 4:33   13. Psalm 51

1. Dependence on offerings

Money and prophecy do not mix. The love of money is the root of all kinds of evil. The unrestrained pursuit of money reveals a deeper lack of dependence on God and His provision. Prophets who tie their gift to money may end up soothsaying and fortune telling. To trust in riches, and beg for cash, is to store up wrath for ourselves on the day of judgement. [14]

2. Creating hype for results

Hyping up the service to obtain results reveals a tendency toward reliance on the flesh instead of the Spirit. We fear that God will not show up and we will be embarrassed. We try to maintain our "reputation". Let's do it Elijah's way – pour some water on the sacrifice and see if God still shows up! [15]

3. Exaggeration

People who are insecure and unstable exaggerate stories of success and manufacture (or inflate) the stories which illustrate their results and fruitfulness. This trait manifests a deep insecurity and fear of man. If exaggeration becomes a pattern in our lives, we must question whether our life is truly hidden in Christ. For if it were, our life would display His glory, and come forth when His light shines. [16]

4. Reliance on methodology

To insist on doing things the same way, or constantly using one method in ministry, may lead to employing witchcraft. The Spirit is like the wind, He will minister as and where He pleases. [17] He is always doing new things, [18] and cannot be manipulated by our

---

14. James 5:3
15. 1 Kings 18:34-16
16. Collosians 3:3
17. John 3:8
18. Isaiah 43:19

methods or manufactured formats. Just as soon as we have camped out at a favourite method, God moves on.

5. Using mystique

People who rely on prophetic mystique manifest a deep lack of trust that people will accept them for who they actually are. This is a classic mistake – to equate gifting with persona – so when people reject the word, they have cause for offense and wounding. Christ was completely down to earth; He had lunch at the pub with sinners and tax collectors. He made no effort to appear super-spiritual; nor should we.

6. Comparison

Comparing ourselves, our ministry, our measure of anointing or our success with others is a fatal snare. It manifests a deeper lack of understanding of our own basic failure, and complete inadequacy without Christ. We should not be high minded, or inflate our self image. Consider others more highly. [19]

7. Dissatisfaction

Being dissatisfied with our present calling, ministry or status leads to competitiveness and inordinate desire for achievement (at all costs). This shows a deeper lack of understanding grace – we are saved by God's impressive mercy, not by our own efforts. We are not promoted in the Kingdom according to our station, success or achievement – we must be satisfied with where He has placed us right now, and work for Him there. [20] Grow where you are planted, like Elisha did, working in his father's field. Do not branch out and establish your "own ministry" until you can be sent out and blessed.

---

19. Romans 12:3   20. Luke 3:14

REFERENCES

Bickle, Mike & Sullivant, Michael. "Growing in the Prophetic." Kingsway, 1995.
Cole, Edwin Louis. "On Becoming a Real Man." Thomas Nelson, 1992.
Hybels, Bill. "Who You Are When No One's Looking." Inter Varsity, 1987.

Chapter Two
THE GIFT, MINISTRY & MANTLE

"So He took the pair of oxen and sacrificed them and boiled their flesh... and gave it to the people and they ate. Then he arose and followed Elijah and ministered to him."
(1 Kings 19:21).

This is the BBQ to celebrate Elisha's calling into ministry, but he had no training (by our standards) for this high calling. He could turn a field with a plow, he could plant and grow corn or wheat, and he could lift a hundred pounds of flour, but could he prophesy? Probably not. Now he was in training, and he had some things to learn. Elijah had to start with what he found in the field of Elisha's life. He had to dig around and found out what natural aptitude Elisha had.

Most growth in the prophetic begins with developing the gift first, then working on the ministry and finding out if the person has a calling to wear the mantle of a prophet. Let's look at the gift first. I define it this way:

> The gift of prophecy is a grace bestowed upon a believer so chosen by the Lord, to communicate what has been heard from God. The words brought will strengthen, encourage and comfort those who hear and receive them. The one who prophesies, builds up the Church. The word so spoken may be fore-telling, forth-telling, expounding, a word of knowledge, a word of wisdom, some instruction, direction, a song, poem or other communication.

John Wimber coined the word "gracelets" to describe the gifts bestowed upon men by God. The Greek word used in the New Testament for gifts is *charismata* meaning: gifts of grace. Gracelets are given freely, just like salvation, and cannot be earned. In other words effort and exertion do not bring us closer to getting gifts, nor does our performance or position before God.

"But to each one is given the manifestation of the Spirit for the common good." (1 Corinthians 12:7). *"To another prophecy [is given]... the same Spirit works all these things, distributing to each one individually as He wills."* (1 Corinthians 12:10,11). These gifts – these manifestations of God's Spirit – are given by Him for the benefit of others. The Spirit works them in us as He wills. They come and go; are strengthened or retire as God wills. So often a gift will manifest because of the need of someone God wants to touch.

PROPHETIC MINISTRY

God places gifts and ministries in people, the gift and the gifted one are inseparable. Once a person is recognised as having received the gift at the level of prophetic ministry, then the gift can be worked on, trained up and honed like any skill. We can recognise a believer at this level from the following definition:

> The prophetic ministry will be recognised and the person commissioned for regular service in the local church setting. Church leaders acknowledge that a person has the ability to discern, interpret and apply revelation. The prophetic minister develops a track record of accuracy and reliability.

The essential difference between the simple gift and the motivational gift is explained by Paul, *"Since we have gifts (charisma) that differ according to the grace given to us, each of us is to exercise them accordingly; if prophecy, according to the proportion of our faith."* (Romans 12:6).

These gifts do not come and go; they are not removed at the will of the Spirit. Rather, they are deposits of His grace in our lives, even from birth. The Scripture tells us **we** must, "Exercise them accordingly." This prophetic gift is **exercised** according to our level of faith. We will see this later explained, in the story of Elisha crossing the Jordan.

THE MANTLE OF THE PROPHET

I define a prophet as:

> A person who serves as a regular and reliable channel of communication between God and humanity. He or she stand before man on behalf of the Lord. Their focus is foundation laying, restoring truth and bringing the light of God's whole counsel to the Church. They act as an eye in the Body of Christ. This mantle includes those who have been labelled as oracles, seers and king's counsellors.

Each prophet is given a mandate *(metron)*; a sphere of influence. The prophet must be careful to stay within these God-given boundaries! For example: Jeremiah was set over nations; Hosea walked out an example of God's grace by marrying a prostitute. Agabus was appointed to the church in Jerusalem; Nehemiah was called to rebuild Jerusalem.

The prophet may major in certain aspects of revelatory ministry such as words of knowledge, wisdom, visions or foretelling of events. The Lord may appoint the prophet to a travelling ministry (itinerant), or appoint him to serve in a particular local congregation with the leadership team. Each portfolio is as different as the prophet. It is like a job description, which may include a variety of activity:

Giving direction: Elisha instructed the kings about battle strategy;[1] Micaiah instructed kings on their plans.[2]
Warning: Agabus warned Paul about Rome;[3] Jeremiah warned Israel of the Babylonians.[4]
Confirmation: Nathan confirmed the temple with David.[5]
Judgement: Samuel prophesied Eli's demise;[6] Peter spoke death to Ananias.[7]
Weather: Elijah commanded the rain;[8] Agabus predicted drought in Judea.[9]
Correction: Nathan corrected David's adultery.[10]
Equipping saints: Bringing the Body to maturity.[11]
Foundation laying: Rightly founding the Body of Christ.[12]

FOUNDATION FOR THE MANTLE

We cannot choose to become a prophet. God distributes gifts according to His grace, He gives **some**, *"to be apostles, some prophets, some evangelists..."* (Ephesians 4:11). It's not something to work up to, or to be promoted into. Being a prophet is something you are, or are not.

---

1. 2 Kings 3:17
2. 2 Chronicles 18:16
3. Acts 21:10
4. Jeremiah. 20:4
5. 1 Chronicles 17:4
6. 1 Samuel 2:27-36
7. Acts 5:1-11
8. 1 Kings 17:1
9. Acts 11:28
10. 2 Samuel 12
11. Ephesians 4:11-12
12. Ephesians 2:20

Recognising a person as a New Testament prophet requires the presence of at least three key attributes:

- Supernatural giftedness – prophets regularly receive accurate **divine** information;
- Godly character – true prophets are becoming truly Christlike; (they are called **holy** prophets in Ephesians 3:5);
- Mature wisdom – true prophets do not just have revelation, they also have wisdom. [13] They have learned from experience and relationship.

There are three phases to the process of maturing into the mantle of prophet: the calling (or anointing), the choosing (or training) and the commissioning (or releasing).

1. Calling

Only God can call a prophet. It is sovereign. This can happen one of three ways. He can call you:

- Before birth – as with Jeremiah [14] and Isaiah; [15]
- Out of a current calling – Amos was called out of fig tree raising; [16]
- Through another prophet – Elisha called by Elijah. [17]

2. Choosing

The period of choosing is the time of training, refining and character development. *"Many are called but few are chosen."* (Mathew 22:14). Will we make the grade? Many don't. God chooses a unique and individualised training regime for each prophet, depending on his or her character, needs, portfolio and public ministry.

---

13. Ephesians 1:17
14. Jeremiah 1:5
15. Isaiah 49:1
16. Amos 7:14
17. 1 Kings 19:19

We can be trained:

- Through trials – as Joseph,[18] Moses[19] and Daniel were;[20]
- Sovereignly by God – as with Jeremiah;[21]
- By another prophet – as with Elisha;[22]
- In a school of prophets – as some did under Elisha.[23]

3. Commissioning

The day we are commissioned is like the day of graduation from school. We are stamped with God's divine authority, and begin a publicly demonstrative ministry. We may have ministered publicly before that, but now all people will see and recognise our office. We will carry authority that we did not have before. Being commissioned is not something a person can hide. The elders and pastors will know you have made it through.

We don't need to work at anything but our obedience and character. Our gift will be recognised, called upon, utilised, admired, spoken about and eventually we will receive the recognition of leaders. Do not pursue the accolades and admiration of people. The love of men is a folly, *"Beware when all men speak well of you, for so they spoke of the false prophets."* (Luke 6:26).

REFERENCES

Bickle, Mike. "Growing in the Prophetic." Kingsway, 1995
Hybels, Bill. "Who You Are When No One's Looking." InterVarsity, 1987.
Sandford, John Loren. Private Conversation on Portfolios of Prophets, April 1994.

---

18. Genesis 37-39
19. Exodus 2:23
20. Daniel 1:3
21. Jeremiah 1:7-8
22. 1 Kings 19-22 and 2 Kings 3:11 as he washed hands
23. 2 Kings 2:16, 2 Kings 4:38, 2 Kings 6:1

Chapter Three
THE MAKING OF A PROPHET

[The Captain said]: *"Elisha the son of Shaphat is here, who used to pour water on the hands of Elijah."* (2 Kings 3:11).

This is one of the most derogatory statements a captain of the army could make about the occupation of another man. Yet in the economy of God, it is **the** qualifier. Service is central to the making, and indeed the keeping, of a prophet.

In the East, thousands of years ago, women were considered second-class citizens. They received no inheritance, could not own land and were generally treated like servants. The work around the house was allocated in a strict pecking order. The "women's work" was ordered according to honour among the women. There were three jobs reserved for the lowest of the low class servant girls: emptying the "black water" pails (toilets), washing down the service areas and pouring water on the hands.

In the East, they ate food with one hand, and did ablutions with the other. Before and after eating, before and after going to the toilet, the members of the house needed someone to pour water on their hands (both left and right). This job, reserved for the least respected woman in the house, was committed to Elisha!

In the East, it was (and is) quite common for a master to give a tyro (learner) impossible tasks to do. In this way they would humiliate, or break the person's natural pride, arrogance and confidence. Elisha did the humiliating, backbreaking servant work, and this qualified him for the mantle of prophet. In the end, a prophet is not just a "platform ministry", gaining reputation for awesome ability to gain supernatural knowledge. No, a prophet is a hand servant to the Bride of Christ, one who washes her with the water of the word of God.[1] So it is today, whether we speak to children or Presidents of nations, we are servants.

WHEN GOD MAKES A PROPHET...

When God makes a prophet, what does He have in mind? According to Ephesians 4:8-11, when He ascended on high, He made gifts of men. He took of His Spirit, and poured Himself (by the Holy Spirit), into men. He manifested His nature in five intrinsic expressions – the apostle, the prophet, the pastor, the teacher and the evangelist. Christ the Chief Apostle; Christ the Prophet mighty in word and deed; Christ the Good Shepherd; Christ the Great High Priest; Christ the Evangelist.

How does God want to express Himself as Prophet in the earth? God has given us examples like Isaiah, Jeremiah, Ezekiel, John the Baptist – He lets us engage their life stories. We should listen carefully to the statements they make about how they demonstrate the prophet's nature through their relationship with God.

Look at how God relates to His servants: how He praises and reprimands them. He builds up the things He wants to see, and He roots out the things He does not want to see. He moulds and shapes them toward His ideal, and at the same time He speaks to them about their adversaries – their anti-types, the false prophets. From these conversations, we can see a pattern emerging. It is from these conversations that we glean the mind of God. Some of the examples are positive, and some negative. There are twelve gifts that God forms in a prophet:

The Making of a Prophet

1. The gift of sight
A prophet is made to see.[2] This is intrinsic and basic to the prophetic gift, the capacity for insight, hindsight and foresight. A false prophet is blind, or cannot see truth.[3]

2. The gift of truth
A prophet is made to tell eternal truth.[4] They see things as black and white issues, they see things in very contrasted ways. They want the truth to be known, and they want to know the truth. A false prophet tells lies,[5] deceives and colours truth.

3. The gift of substance
A prophet is made to carry and bring words of substance.[6] Their words carry weight; their words are the word of the Lord and carry gravity. A false prophet's words are empty like the wind.[7]

4. The gift of value
A prophet is made for the profit of God's people.[8] Their presence in the Body of Christ adds value, promotes prosperity and blessing. A false prophet makes God's people worthless,[9] and bankrupts their soul.

5. The gift of purity
A prophet is made to model purity in the fear of the presence of God.[10] They love and value purity and seek righteousness. They try to help the Bride become spotless and without wrinkle. A false prophet pollutes the land,[11] and infects the people.

---

1. Ephesians 5:26
2. Numbers 12:6, Hosea 12:10
3. Isaiah 29:10
4. Zechariah 1:6, Daniel 9:10
5. Jeremiah 14:14, Isaiah 9:14,15
6. Hosea 6:5
7. Jeremiah 5:13
8. 2 Chronicles 20:20, Ezekiel 22:25
9. Jeremiah 23:16
10. Haggai 1:12
11. Jeremiah 23:15, Zechariah 13:2

6. The gift of disillusionment

A prophet is made to bring holiness and morality. [12] The result of sharing moral truth is that people become disillusioned – they let go of their current values. The extent to which we are under an illusion, or a deception is the extent to which we will experience a "beautiful letdown". A false prophet deceives, excusing sin and reinforcing illusion. [13] They give false hope.

7. The gift of friendship

Prophets model intimacy and friendship with God. [14] Their favourite "tourist destination" is the secret place of the Most High. A false prophet is not intimate with God and is not His friend. [15]

8. The gift of spirit seeing

A prophet is Spirit led, not by sight or outward senses. [16] He walks with integrity in the spirit realm and model for others how to value what cannot be seen, as Elisha when he saw the chariots of fire. A false prophet follows his own spirit, and is therefore blind. [17]

9. The gift of provision

A prophet demonstrates God's faithful provision. [18] Miracles follow his life; he stands at the tap of heaven and turns it on for the Church. His provider is God; his source is God's strength. A false prophet will lean on men for money. [19]

10. The gift of power

A prophet is full of power, a man of the Spirit. [20] A prophet demonstrates Heaven, with God's backing. He has a pass that reads, "access granted". Prophets usher the Spirit into a hopeless situation.

---

12. Amos 2:11 MSG
13. Isaiah 30:10
14. Amos 3:7
15. Jeremiah 23:22 & 30
16. Isaiah 42:19
17. Ezekiel 13:3
18. Habbakuk 3:17,18
19. Micah 3:11
20. Micah 3:8 and Isaiah 44:26

But a false prophet is full of himself, and inspired by wine.[21] His words are always frustrated by God.[22]

11. The gift of yieldedness

A prophet is a faithful, yielded servant ready to go wherever he is sent.[23] He is broken and humble, because God has brought an end to his "self" life. A false prophet is unfaithful and unreliable,[24] like a treacherous swamp, a filthy place of refuse.

12. The gift of integrity

A prophet is a model of reliability and integrity.[25] You can always rely upon him; his character can be depended on implicitly. Prophets will come through in a time of stress or duress. A false prophet is insolent and treacherous.[26]

ENTER THE PROPHET

These lessons are not learned in the courts of the king. They are learned as you obey your parents, work hard in a secular job (no matter how back breaking or servile), in the marketplace. For Elisha, they were learned first on his father's farm, and then as a hand servant to Elijah.

St Patrick gives us an example of these aspects.

Time will not allow for a full and proper account of Patrick of Ireland (398-471 AD). Suffice it to say, the prophetic was both evident in his ministry and prospered the apostolic work in Ireland. Saved from slavery by a dream, commissioned by an angel into apostolic work, ordained by Germans as a monk. Patrick knew the power of the prophetic.

---

21. Isaiah 28:7
22. Isaiah 44:25
23. Jeremiah 7:25
24. Jeremiah 6:13
25. Ezra 5:2
26. Jeremiah 43:2

His co-worker Kieran was commissioned to go before him through Ireland, establishing communities and monasteries. This team planted more than 300 churches and baptised over 120,000 people.[27] He prophesied the conversion of Dublin, raised King Alphinus' son, Eochadh, from the dead, saw miraculous provision of food and water and was often guided by dreams and visions.[28]

The prophetic was powerfully coupled with ascetic holiness, as his communities practised prayer, abstinence, generous and sacrificial giving, acts of service and protection of the poor. Patrick, and men like him typify for us the power of one holy, prophetic life.

REFERENCES

Denten, Kerry. "The Beautiful Letdown." The Gathering, Sept 2, 2004 audio recording.
Ryle, James. "A Dream Come True." Creation House, 1995.
Walters, Kathie. "Celtic Flames." Good News Ministries, 1999.

---

27. Fulton, J Sheer. "The World Book Encyclopedia", Vol 15, Pg 174. World Book, 1969.
28. Maison, R.P.C. "The Life and Writings of Historical Saint Patrick.", Pg 86-88. Seabury Press 1983.

Chapter Four
BASIC PROPHECY

"When they came to the Jordan, they cut down trees. But as one was cutting down a tree, the iron ax head fell into the water... so [Elisha] cut off a stick, and threw it in there; and he made the iron float." (2 Kings 6:1-7).

This vignette is taken from the latter part of Elisha's life. He is mature and has young prophets to teach. They are probably living in community, and come to their spiritual father, asking permission to move to a broader place. They obtain his blessing, and then ask him to come with them.

In the midst of building the new community, an accident happens, and they cry out to Elisha for help. They call upon the prophetic gift in their midst. They do not know what to do, for the axe head was borrowed, and they despair. But Elisha offers practical help – like Samuel finding Saul's missing donkey – Elisha retrieves the axe head. He utters a prophetic declaration – he speaks change into his environment.

How did Elisha understand God's will? He asked God, and listened to the whispering voice of the Spirit. How did he know what to do? He did what he saw his Father doing. Jesus said, *"My sheep hear my voice."* (John 10:17). When you hear the Voice of God, He will often speak to you about helping your neighbour! Apply your gift very practically to life and family. It is here we must begin, whether we are called to the gift, the ministry or the mantle of prophet. That's the kind of gift Paul told us to earnestly desire in 1 Corinthians 14:1.

EDIFICATION, EXHORTATION AND COMFORT

The first role of basic prophecy is to strengthen, encourage and build up the believer, especially those who have backslidden or become discouraged. *"He who prophesies speaks edification [strengthening] and exhortation [encouragement] and comfort [building up] to men."* (1 Corinthians 14:3 NKJV).

It is incredible that such a clear passage of Scripture should be applied incorrectly so often in the Church today. Many churches insist that prophecy must be positive, uplifting, happy, generous, kind, strengthening and **always** upbeat. This makes for insipid stuff; of no lasting use in building the Church. God loves us too much to leave us the way we are. Prophecy was intended by God to challenge, stir, inspire and undergird. So if the wood needs sanding, then get the sandpaper. If the metal has rust, pour acid on it. If the walls were eaten by white ants, rip out the old wood and restore it. This is the sentiment contained in the words, "edify, exhort and comfort". Strong stuff. Look at some other uses of these adjectives:

1. Comfort comes first...

"Comfort, O comfort my people, says your God, speak tenderly to Jerusalem and proclaim to her... that she has received from the Lord's hand double for all her sins." (Isaiah 40:1,2).

Comfort her, by proclaiming that justice will come in the form of double penalty for her sin! Lest we dismiss this as being, "Old Testament, law," it is from this very passage that the call of John the Baptist arises, *"The voice of one crying in the wilderness"* (vs 3). What was John's first message of comfort? *"Repent, for the kingdom of heaven is near,"* (Mathew 3:3) followed by, *"You brood of Vipers"*!

Let us, look a little deeper. Repentance leads to restoration of relationship with God. Very comforting ministry from John!

2. How about exhortation?

That word turns up in John's life too, *"And with many other exhortations he preached to the people."* (Luke 3:18). What did these exhortations contain? Instructions to the rich to share their wealth, to the tax collectors not to steal, to the soldiers not to intimidate and to adulterers not to sleep around. These topics dealt squarely with sin, and exhorted people toward righteousness.

Peter was good at exhortation too. On the day of Pentecost, Peter rebuked the crowd for crucifying Christ, pleaded with them to repent, invited them to receive the Holy Spirit, and welcomed the humble to join them. Scripture says, *"With many other words he testified and exhorted them saying 'be saved from this perverse generation'."* (Acts 2:40). Exhortation is a strong word too. There is no implication of platitudes lulling us to sleep with "feel good" messages.

3. Now it's time for edification

Edification in Greek (*oikodome*) means the act of building a house, roofing an apartment, constructing from the foundations. Our words should carry constructive power and resurrection life. Paul said, *"Be zealous for spiritual gifts, let it be for the edification of the Church that you seek to excel."* (1 Corinthians 14:3). Can you hear Paul's heart? His zeal is aimed at building excellence, ambitious to achieve, hungry to promote other people. *"Our authority, the Lord gave us for edification and not for destruction."* (2 Corinthians 10:8). The power, the authority and strength of prophetic leadership is not to destroy, but to edify.

Paul says, *"Let no corrupt word proceed out of your mouth, but what is necessary for edification, that it may impart grace to the hearers."* (Ephesians 4:29). Just imagine what might happen to ordinary believers if we edified them in this way!

CONVICT AND CONVINCE

The second role of basic prophecy is to convict the unbeliever, the lost person, and the sinner of wrongdoing and convince them to lead a holy life.

"If an unbeliever or someone who does not understand comes in while everybody is prophesying, he will be convinced by all that he is a sinner and will be judged by all, and the secrets of his heart will be laid bare. So he will fall down and worship God, exclaiming, 'God is really among you!'" (1 Corinthians 14:24-25).

INSTRUCT AND TEACH

The third role of basic prophecy is to instruct and teach the new believer. *"For you can all prophesy one by one so that everyone may be instructed and encouraged."* (1 Corinthians 14:31).

Prophecy intrinsically contains instruction, or better said, by prophecy we learn. It gives us God's perspective on a matter. It leads us to understanding. Prophecy is the key of knowledge (more on that later). The word for instruction (*manthano*) means to learn, be educated, receive, so that you may be encouraged.

Herein lies the difference between ordinary teaching and prophetic teaching. There is urgency to the instruction brought by prophetic means. The Spirit – our *parakletos* – is urging us to do something. His instruction is time specific, it is serious and urgent, pushing toward an outcome. It is not knowledge to be understood but <u>obeyed</u>; not to be obtained but <u>followed</u>; not to be certified but <u>guaranteed</u>.

SOME ORDER PLEASE!

I was brought up in the home of a high-ranking Navy Officer. We had many "visiting firemen." My parents taught me that it is not polite to interrupt a person whilst they are speaking. That went particularly for our visiting dignitaries. We should not interrupt the Apostle Paul at the end of v 31 either. At the end of his statement about all prophesying one by one there is a semi colon. His very next statement is this:

"The spirits of the prophets are subject to the prophets."
(1 Corinthians 14:32).

There are at least three ways of interpreting this statement:

- The conduct of everyone prophesying (those he has just been speaking about) is subject to the prophets (a group of leaders) in the Church; OR

- You (the individual prophesying) are subject to other prophetic people (your peers) in the group prophesying (meaning co-accountability); OR

- You (the prophet) are subject to yourself (display some self control please)!

Which ever way we choose to interpret this, we must be subject to authority and exercise self control! Paul continues his thoughts; *"For God is not a God of confusion but of peace, as in all the Churches of the saints."* (1 Corinthians 14:33). One way or another, basic prophecy is not practised in disorder, nor does its expression bring disorder, nor does the fruit produce chaos. This gift is from God, and God is a God of peace not confusion.

BACK TO ELISHA

Basic prophecy then, is for practical building up of people. As practical as saving an axe head, or healing a sick mother-in-law, or restoring a dead child.

Like the day I told a man in a remote Indian village, in Tamil Nadu that his wife would return to him. She had left two years earlier over his infidelity. She was missing. I told him, "If you have truly repented, and if we pray right now, your wife will come back." He did, and to the amazement of the Hindu elders, she came back that very afternoon! As a result, our team were asked to share the gospel at the village square. Guess what we preached, repentance of course!

REFERENCES

Austin Sparks, T. "Prophetic Ministry." Destiny Image, 2000.
Bevere, John. "Thus Saith The Lord?" Creation House, 1999.
Clark, Jonas. "Prophetic Operations." Spirit of Life, 1996.
Denten, Kerry. "The Green Tree." Prophetic Modules, Level One. 1998.

Chapter Five
HEARING GOD'S VOICE

"Then Elisha spoke to the woman whose son he had restored to life saying, 'Arise and go, you and your household, and stay wherever you can; for the Lord has called for a famine and furthermore, it will come upon the land for seven years'." (2 Kings 8:1).

This is such powerful insight, and helpful advice coming from Elisha. This is practical revelation – stay where you can, in the knowledge that there is a seven year famine coming. Bunker down; get prepared. Elisha listened to God's voice, and brought it to the people who needed help. How did Elisha hear? How does anyone hear the voice of God? This passage does not specify, but the Old and New Testaments are full of examples of how people heard God.

There are more than 60 ways God gives guidance in the Bible. Most of them are explicitly mentioned, and many of them are ignored or poorly understood in the Church today. There is a solid focus on reading God's word, understanding dreams, and in some circles, of receiving and sharing visions and prophetic utterance, but the rich diversity of God's communication goes well beyond this.

PERCEIVING GOD

Because God is God, He speaks as He chooses, when He chooses, to whom He chooses. We do not necessarily start in the "impression" category and work our way up to open visions. People at any level of maturity can see a vision, and even the most mature saint will still receive impressions from God.

Sometimes the language of the Scripture is indistinct – it does not readily allow us to understand the mechanism by which the person is hearing God's voice. For example, Paul *"decided in the Spirit"* (Acts 19:21) but we are not told how. Some of the most important theological decisions made in the New Testament do not include the how of hearing. For example, when *"The Spirit set apart Paul and Barnabas"* (Acts 13:2) and, *"It seemed good to the Holy Spirit and also to us."* (Acts 15:28).

We must not try to categorise such events, important as they are, because God has not told us the media or the method of communication. The purpose of this chapter is to distinguish what God is communicating from that which we ourselves are inventing (with our mind or soul).

1. IMPRESSIONS

1.1 A simple impression

A simple impression can easily be mistaken for indigestion! It is a very quiet perception inside; so quiet we may not notice it, unless we know it might be God. That impression may be, "Turn left at the next intersection," or simply, "Call your wife," and it comes with an urgency or desire rising up to do something. Elijah may be referring to such a still and quiet voice in his encounter with God on the mountain, *"And after the fire came a gentle whisper, and Elijah perceived it."* (1 Kings 19:13). Impressions are fleeting; they are easily missed or written off as our imagination. I had an impression one day to drive a different way to work. I found out when I got there, that the road I would normally have used was flooded.

1.2 A strong impression

A strong impression comes as a moving of God upon our instincts, a rush of adrenaline, an impulse from the Spirit to do something. It is stronger than an impression; there is urgency, a pressing. We are not told how, but Paul and his friends were, *"Kept by the Holy Spirit from preaching the word in the province of Asia."* (Acts 16:6). One can take the blowing of the wind as a sign of its presence, though you cannot see it.[1] People born of the Spirit are like a boat pushed along by the breeze. Strong impressions are more difficult to ignore but are usually dismissed.

1.3. Compelling/ impelling

We can be outwardly compelled, or inwardly "impelled" to do something. When people speak of "being led," they are referring to the Word of the Lord impelling them to do something. *"Jesus was led by the Spirit into the wilderness."* (Mathew 4:1). Likewise, *"The two of them were sent on their way by the Holy Spirit."* (Acts 13:4). Being impelled is like having an inward pulling, as though God had put a rope through a nose ring and was leading us forward. We are urged forward, our feet walk before our mind has really connected and evaluated the situation. Jeremiah described the fire in his bones, impelling him to speak,[2] and Hosea said when the lion roared he was compelled to speak.[3]

2. CASTING LOTS

I include this for completeness. The practice of casting lots is not widely encouraged in the Bible. Of the 25 times it is referred to, only twice is it a godly thing. Only once does God command a person to cast lots.[4] The modern day equivalent would be to toss a coin. This form of guidance is fraught with danger, and the possibility of divine intervention remote. But nevertheless God used it once as a way for men to discern His instruction. There is much debate as to the way the Urim and the Thummim were used, but on occasion they

---

1. John 3:8
2. Jeremiah 20:9
3. Amos 3:8
4. Leviticus 16:8

were clearly useful in "making judgments".[5] The process of using these articles is not well understood, and speculation is not helpful.

3. CIRCUMSTANTIAL LEADING

Many people rely upon circumstances lining up to lead them. Though we may not hear God's voice in our spirit, we trust He will shape events to lead us. We rely on the fact that, *"The steps of a righteous man are ordered by the Lord."* (Psalm 37:23). The beggar who sat at the temple gate Beautiful all his life must have seen the Lord Jesus come and go on numerous occasions. One day, *"When he saw Peter and John about to enter, he asked them for money."* (Acts 3:3). This act led to his healing. I do not believe in coincidence; I believe in God's orchestration. Do remember, however, the devil can also orchestrate events, making it appear that things are lining up. Using circumstance alone to guide us is not infallible.

4. ENIGMATIC SAYINGS

4.1 Dark speech

When Aaron and Miriam were railing against their brother, the Lord defended His servant, saying He spoke with Moses face to face as a friend. Conversely, He spoke to the prophets, *"In dreams, in visions, and dark sayings."* (Numbers 12:6). This is otherwise translated dark speech or mysteries. *"It is the glory of God to conceal things, but the glory of kings is to search things out."* (Proverbs 25:2). There have been many times the Lord has dropped just one word into my heart. At other times I have received a phrase used in the military, such as "lock and load" and I have had to search out its meaning.

---

5. Exodus 28:30

4.2 Parables

To have seen Jesus was to have seen the Father, and to have heard Jesus was to have heard God. A parable is a kind of mystery. Jesus made extensive use of parables in His teaching style. *"I will open my mouth in a parable; I will utter dark sayings of old."* (Psalm 78:2). Samson used a parable to fool his detractors. Parables are given so that those who have no particular interest to learn will walk away, *"To you it has been given to know the mystery of the kingdom of God; but to those who are outside, all things come in parables, so that, 'Seeing they may see and not perceive, and hearing they may hear and not understand'."* (Mark 4:11,12).

4.3 Word plays

There are several times in Scripture in which the Lord uses a word play. For example, He says, " *'Jeremiah, what do you see?' And I said, 'I see a branch of an almond tree.' Then the LORD said to me, 'You have seen well, for I am ready to perform My word'."* (Jeremiah 1:11,12). Jeremiah says he sees an almond branch (*shaqed*) and God says He is ready to perform (*shaqad*) His will. These two words are pronounced the same way. A modern day example would be for God to say, "What do you see," and for you to reply, "I see a watch," to which God would say, "You have seen well for I am watching over my word."

4.4 His disguised voice

God sometimes disguises His voice, by speaking to us through another person. God particularly rejoices in using unsaved or unsanctified people. Hollywood (at times) speaks the word of the Lord loudly. Movies like Braveheart, or the Matrix spoke to the Church strongly. God called the king of Babylon "My servant" (Jeremiah 27:6). Pilate's wife rebuked him after having a vexing dream about Jesus [6] and King Abimelech rebuked Abraham for deceiving him.[7]

---

6. Mathew 27:19   7. Genesis 20:3-9

In modern times we must be prepared to hear the Lord speaking through a boss, co-worker or political leader – even when they might not be aware of it themselves.

5. CONFIRMING SIGNS

God can respond to a request for confirming signs. Gideon was fearful, though he heard God clearly and was visited by an angel. He asked for signs to confirm God's will.[8] Today we refer to this as "putting out a fleece". My wife and I have had to rely upon this method on two occasions, when our emotions clouded our ability to hear or think clearly on the issue of moving house.

We must take care not to fall into the realm of testing God. The Bible teaches us, *"Do not put the LORD your God to the test, as you tested him at Massah."* (Deuteronomy 6:16). Massah was the place Israel demanded a miracle from God to bring forth water. Nevertheless, God is not threatened by our honest, searching, heart-felt questions.

6. CREATIVE ARTS

6.1 Interpreted musical prophecy

God speaks through music. Somehow music taps straight into our spirit, and speaks directly (and often wordlessly) to our heart. *"You will sing as on the night you celebrate a holy festival; your hearts will rejoice as when people go up with flutes to the mountain of the LORD, to the Rock of Israel. The LORD will cause men to hear His majestic voice and will make them see His arm coming down."* (Isaiah 30: 29-30). God can speak to us through music. Sound and light are on the same electro-magnetic spectrum – it is possible to "see" pictures created in music.

The Psalms were written to be sung to music. In them, we often come across the untranslatable Hebrew word, *"selah."* There are all sorts of opinions about the significance of selah. Ray Hughes has suggested, it was a musical interlude in the Psalm.[9] It was the 'space' God used to turn the heart of the musicians and the writer to Himself, the phrase or pause in which He ministered.

6.2 Prophetic dance and drama

On several occasions in the Bible we see people expressing their gratitude, understanding, or praise to God through dance. Moses, Miriam and David danced. We are told that the Lord rejoices over His works, *"May the glory of the LORD endure forever; may the LORD rejoice in his works, who looks on the earth and it trembles."* (Psalm 104:31,32). The word used for rejoice (*samach*) literally means to be gleesome, glad, merry and spin like a top. In modern times, dance has been renewed as a form of bringing God's instruction and celebration to the people. Dance and drama are valid forms of expression, and God uses them to speak to people.

6.3 The song of the Lord

Spontaneous prophetic song is another way God speaks to us, or through us to others. We may have a sense of music playing in our inner ear. We are hearing, or seeing the notes in a melody. The Lord releases songs through which He communicates. A song may be used as a vehicle for salvation, deliverance or healing. David understood the power of music and prophecy, *"Moreover, David and the captains of the host separated for service, the sons of Asaph, and of Heman, and of Jeduthun, who should **prophesy** with harps, with psalteries, and with cymbals."* (1 Chronicles 25:1 KJV emphasis mine).

---

8. Judges 6:37   9. "Selah." Audio Message, The Minstrel Series.

7. DREAMS

7.1 Normal Dreams

If dreams were removed from the Bible, more than half of its significant turning points would be removed, and nearly a third of its revelations. God speaks through dreams. In Genesis 40:5, the butler and baker had a normal dream in jail. These sort of dreams are allegorical, mysterious and usually contain type or symbol.

Dreams must be interpreted because they come shrouded in a language hard to understand. People say that God does not speak to them, but ask if they dream and invariably the answer is, "Sometimes." Secular research shows that we actually dream almost every night, though we may not recall them when we wake up. Dreaming occurs during "beta" sleep If we do not reach the "beta sleep" stage, we do not feel rested the following day. Anyone who has slept properly will have dreamed, even if they do not remember it.

Writing the dream down immediately after we wake up is helpful, both in remembering and in interpreting dreams. Over time we will develop an understanding of God's "dream language" for us. Symbols, types and parables become familiar as we learn to understand our own dreamscape. There are a number of good types and symbols books available on the market to assist new dream interpreters.

7.2 Second heaven dreams

When people start hearing God, they very often have a particular type of dream, referred to as second heaven revelation. This is, seeing into the realm of the air (second heaven). The dreamer may see elements of the enemy's plans, purposes and strategy – like Elisha seeing into the planning chamber. [10]

---

10. 2 Kings 6:8-20

The colours are often stark, black and white or sepia. There may be a foreboding sense of terror or excessive violence. We may mistake them for nightmares, but they are not. King Nebuchadnezzar of Babylon described his reaction to a dream given by God this way, *"The dream frightened me... the visions of my head sore terrified me."* (Daniel 4:5). God may allow the person to see what the enemy has in mind. The dream is often symbolic and allegorical, needing prayer to comprehend its meaning, such as the king of Babylon looking to the wise men and prophets to interpret his dream,[11] or Pharaoh calling upon Joseph.[12]

7.3 Third heaven dreams

Once exposed to the heavenly realm, a person may experience another type of dream referred to as a third heaven revelation. This is seeing into the lower realms of heaven. There is substantially more clarity, the colours are divine, and there is full emotion, sight, smell and almost sensory overload. There is far less mystery and symbolism. However such dreams also overload or overwhelm our human frame – and can bring a sense of terror. Job testified, *"When I think my bed will comfort me and my couch will ease my complaint, even then you frighten me with dreams and terrify me with visions."* (Job 7:13). Daniel declared, after having such a dream, *"My spirit was sore troubled within me."* (Daniel 7:15). It is not easy for human beings to experience heaven before we have received our new bodies!

7.4 Dream in a dream

Whilst there are no examples in the Bible, scientific and psychological research shows us there is another form: having a dream inside a dream. A person dreams that he is having a dream, and the "inside dream" is often less cryptic and more realistic. This kind of dream is rare. It would be hard to emulate, or to make up

---

11. Daniel chapter 2   12. Genesis 41:15,16

with the carnal mind. Job tells us, *"God does speak—now one way, now another—though man may not perceive it. In a dream, in a vision of the night, when deep sleep falls on men as they slumber in their beds, he may speak in their ears."* (Job 33:14,15). You will know you have had one if you wake up from a dream, **then** wake up from a dream! Usually physical healing, prophetic guidance, a visitation from God, strengthening, encouragement, or a revelation occurs in the inner dream.

In one such dream I had, I was given the keys to understand the outer dream – in the inner dream. When I woke from the outer dream, I was able to understand it – because of the second dream inside it!

8. WORDS

8.1 A word from Scripture
Logos is the Greek word for the revealed word of God, and for written or scribed truth. God uses His word as a primary way of communicating His will to us. *"Indeed, the word of God is living and active."* (Hebrews 4:12). It is useful for every good thing, *"All scripture is inspired by God and is useful for teaching, for reproof, for correction, and for training in righteousness."* (2 Timothy 3:16). So the word of God is a primary way by which God speaks to us, and all other prophecy must be in line with the teaching of scripture.

8.2 A spoken word
Rhema is the Greek word meaning: an utterance, narration, counsel or command. The Hebrew equivalent is *daubah*. It can be the quickening of Scripture to us, or hearing His counsel according to the light of Scripture. Daniel was reading scripture when suddenly he, *"Understood from the Scriptures, according to the word of the LORD given to Jeremiah the prophet."* (Daniel 9:2).

He had *rhema*. For the first time he understood the timing of Jeremiah's prophecy, was given the counsel of God on the matter and was led to pray and fast. David said God's spoken counsel (*daubah*: word) was a lamp unto his feet. [13]

8.3 An understanding of seasons

Kairos is the Greek word for season. The Hebrew equivalent is *zeman*: a time for everything under the sun. Solomon said, *"For everything there is a season, and a time for every matter under heaven."* (Ecclesiates 3:1). I Chronicles 12:32 tells us, *"The offspring of Issachar, [were] those who had understanding of the times, to know what Israel ought to do."* [14] We will examine this further in chapter 29. They knew what God's heartbeat was for the country, when to move forward and when to retreat Knowing the season of God, sensing the time of His visitation, knowing when He is prevalent to succeed in a venture is vital for prophetic people.

9. MEMORIES

Jesus spoke of the Holy Spirit "bringing to remembrance" all the things we would need to say when under pressure. [15] The process described in the passage says first, *"The Holy Spirit will teach us"* and then *"He will remind us."* The original language implies that God will remind quietly, gently suggest to the memory, put in mind and keep bringing up. We cannot rightly remember if we have not first heard a matter. This is another way the Lord speaks. Be aware of memories which suddenly pop up unprompted – they may well be of the Lord. If you have no other reasonable reason for remembering a matter, it could be the Spirit prompting you.

---

13. Psalm 119:105   14. Mathew 16:3
15. John 14:26

Our minds have three levels at which they operate:
- The unconscious – physiological, biological operations;
- The subconscious – memories, feelings, emotions;
- The conscious – awake and alert, aware thought.

This process is one of the Lord bringing our memories up from the subconscious into our conscious mind. Job 33:14-18 puts it beautifully. God trys to speak to people in one way, and in another way. He tries to drop things to our conscious mind, but is often forced to speak to us while we sleep. This conscious/sub-conscious dynamic is played out in the difference between memories, dreams, visions and daydreams.

10. JOURNALLING

The practice of writing down what we believe God is saying to us often sparks a dialogue with God and inspiration starts to flow. Diarising, journalling or writing may catalyse a prophetic flow or discussion. There are several instances in Scripture where someone was told to, "Write it down, and make it plain" in the Bible. Journalling is a valid practise for receiving God's guidance. Habakkuk shows us the process in Chapter 2:1,2:

I will stand on my watch post – find a quiet place to hear God;
I will keep watch and see – be expectant for God to speak;
Record the vision – write it down in a journal or diary.

11. TONGUES

Speaking in tongues is a contentious issue in the Church. But, tongues are mentioned as part of Christian life in the New Testament. It is the author's belief that they still exist today, along with the gift of prophecy!

11.1 Tongues interpreted

Tongues alone do not constitute hearing God's voice. But with interpretation, tongues can communicate a distinct message to the local church. We are told that, *"A man edifies himself"* (1 Corinthians 14:4), or builds up his spirit through a private prayer language. Ordinarily tongues are a private matter between us and God, but on occasion the Lord prompts us to speak it out loud.

Paul distinguishes interpreted tongues from ordinary prophecy as another way the Lord can speak. Paul counsels us, *"If anyone speaks in a tongue, two—or at the most three—should speak, one at a time, and someone must interpret. If there is no interpreter, the speaker should keep quiet in the church and speak to himself and God."* Sometimes He will give the interpretation to the one who spoke in tongues, sometimes it is given to another person. [16] This process may involve two people and therefore the prophetic word has a higher risk of being warped or distorted in the process.

11.2 Tongues (foreign language)

Occasionally, someone supernaturally speaks in a foreign language – a language not acquired through natural learning or education – and is understood. This happened on the day of Pentecost in Acts 2:4-7. Inwardly, the people receiving this revelation may not know they are speaking an actual language. They may simply feel the flow of the Spirit through them as they speak. The hearers (on that day) exclaimed, *"These men are praising God,"* (Acts 2:11) and they brought a testimony of Christ – which is one of the defining characteristics of prophecy. [17]

---

16. 1 Corinthians 12:10   17. Revelation 19:10

12. PROPHECY

12.1 Spontaneous prophecy

This form of prophecy bubbles up from the spirit of a person. The Hebrew word *naba* describes a kind of prophetic utterance that springs forth spontaneously by inspiration. It is, therefore, critical to allow it to manifest spontaneously. Such words often come during worship, prayer, and intercession times. An example of this is in 1 Samuel 10:6, *"The Spirit of the LORD will come upon you in power, and you will prophesy with them."* Saul prophesied spontaneously when the Spirit came upon him – or moved him immediately to speak. The Hebrew word used for the satanic or false prophecy is *ziyd,* meaning to boil up. True prophecy bubbles up and gushes out; false prophecy boils up inside and is "cooked up"!

12.2 Gradual prophecy

This form of prophecy distills gradually in your spirit. The Hebrew word *nataph* means a forming, developing word, like ruminating on food. This form of prophetic utterance is slow to develop and comes like the dawn. It is possible to write such inspiration down and deliver it. An example of this is found in Job, *"After I had spoken, they spoke no more; my utterance fell gently on their ears."* (Job 29:22). As he spoke, they had unfolding revelation or understanding of God's word to them.

13. ORACLES

13.1 Visual oracles

This form of prophecy comes in a visual fashion. The Hebrew word *massa'* relates to declaring an oracle that comes by vision. *"The oracle concerning the valley of vision."* (Isaiah 22:1). It relates to an inspired, non-premeditated utterance. Spontaneity is critical. It may be given voice as a song. Isaiah tells of the way a vision is told to him, *"The oracle concerning the wilderness of the sea. As whirlwinds in the Negeb sweep on, it comes from the desert, from a terrible land. A stern **vision** is told to me."* (Isaiah 21:1 emphasis mine).

13.2 Auditory oracles

This form of prophecy comes in an auditory fashion. The Hebrew word *ne'um* refers to the process of **hearing,** then speaking an oracle. This form of prophecy almost always comes as a spoken word. *"The oracle of one who hears the words of God,"* (Numbers 24:4) is an auditory oracle. *"Now these are the last words of David: The oracle of David... The spirit of the LORD speaks through me, His word is upon my tongue."* (2 Samuel 23:1). David could say that, *"My tongue is the pen of a ready writer,"* (Psalm 45:1) that what he sang or spoke was the Lord's pen, used to write the word of God.

14. VISIONS

14.1 Ordinary vision

The most basic form of vision is seen within the human spirit. The Hebrew word *chazah* means: to perceive or envision. It is to gaze at or perceive prophetically, to have a vision of something in our spirit. *"Isaiah son of Amoz saw concerning Judah and Jerusalem."* (Isaiah 2:1). David had this kind of experience on several occasions, *"In righteousness I will see your face; when I awake, I will be satisfied with seeing your likeness."* (Psalm 17:15). *Chezev* is the Chaldean equivalent to this (Daniel 2:19), meaning a sight or insight into the spiritual realm.

14.2 Gazing vision

The Hebrew word *ra'ah* is often used simply to mean "gaze" in an ordinary sense. In some cases, however, this Hebrew word is used to describe an appearance by revelatory discernment (like seeing an angel).

seeing an angel). It is spiritual gazing – seeing into the spirit realm. The person perceiving will usually be present in the vision, in other words you will be looking in at yourself: *"In the vision I was looking and saw myself in Susa the capital."* (Daniel 8:2). *"The glory of the God of Israel was there, like the vision that I had seen in the valley."* (Ezekiel 8:4).

14.3 Day vision

The Hebrew word *chaza'* means to mentally dream while awake, to gaze spiritually, in your subconscious, while you are awake. This is having a day vision. They are easily confused with "day dreams", images cast upon the mind by our own imagination. In a day vision we are conscious but in a dream-like state having a vision. We often look, or watch in the vision we are having, *"You were looking, O king, and lo! there was a great statue."* (Daniel 2:31). This is Daniel, seeing the king, seeing himself.

It also means to wake up, and gaze upon something. *"Immediately the fingers of a human hand appeared and began writing on the plaster of the wall of the royal palace, next to the lampstand. The king was watching the hand as it wrote."* (Daniel 5:5). The king perceived while he was awake, but he was in a drunken stupor.

14.4 Night vision

The Hebrew word *chizzayown* means a revelation, a dream-vision, or a vision of the night. There is a condition, half way between waking and sleeping, when the conscious mind has not quite been stirred. In that place we may have revelation. It usually occurs at night or early in the morning. The vision Nathan had, which brought correction to David, was such an experience: *"But that same night the word of the LORD came to Nathan... In accordance with all these words and with all this vision, Nathan spoke to David."*

(2 Samuel 7:4 and 17). Job also speaks of having such visions: *"They will fly away like a dream, and not be found; they will be chased away like a vision of the night."* (Job 20:8).

14.5 Abstract vision

The Bible only once uses the term *ro'eh* or abstract vision as it specifically relates to the experience of revelation. Such a vision may be obscure in meaning and highly symbolic. The only reference we have is in Isaiah 28:7. The abstract vision is compared to being drunk or hallucinating. Such an abstract vision blurs the line between dreams and visions. Alcohol, drugs, food and lack of sleep can often contribute to such "revelation", which should thus be ignored.

14.6 Open vision

The Hebrew word *machazeh* means a spiritual sight with the eyes wide open or uncovered. Abraham had such a vision of the Lord. [18] *"One who hears the words of God, who sees the vision of the Almighty, who falls down, but with eyes uncovered."* (Numbers 24:4). The eyes of the physical body see into the realm of the spirit, as Elisha's servant did on the day he saw the chariots of fire. [19] The vision itself is external to the person, not simply experienced within our spirit. People describe this as a kind of panoramic or movie style vision. A movie screen opens up before our eyes and we observe it. On the occasions I have had such visions, I have been able to see and respond to the physical world without interupting the vision at all.

14.7 Looking glass vision

The Hebrew word *mar'ah* was commonly used for a mirror or looking glass. But in some contexts, it related specifically to seeing something no one else sees. It is obtaining a reflection in the spirit, or discerning a presence when everyone else is oblivious.

---

18. Genesis 15:1   19. 2 Kings 6:17

"As I was among the exiles by the river Chebar, the heavens were opened, and I saw visions of God." (Ezekiel 1:1). *"I, Daniel, alone saw the vision; the people who were with me did not see the vision, though a great trembling fell upon them."* (Daniel 10:7).

One day during a worship service in Sydney, I was singing with my eyes open. My vision flickered and the whole scene switched to photographic negative. I shook my head, thinking there was something wrong with me, and then noticed an angel standing behind the pastor. I do not think anyone else saw him. For the church at the time, was a good sign, but the message the pastor spoke was clearly underlined by the presence of that angel!

14.8 Book vision

The Hebrew word *chazuwth* relates to the signing of a pact, making an agreement, or writing a book. In the context of certain passages it is takes the meaning of seeing a book. It calls atention to the striking appearance of a document, *"The vision of all this has become for you like the words of a sealed document. If it is given to those who can read, with the command, 'Read this,' they say, 'We cannot, for it is sealed'."* (Isaiah 29:11).

Our lives and all we do are recorded in the books of life [20] and these will be opened at the judgement day. We may be given revelatory knowledge, by being allowed to read these books of life. I have experienced this on several occasions while ministering in a congregation. I have been permitted to see a person's book, and read from selected chapters, or certain pages. This gives me information about the person's past (facts and details) and enables me to unlock a situation in their present.

---

20. Daniel 7:10

14.9 Countenance vision

The Hebrew word *mar'eh* usually means "sight" or "to see." But in the context of revelation it means to see countenance. Have you ever looked at someone, and thought for a moment she was someone else? For a moment the person had the countenance or look of another person. You were reminded of some aspect of another person. Such an experience is a countenance vision. This will often unlock information to you about the person you are looking at physically. Ezekiel was standing by the river Chebar, and he saw the Lord, like a mighty river. His glory sounded like mighty waters and His glory flowed all about. *"This was like the vision that I had seen by the river Chebar; and I fell upon my face."* (Ezekiel 43:3). Very often we need help to understand or interpret the connection.[21]

14.10 Expansive vision

Large, unfolding, expansive, ongoing visions are referred to as *chazown* visions. They are very long and large, encompassing and complex. Isaiah had such a vision, describing the life of Hezekiah, mentioned in 2 Chronicles 32:32. They may involve a full range of senses which result in a vision or view, an outlook or understanding. Daniel, after having many revelations and visions, was told, *"The vision of the evenings and the mornings that has been told is true. As for you, seal up the vision, for it refers to many days from now."* (Daniel 8:26).

The Revelation given to John, was such a vision. He was also told not to write down certain "chapters" of the information he was given. James Ryle's three part vision of the "Sons of Thunder" was such a revelation, as was Rick Joyner's "The Final Quest".

---

21. Daniel 8:16

14.11 Visions in a dream
Jacob, *"Had a dream in which he saw a stairway resting on the earth, with its top reaching to heaven, and the angels of God were ascending and descending on it."* (Genesis 28:12). He had a vision in a dream. Just as we can have a dream in a dream, we can have a vision, an open vision or a night vision in a dream. We can have any of the above forms of vision in a dream!

I used to lead worship at a regular Friday night gathering in Sydney. One evening three witches attended the meeting, and proceeded to curse the leaders. I suffered a stinging, itchy rash all over my body for ten days. It started at 9pm and departed at 9am everyday. No amount of faith, prayer or anointing with oil would heal me. Then one night I had a dream. I was standing on the stage at the Friday gathering, and in the dream I had an open vision. In that vision, I saw these three ladies, and where they each lived. I came out of the vision, and in the dream told them, "I know where you live, your power is broken." When I woke up, I was completely healed!

15. WORDS

15.1 Word of knowledge
A word of knowledge (*gnosis*) comes by revelation direct to the spirit of man. It is a piece of information, a divine sliver of knowledge, a token given to us about something or someone else. We have no natural way of knowing that information. It is usually very specific, relating to a person's past or present. Knowledge relates to what and who rather than how or why. The Bible distinguishes word of knowledge from other forms of revelation.[22] A word of knowledge is rarely just one word however! It may be a sentence, an impression or a visual cue. One day I was ministering to a lady in Johannesburg, with Kylie Fogarty, a co-worker. We had come to a lull in the session when

---
22. 1 Corinthians 12:8

an unusual Afrikaner name dropped into my mind (a name I was not familiar with). I pronounced it how I heard it, and she looked stunned. "I haven't seen him for years! That man was my pastor ten years ago." It was a word of knowledge.

15.2 Word of wisdom

A word of wisdom (*sophia*) is also a divine piece of information that can not be gained by natural means. Wisdom is applied knowledge. Wisdom relates to how or why rather than who or what. It is wisdom given for a circumstance or situation. It may involve righteous judgement or discernment. It may be an instruction, direction or piece of advice given by God. A pastor, counsellor or psychologist often receives such wisdom in order to help a person unlock the past, or obtain healing in their present situation.

16. SPIRIT TO SPIRIT

Psychics and telepaths develop the ability to communicate spiritually, apart from God. The English word psyche comes from the Greek word *psuche* – which is the soul. Psychics operate in the realm of the soul. They obtain valid (meaning accurate) information from the spirit world by invalid (illegal) means. But God is not their source and we are forbidden to operate like psychics! We are to communicate from our human spirit to God's Spirit within us.

Paul makes it clear that the carnal mind cannot understand the hidden things of God. The Spirit of God searches the things of God and communicates them to the spirit of man. *"These things God has revealed to us through the Spirit; for the Spirit searches everything, even the depths of God. For what human being knows what is truly human except the human spirit that is within? So also no one comprehends what is truly God's except the Spirit of God."* (1 Corinthians 2:10,11).

17. GOD'S REASSURING PRESENCE

God can communicate an enormous amount just by giving us a reassurance of His nearness to us. He can communicate His love through an experience of His presence. Paul knew this comfort in prison, *"The following night the Lord stood near Paul and said, 'Take courage!'"* (Acts 23:11).

Such a feeling brings a calming effect, immediate assurance and peace. This presence, this spiritual act of touch, brought me very great peace one day. I had been misunderstood and devalued in a relationship, I felt tossed aside. I went into a forest to be alone, and sat by a stream weeping. There, instead of giving me "revelation", God touched me, reassuring me of His love. Hundreds of things were non-verbally communicated to me. I felt much better. This experience of God isn't the same as seeing the form of God, or an event when God steps physically into time and space.

18. WRITING ON THE WALL

When spiritual beings enter physical time and space, dynamic things happen. An angel visited Gideon, making the sacrifice burst into flame and be consumed.[23] These supernatural occurrences fall into the category of "writing on the wall". God manifesting His communication physically, *"Suddenly the fingers of a human hand appeared and wrote on the plaster of the wall, near the lampstand in the royal palace. The king watched the hand as it wrote."* (Daniel 5:5). The hand wrote a message to the inebriated king and his followers. God was about to end that reign! The Christians in Jerusalem in AD 69 saw the writing in the sky warning them to leave. More on that in chapter 11.

---

23. Judges 6:21

19. NATURE'S VOICE

19.1 Nature speaks

God declares His majesty, beauty and power through creation, *"The heavens declare the glory of God; the skies proclaim the work of His hands. Day after day they pour forth speech; night after night they display knowledge."* (Psalm 19:1,2). Job goes further with this thought: *"Ask the animals, and they will teach you, or the birds of the air, and they will tell you;... or let the fish of the sea inform you."* (Job 12:7-9).

Animals do not ordinarily speak. What Job and the Psalmist point to, are the truths animals communicate about God in other ways. King Solomon, for example, could point to the behaviour of ants as a lesson in being prepared.[24] The animal kingdom and nature itself speaks and instructs us. It leaves all of humanity without excuse.[25]

19.2 Animate objects

The donkey spoke to Balaam,[26] which is very different from the comments made by Job about the fish and animals teaching us. In the case of Job, the animal kingdom communicates truths about God to us. We do not know if Balaam was like the "Dr. Dolittle" of his day, understanding what the animal said; or whether the Lord caused the donkey to speak Aramaic. Either way, an animal spoke something from God and it was clearly understood. There are numerous stories of dogs alerting others to the injury of a loved one, or of animals seeming to communicate in a human way.

---

24. Proverbs 6:6   25. Romans 1:20
26. Numbers 22:28

19.3 Inanimate objects

Animists believe that plants, animals and non-living objects have souls, emotions, and even a collective consciousness – this is not a Biblical view. However, there are a number of references to God speaking through His inanimate creation. Moses heard when, *"God spoke from within the bush,"* (Exodus 3:4). Jesus stated that, *"If the children keep quiet, the stones will cry out."* (Luke 19:40). So God can speak through inanimate objects as well.

20. ANGELIC VISITATIONS

20.1 Angelic visitation in a dream

Angels can visit us in many ways. Amongst other duties, they can bring encouragement, instruction, direction or warning. For example, *"After [Joseph] had considered this, an angel of the Lord appeared to him in a dream."* (Mathew. 1:20). An angelic visitation in a dream can be very real. An angel convinced Joseph not to believe his common sense, but marry Mary.

Jacob met an angel of the Lord in a dream and wrestled with him until dawn. [27] That wrestling caused his hip to be displaced!

20.2 Angelic visitation in a vision

Angels may appear and deliver their message in vision. They may appear with wings, or in the form of a man. No matter which way the angel appears, the viewer knows they are seeing one! [28] Peter, *"At three in the afternoon had a vision. He distinctly saw an angel of God, who came to him."* (Acts 10:3). David looked up and saw in a vision the angel standing between earth and heaven. [29] Though it was a vision, that angel carried a deadly weapon he was about to use, to destroy many in Israel.

---

27. Genesis chapter 32
28. Zechariah chapter 1
29. 1 Chronicles 21:1

20.3 Angelic visitation physically

Jacob met angels at Mahanaim.[30] Gideon physically met an angel under a tree, *"The angel of the LORD came and sat down under the oak in Ophrah... where Gideon was."* (Judges 6:11). Angels visiting in physical form often appear as men. Gideon's angel caused the offering to be consumed with real fire, and only then did he realise it was an angel! The New Testament warns, *"Do not neglect to show hospitality to strangers, for by doing that some have entertained angels without knowing it."* (Hebrews 13:2).

21. A VISITATION FROM GOD

A person may have a visitation from God, which is more than a reassuring touch from God. This experience is usually marked by being allowed to see God. We are told that, "No man shall see God and live," (Samuel 6:20) for our flesh would flee (being sinful) before a holy God. In vision or dream, however, we may see the Lord's form and live. (1 Samuel 6:20). Micaiah saw the Lord in a vision[31] and Isaiah saw the Lord on His throne.[32] God may visit us at night, *"One night the Lord spoke to Paul in a vision."* (Acts 18:9). When God visits, rather than only speaking to our spirit, the impact of the message He brings is usually great. In Isaiah's case, he was commissioned for ministry. In Paul's case, he received a promise that no one in that city would hurt him.

22. BEING TAKEN UP

22.1 In the Spirit

John uses interesting wording in Revelation to describe his experience. He says, *"On the Lord's Day I was in the Spirit."* (Revelation 1:10). His wording is identical to Paul's in his letter to the Ephesian church, *"Pray in the Spirit."* (Ephesians 6:18).

---

30. Genesis 32:1   31. 1 Kings 22:19
32. Isaiah 6:1

John repeats this phrase saying, *"Instantly I was in the Spirit,"* (Revelation 4:2) and talks of being, *"Carried away in the Spirit."* (Revelation 17:3 and 21:10). His spirit is alive and he is more aware of the spirit realm than the earthly realm. Reading the diary of Jeanne Guyon or David Brainerd will give ample modern day examples.

22.3 Trance

The Bible owned trances long before New Agers grasped the concept, way before hallucinogens were discovered. A trance may be induced by drugs or false worship of demonic gods, but may also be induced by the Spirit of God. Those who worshipped Baal worked themselves up into a trance-like state and cut themselves with knives.[33] Christians should never try to "work up" a trance; nor should we practice Eastern methods of relaxation and emptying the mind to go into a trance-like state. Peter, *"Was praying at the temple, and fell into a trance and saw the Lord speaking."* (Acts 22:17 c.f. Acts 10:10).

The word he used here is *ekstasis*, which according to W.E. Vine means, *"A condition in which ordinary consciousness and perception of the natural is withheld, and the soul becomes susceptible only to visions imparted by God."* It is a literal displacement of the mind. We lose our ordinary faculties during the period of the trance, but do not leave the body.

It is a state we can snap out of at any point, by the exercise of our will. One day I was caught into a trance at the dinner table. My wife was unaware that I was "somewhere else" though I could see her, and experience the trance at the same time. She called my name, strongly, and I chose to "snap out of it". Then I wrote down what I saw. Interestingly enough, I could not "return" to the trance.

---

33. 1 Kings 18:28,29

22.4 Out of Body

The Bible mentions "out of body" experiences on several occasions. There are two terms used for it. Paul refers to being out of the body [34] where he "was caught up to the third heaven". He uses the word *harpazo*, meaning to seize, catch away, pluck up, pull out or take by force. He heard inexpressible things; things that man is not permitted to tell.

Ezekiel had a similar experience, *"The hand of the LORD was upon me, and carried me out in the Spirit of the LORD, and set me down in the midst of the valley."* (Ezekiel 37:1 KJV). The Old Testament equivalent is *yatsa'*, meaning to force out, break out, carry away, extricate. The defining characteristic is translocation. We are physically, or temporally present in another place.

23. AUDIBLE VOICE

23.1 Thunder

Sometimes God speaks with a sound like thunder. He roars from heaven, and it sounds like thunder or trumpeting in the natural realm. No one present will deny that He has spoken, but no words are understood. *"The crowd standing there heard it and said that it was thunder. Others said, 'An angel has spoken to him'."* (John 12:29 NRSV).

The effect may be fear, awe and surrender, but usually not frivolity or fun. *"The LORD thundered from heaven; the voice of the Most High resounded."* (2 Samuel 22:14). It sounds just like thunder and it may have physical repercussions. In 1 Samuel 7:10 we read, *"But that day the LORD thundered with loud thunder against the Philistines."* The enemy was totally defeated!

---

34. 2 Corinthians 12:2

23.2 Voice like many waters

Have you ever stood right beside a waterfall as it roared into a canyon or riverbed? Or heard a screaming jet as it took off? This is not background noise – it's in your face, overwhelming white noise! This is like the audible voice of God – but its wavelength is jammed somewhere between thunder and the intelligible-audible voice of God. John heard the Lord speaking in this way – and there were distinct words, *"Like many waters."* (Revelation 14:2). John was able to communicate what he heard in the waters.

23.3 Intelligible-audible voice

The Lord can speak directly, physically, and audibly to one or more people simultaneously. *"And a voice from heaven said, 'This is my Son, whom I love; with Him I am well pleased'."* (Mathew 3:17). Some will hear and understand, whilst others will not – as with Saul on the road to Damascus.[35]

24. GOD COMES DOWN

When God Himself steps down and enters the realm of human life the phenomenon goes beyond sensation or a brief visual encounter. Mountains melt like wax,[36] thunderstorms arise,[37] the temple fills with smoke,[38] or the place is set on fire! *"The LORD descended to the top of Mount Sinai,"* (Exodus 19:20) and Mount Sinai was covered with smoke, because the LORD descended on it in fire!

It was God's intention to speak to the people from this state, but they would not have it. It was man, not God, who withdrew from intimacy and communication with God. *"When all the people*

---

35. Acts 9:7
37. 2 Samuel 22:10
36. Psalm 97:5
38. 1 Kings 8:10

witnessed the thunder and lightning, the sound of the trumpet, and the mountain smoking, they were afraid and trembled and stood at a distance, and said to Moses, 'You speak to us, and we will listen; but do not let God speak to us, or we will die.' Moses said to the people, 'Do not be afraid; for God has come only to test you and to put the fear of Him upon you so that you do not sin.' Then the people stood at a distance, while Moses drew near to the thick darkness where God was." (Exodus 20:18-21).

CONCLUSION

What a diverse range of ways our God speaks! Impressions, dreams, visions, angels, a voice like thunder... and many other ways. It takes time to recognise God's voice, and distinguish it from others, but once we do, another important element is also needed – confidence.

We might find ourselves walking into a room, when the hair on our arm stands up; or we get a shiver down our spine. How can we tell if this is the Spirit, or if it is a demonic presence. That takes the gift of discernment, which we will look at in chapter 18.

We may have a strong impression that someone is in sin, or needs our help. But if we lack the confidence to act on that impression, nothing will happen. Confidence takes time to build up. We need a track record of successes, to help us be sure we heard from God.

I would caution not to take things too seriously at first. Our ability to hear God is often flawed by sin, skewed by desire or clouded by ambition. We may be asking God about a certain decision and receive several Scripture verses during prayer.

I would caution not to take things too seriously at first. Our ability to hear God is often flawed by sin, skewed by desire or clouded by ambition. We may be asking God about a certain decision and receive several Scripture verses during prayer. We might be tempted to work hard to make them "line up" as direction from God.

I knew a woman once, whose faith in God was deeply shaken because she got one detail of a prophetic word incorrect. The majority of it was right, but the sex of a child was wrong. She said, "All of it was God, it was all the same voice. If I got that detail wrong, then the voice I heard was not God. And if that was not God... then I never have heard from Him at all!"

Don't throw it all away because of error. Things can creep in along the way (more on that in chapter 22). Just keep trying, keep listening, keep writing and grow in your confidence to hear His voice!

REFERENCES

Goll, Jim W. "The Seer." Destiny Image, 2004.
Guyon, Jeanne. "An Autobiography." Whittaker House, 1997.
Howard, Phillip E. "The Life & Diary of David Brainerd." Baker Bookhouse, 1992.
Hughes, Ray. "The Minstrel Series." Audio Tape 7. EagleStar Publishing, 2000.
Jackson, John Paul. "Dreams Part I." Article, Streams of Shiloh, 1994.
Ryle, James. "A Dream Come True." Sovereign, 1999.
Virkler, Mark. "Dialogue with God." Peacemakers. 1985.

Chapter Six
WEIGHING & TESTING PROPHECY

"A letter came to [Jehoram] from the prophet Elijah, saying: "Thus says the LORD, the God of your father David: Because you have not walked in the ways of your father Jehoshaphat... the LORD will bring a great plague on your people, your children, your wives, and all your possessions."
(2 Chronicles 21:12-14 NRSV).

Joram is the king of Israel, Jehoram son of Jehoshaphat is the king of Judah, and Hazael is on the throne in Syria. Elisha has an active prophetic ministry to all three of these kings, and has helped them in battle against the Edomites and Moabites. Six to ten years after Elijah's death, a letter arrived from Elijah to the king in Judah! Not just any letter, it is a letter written in the days when his father Jehoshaphat was still on the throne. Jehoram may have known Elijah. He was certainly familiar with the devastating effects of "crossing" the prophets – having witnessed the fire from heaven on the captains of his father's forces. Now he is on the throne and a strong word comes against him from the grave! How does one weigh and test a word that finds life even after the speaker is gone?

Jehoram was not a particularly godly man. He had killed his six brothers and a number of other relatives in a spate of paranoid psychosis. He was ambitious, idolatrous and disobedient to the law of God. Elijah had foreseen this, and judged Jehoram's rebellion, years before it happened. Perhaps he had observed the young man in the courts of his father? Perhaps the would-be king had crossed words with the prophet?

Clearly Elisha had no regard for him, seeming to even despise his presence (see 2 Kings 3:14). Would Jehoram's idols answer him now?

SOURCES OF REVELATION

There are three potential sources of revelatory information or guidance: God, the devil and ourselves. If we are receiving revelation, we need to know how to test what we are receiving, to see if it is from God. Satan has always tried to deceive the elect.[1] So we must weigh[2] and test[3] all revelation and the spirit behind it. There is no doubt that we are to look to God for guidance, which may well come through other people. When it does, however, we have to remember that the human vessels God uses will always be cracked. Hence, Paul said, we will always bear the stain of sin.[4] Therefore Paul said, *"Do not treat prophecies with contempt. Test everything. Hold on to the good. Avoid every kind of evil."* (1 Thessalonians 5:21,22). As John Sandford puts it, *"Chew the meat and spit the bones."* There are always going to be bones in meat – that is the way it comes, but spit out the bones; discard the evil. I am indebted to Dr John White for the following seven points:

SEVEN WAYS TO TEST REVELATION

Revelation and Scripture
We must ask if the communication squares with Scripture. That is the first base, and the most fundamental test. It must line up with, or be within the riverbed of Scripture.[5] Does it claim to add to Scripture?[6] Does it contain slander or accusation? Then we must

---

1. Mathew 24:24
2. 1 Corinthians 14:29
3. 1 John 4:1
4. 1 John 1:8
5. 2 Timothy 3:16
6. Revelation 22:18,19

disregard it. What do we do, then, when the matter is not specifically addressed by Scripture (for example smoking)? How do we test revelation which says, "Turn left at the next set of traffic lights"? For these situations we must have other tests.

Revelation and fulfillment

Suppose we receive a prophecy – perhaps an impression, or a word from the Lord. A sure sign of its veracity is its accuracy [7] – it comes to pass! Suppose it does not come to pass? The first response we have is – false prophecy! Perhaps not. The fulfillment of prophecy is contingent on our response to it – if we respond in a certain way, it will not come to pass! The Ninevites repented when warned by Jonah, and his predications did not come to pass. [8] Although this caused loss of face for the prophet, the heart of God was towards the repentant Ninevites. In exactly the same way, we can not judge prophecy we give or receive by its fulfillment alone – there are other factors at work.

For example, in 2004 I gave a prophetic word in Kitwe, Zambia about a coming mine disaster, and deaths resulting. The church repented and prayed earnestly for the disaster to be averted. In 2005 an explosion and flood took place in one of the mines, but there were no casualties. I see this as an accurate word, with an adequate response. So the word was certainly true.

Revelation and character

Sometimes a prophecy will tickle our flesh and carnality. [9] It could send us scurrying after idols, or lead us to worship or pay homage to someone other than God. [10] It might tempt us to sin and walk away from God's clear instructions in the Bible. [11] If prophecy

---

7. Deuteronomy 18:22
8. Jonah 3:4,5
9. 2 Timothy 4:3
10. Deuteronomy 18:20
11. Isaiah 28:15

does any of these things, then we must discard it out of hand! Revelation must lead us toward love. [12] It should sharpen our spirit, not lead to sluggishness. [13] It should result in exposing, not protecting sin, and drive us toward holy living. [14] It should generally encourage, edify, and comfort. [15] It should build more of the character of Jesus into us.

Revelation and fruit

Revelation never exempts the recipient or the deliverer from bearing good fruit. Revelation should always result in good fruit – the fruit of the Spirit [16] and not the works of the flesh. Does the revelation cause evil? Does it result in an heretical stance being taken by the Church? Then discard it, even if it is accurate. It must result in bringing glory to God and not ourselves. [17] We have been appointed by God to bear fruit, good fruit for the Kingdom, and any God-given revelation should move us in that direction.

Revelation and the spirit behind it

We are told to test the spirits to see if they are of God. [18] To do this, we must use the spiritual gift of discernment [19] and our own wisdom – developed over years of testing. [20] These two kinds of discernment – the spiritual and the natural – protect us from evil. We pray: "Lead us not into temptation, but deliver us from evil," which is a promise we can rely on. But He also gave us faculties of discernment, and promises to give wisdom to all who ask. [21] True revelation will testify of Jesus [22] and will result in love. Those who are spiritual discern all things. [23]

---

12. 1 Corinthians 13:2
14. Lamentations 2:14,15
16. Galatians 5:22,23
18. 1 John 4:1
20. Hebrews 5:14
22. Revelation 19:10
13. Romans 11:8
15. 1 Corinthians 14:3
17. Mathew 7:16
19. 1 Corinthians 12:10
21. James 1:5
23. 1 Corinthians 2:15

Revelation and hope

Prophecy will never result in the loss of hope. Faith, hope and love are fundamental to our relationship with God. Prophecy may indicate hard times are coming – but it will always point to God's promise in the difficulty – which leads to hope. [24] Regrettably, some prophecy gives us false hope and makes our hearts sick with waiting. [25] Jeremiah invites us to discard the false hope offered by false prophecy [26] that makes us worthless.

Revelation and authority

Donald Bridge points out, "Prophecy carries the same authority as any other Christian endeavour like leadership, counseling, teaching, preaching, and worship. If it is true, let it prove to be so." [27] Revelation must be exercised in an orderly manner – and it must not bring confusion. [28] It should not result in submission to ungodly authority, [29] and it should not create the wrong impression of leadership. It should never move into the realm of dictating – telling people what they **must** do "or else". We must not threaten or use relational violence.

GETTING STARTED

Now we are familiar with the potential for mixture and we have in place some tests, checks, and balances. How are we to make a start? If we are already hearing His voice, how are we to grow? I believe the answer lies in abiding rather than striving. We must come into a place of being able to abide in Him and hear His voice for our lives – at all times. It leads us to finding rest, not running; abiding instead of chasing; not sweating and striving, but finding Christ in everyday serenity. If we are not at rest, abiding in His life, we might bring mixture into the prophetic word.

---

24. Romans 5:3-5
25. Proverbs 13:12
26. Jeremiah 23:16
27. "Signs and Wonders Today." pg 203.
28. 1 Corinthians 14:40
29. Hebrews 13:7

If we are not at rest, abiding in His life, we might bring mixture into the prophetic word. It will be blunt instead of sharp. It will not be up to the standard to Christ. Let's look at six kinds of poor or diminished prophecy, to see what misrepresentations we may be receiving...

Classifying Prophecy

Prophecy can be essentially accurate – but badly conceived. It can be essentially inaccurate but well delivered. Or it can be both inaccurate and badly delivered! By listening to the person who is prophesying, we can discern what we are hearing.

Old prophecy
Religion is a funny thing. We become staid, and comfortable in our ways. When this happens, we can prophecy in a very well rehearsed way. There is a distinct lack of power, and a lack of the genuine ring of heaven to the timbre of the message. It may be without anointing, and as a result, the words will have no affect whatsoever on the hearers. It is usually old seed, old words with no life. It is recycled, reused, and has lost its flavour.

Weak prophecy
Sometimes the person hearing from God lacks confidence, or has only received the first few words and does not have the faith to continue as it is delivered. The result is broken, stammering or halting delivery. They will usually ask questions, "Do you have a child?" then "Is it a son?" They will build their prophetic word from the conclusions. This is not good prophecy, and the likelihood of error is greatly increased as the speaker continues.

Impure prophecy

This is true prophetic utterance mixed with the thoughts of the deliverer. This frequently happens with immature believers, or when we know the recipient. It results in God's word being altered or distorted. Often the message is coloured by the prejudices of the deliverer. This form of prophecy can be quite dangerous if not weighed carefully. Those who prophesy should always split interpretation away from revelation.

Flattering prophecy

Many times people receive the sense of a word, and overstate it to flatter the hearer. Perhaps the person prophesying receives an impression that travel is on the cards. But they say to the recipient, "God is calling you to an international ministry!" Flattery is never from God and, in fact, is the first sign of a prophetic person going off the rails. It is better to pitch the word down, than to inflate it.

False prophecy

Mathew 7:15 warns us against false prophets who come as wolves in sheep's clothing seeking whom they may devour. Question peoples motives, their reasons for coming. If it is to get (prestige, finances, the people's hearts, establish their own power) then they are displaying "wolf like" behaviour. It will happen, it does happen! Many have been damaged and even destroyed by it! This sort of false prophecy was evident when Micaiah challenged the 400 prophets of Israel before the kings, and when Jeremiah challenged the prophet Hananiah (read the story in 2 Kings 22).

Embellished prophecy

"When words are many, transgression is not lacking, but the prudent are restrained in speech." (Proverbs 10:19). Many times the prophetic person goes on and on, needlessly embellishing the

True prophecy

Have you ever seen an instrument, such as a guitar, placed infront of a fold-back speaker? If someone in the auditorium sings a note (like "E"), an interesting thing happens. The E string on the guitar resonates, by itself, in the key the person sings. There is an intuitive, sympathetic vibration. When we receive a true prophetic word the same thing happens. You really "witness" with it.

REFERENCES

Bridge, Donald & Phypers, David. "Spiritual Gifts and the Church." IVP, 1973.
Bridge, Donald. "Signs and Wonders Today." IVP, 1985
Grudem, Wayne. "The Gift of Prophecy." Kingsway, 1988.
White, John. "Discerning Prophecies." Appendix B in, "Some Said It Thundered." Oliver Nelson, 1991.
Yocum, Bruce. "Prophecy: Exercising the Prophetic Gifts." Servant Publications, 1993.

Chapter Seven
PROPHETIC ETIQUETTE

"Elijah said to Elisha, 'Stay here please for the Lord has sent me as far as Bethel.' But Elisha said, 'As the Lord lives and as you yourself live I will not leave you.' So they went down to Bethel. The sons of the prophets who were at Bethel came out to Elisha and said to him, 'Do you know that the Lord will take away your master from over you today?' And he said to them, 'Yes I know; be still'." (2 Kings 2:2,3).

The royal houses of Europe are still strong on etiquette – a set of rules that govern acceptable behaviour: the queen walks four steps behind the king; the princes walk two steps behind their mother; the dukes sit here and the earls sit there; everyone stands when the king stands, no-one speaks to the king unless invited to – and so on. Anyone who is not familiar with the etiquette will probably put their foot in it so royal visits are always preceded by a talk from a courtier who explains to hosts how they should behave in the presence of visiting royalty! In exactly the same way, there is etiquette in the kingdom of God. In the passage above we have an example of etiquette between a master prophet and a tyro prophet. We have dialogue between them, as they decide to move to a new city. In that new city there are the sons of the prophets; men raised up in a school of the prophets.

Elisha will not be persuaded to leave Elijah. Bethel, Jericho, and Jordan repeat the story three times, but Elisha is hot on the heels of his spiritual father. Elijah tries to dissuade him from following. The sons of the prophets use the word of the Lord to remind Elisha that their master is about to be taken away. It would seem they are all claiming the higher ground, manipulating by prophetic revelation.

But they are not. In actual fact they are dancing a very clear and defined path of socially acceptable etiquette for their day. To us it may look as if they were in conflict, because we do not know the rules. What are some of the rules governing the gift, the person with the gift, and how to use it today?

OUR SPHERE OF MINISTRY

Each person who is functioning in the prophetic realm has a specific sphere of ministry with its accompanying level of faith. Be careful not to go beyond your God ordained sphere of influence! *"We have different gifts, according to the grace given us. If a man's gift is prophesying, let him use it in proportion to his faith."* (Romans 12:6). The word used for proportion is 'ana-logia'. Ana = repetition, up, increase. Logia = quality, contribution, gathering, intensity. Paul not only meant that the volume of prophecy would increase according to faith, but also its intensity, its value, and its contribution would increase.

SENSE THE FLOW

How do we respond when we receive a word from the Lord? As prophetic people, we need to be sensitive to the flow of a meeting, or the flow of the Spirit in the marketplace. If it becomes apparent that the direction of a meeting is contrary to what we are hearing from God, we should hang on to the word and wait. See if another time is more appropriate. The fundamental rule is love, *"Bear with each other and forgive whatever grievances you may have against one another. Forgive as the Lord forgave you. And over all these virtues put on love, which binds them all together in perfect unity. Let the peace of Christ rule in your hearts, since as members of one body you were called to peace."* (Colossians 3:12-17).

Control and Manipulation

Unfortunately many ministers have compromised in the area of control, extorting affection, favour, honour, prestige, money or commitment from people by means of their strength of personality, charisma, giftedness, exaggerated testimonies or through intimidation. Paul tells us what true ministers are like, *"Since through the mercy of God we have this ministry, we do not lose heart. Rather, we have renounced secret and shameful ways; we do not use deception, nor do we distort the word of God."* (2 Corinthians 4:2). Our ministry is based upon mercy and grace. Freely we have received, so freely we give. We are ministering to the Lord's own Bride, therefore we take great care in our behaviour. We are careful not to abuse our brethren, who are the Lord's own children.

Oracles of God

We must be careful in the use and selection of our words. We need to be careful not to use words that are condemning or condescending, especially if our emotions are out of control. It is right for leaders to ask us to take a back seat, after the death of a loved one, or during tough financial situations. It's not true that prophetic people are called to prophesy **regardless** of how they feel, *"The spirit of the prophet is subject to the prophet."* (1 Corinthians 14:31-33). Our emotional state will affect the utterance. *"We speak as men approved by God to be entrusted with the gospel. We are not trying to please men but God, who tests our hearts. You know we never used flattery, nor did we put on a mask."* (1 Thessalonians 2:4,5). Our words are like the oracles of God.[1] A friend of mine only took three months off work and ministry after the death of her father, and she regrets being forced

---

1. 1 Peter 4:11

back "into the saddle" after such a short period of time. We are human after all!

THE WORD IS NOT THE PERSON

There are times for every prophetic person when someone does not receive, understand, or identify with our word. Rejection of the word does not imply rejection of the person who gave the word. We need to separate action from motive; message from messenger. Our responsibility is to give the word, to sound the clarion call, to blow the trumpet with as much clarity as we possibly can. Paul used the analogy of a resounding cymbal.[2] Ezekiel used the analogy of sounding the alarm (using a trumpet or shophar). *"Son of man, I have made you a watchman for the house of Israel; so hear the word I speak and give them warning from me."* (Ezekiel 13:17). That is where our responsibility ends. Do not rush to defend a word which has been rejected. If it is true, then it will surely come to pass!

ADDICTED?

An addiction is a dependency, being abnormally reliant on something that is psychologically habit forming, or craving for a substance. God wants us addicted to Him, not to His word. Seek Him, not just His prophets. Find Him, do not crave for yet another prophecy. Some churches often end up seeking one aspect of truth, and neglect the rest of the treasure house of God's truth.

This is never truer than for charismatic groups, who have a penchant for seeking after exciting spiritual gifts and manifestations. This explosive mixture coagulates in the prophetic. The results can be powerful, and sometimes toxic cultish. *"It is good that you grasp*

---

2. 1 Corinthians 13:1

one thing, and also not let go of the other; for the one who fears God comes forth with both of them." (Ecclesiastes 7:18). It is best to stay in touch with both sides of an issue. Maintain perspective. James Ryle once defined balance this way, "True balance is not to walk the path between two alternatives, but to hold onto two extreme truths at the same time."

EMPOWER THE LISTENER

It can be emotionally intoxicating to receive revelation. It can also be a power trip to give revelation, then use it to gain authority over a person. Our God-given task is to deliver the word in obedience to the Lord, in way that empowers the recipient. Make every allowance for misunderstanding, speak clearly, use figurative words rather than definitive and closed words. Ask questions instead of making bald statements. Avoid "says the Lord" where possible. Ask the recipient "Does what I am saying make sense?" Leave the hearer to find an application, unless the person asks for help.

HUMILITY WINS THE DAY!

If, for whatever reason, we've done or said the wrong thing, or spoken at the wrong time, don't be afraid to be humble and admit our error. Having done so, we should request restoration, both in our ministry and our relationships. If we've been excessive, we must be prepared to receive some godly counsel from leaders.[3] If we are not prepared to humble ourselves and listen (without argument), the result will be strife! *"Pride only breeds quarrels, but wisdom is found in those who take advice."* (Proverbs 13:10).

---

3. Galatians 2:11-16

AN EXAMPLE

There is a marvellous but rather old story about a prophetic minister called Ed Traut, from South Africa. One day Ed was ministering at a church, when he received a word of knowledge for a man seated at the back of the auditorium. He stopped his message, and asked the man to stand up. He spoke a word, blessing the man, and said God was going to raise him up and promote his ministry.

As it turned out the man was the ex-assistant pastor who had snuck in unnoticed to come and hear Ed. He had been thrown out of the church and was living in sin. Ed got hauled over the coals by the local leadership, told he had received a false word, and was summarily dismissed.

Ed humbled himself, accepted the criticism, and bided his time. He did not rise up to defend himself, nor did he contact the man in question. Time went by, and Ed had reason to return to that church. Events had unfolded just as the Lord had said, even restoring the man to the congregation. God fulfilled everything he had said, and vindicated His servant. The most beautiful thing about this story, is that Ed did not then say, "I told you so," or boast, or become prideful about it. He got on with serving the Lord.

REFERENCES

Denten, Kerry. "The Green Tree." Prophetic Modules, Level One. 1998
Grewal, Brian. "Guidelines for the Prophetic", Bible College Notes, Kempsey, NSW. CCC, 1994.
Ryle, James. "The Prophetic Gift." Audio Message, Thunder Down Under, 2001.
Sullivant, Michael. "Prophetic Etiquette." Creation House, 2000.

Chapter Eight
THE KEY OF KNOWLEDGE

[Elisha said to Elijah], *"please let a double portion of your spirit rest on me."* (2 Kings 2:9).

Before Elijah's ascent to heaven, Elisha doggedly stuck with his master, pursuing him through Bethel and Jericho and across the Jordan River. He heard three times from the sons of the prophets that Elijah would be taken away, and he replied, "Yes I know, be quiet." How did they know Elijah was leaving? How did Elisha know? What did that knowledge do for him? It generated a desire, a deep yearning, to be with his spiritual father at the time of his departure.

Elisha had gained a key insight about the future, and it generated his response to Elijah's question. Looking into his father's face, he said, "What can you do for me? You can give me a double portion... that's what!" He had asked a difficult thing. To receive his inheritance, a Hebrew son had to see his father die, kissing him and closing his eyes. The son buried the father, and having returned him to "sleep with his fathers" he would mourn, and then distribute the inheritance. If the son, however, was unable to attend his father's funeral, or unwilling to bury him, he would forfeit his birthright. Elisha was determined to be present at Elijah's "crossing over". He would perform the duty of a son, and receive his inheritance.

The double portion, the spiritual inheritance, is not an easy thing to gain. Elisha only received his double portion because he pursued Elijah, even as his father told him again and again to stay behind. This key of knowledge, this prophetic insight caused him to perservere despite all discouragements. It would forever change his life.

Meanwhile, in another part of the galaxy...

Jesus was speaking to a crowd one day, when lawyers came to trap him with intellectual questions. Jesus replied, *"Woe to you, because you build tombs for the prophets, and it was your forefathers who killed them... Because of this, God in his wisdom said, 'I will send them prophets and apostles, some of whom they will kill and others they will persecute.' Therefore this generation will be held responsible for the blood of all the prophets that has been shed since the beginning of the world... you have taken away the key to knowledge. You yourselves have not entered, and you have hindered those who were entering."*
(Luke 11:47-52 NIV).

He addressed not only the lawyers, He addressed every person in the crowd, who would one day call for His crucifixion, who would one day kill the Prophet. Jesus accused them of building the tombs of the prophets (past), and predicted that they would also slay the apostles and prophets (present) in their midst. He said that as a result, the blood of all the prophets killed from creation to that day, would be held to their account (in the future).

In legal terms, Jesus leveled **complicit** guilt against them. To be complicit is to be an accomplice, a partner in wrongdoing, to be as guilty as the person who commits a crime. It is as though we hold the gun, whilst someone else pulls the trigger.

As a result of this murder, He says the key of knowledge would be taken away, and they would hinder those who were entering the kingdom of God. To kill the prophets is to destroy the key by which we enter into understanding (c.f. Mathew 23:13-34). Elisha had found a key of knowledge, which brought him inheritance. The Pharisees had lost one... what about you?

COMPLICITY

I was preaching in Auckland, New Zealand one day about the role of prophets. As I made this very point, a brother called out, "But I've never killed a prophet!" He was saying, "How can the blood of all the prophets be laid at our feet, when we have not built their tombs? I don't even know where a prophet is buried!"

When Jesus accused the Jews of murdering prophets, He was speaking allegorically to them. Perhaps those in the crowd had never actually taken a paintbrush and painted the tombs. Certainly not everyone in the audience that day could have decorated the prophets' tombs, carved out of the stone of the hillsides around Jerusalem. Nevertheless Jesus lays the bloodshed at their feet. If they walked in the ways of their fathers, in the ways and teachings of those who killed the prophets, they were showing their agreement with those actions.

"But we welcome the prophets, we honour them, we hold conferences, and give them ample time and space to speak in our midst," another person might object. So did the crowd facing Jesus that day. Messiahs, pariahs and prophets abounded in Israel at that time. There were many documented "voices" crying to the people. Such defenses excuse no one before the judgement seat of Christ. They do not make for good defense, because...

1. It is possible to hear the voice of the prophets but never really listen to them

"The people... did not recognize Jesus, yet in condemning Him they fulfilled the words of the prophets that [were read to them] every Sabbath." (Acts 13:27). The people heard the prophets weekend after weekend, yet they never understood how the message of the prophets applied to them. Words flowed over them but never penetrated their hard hearts.

2. It is possible to have prophets among us and not do what they say

"Day after day, again and again I sent them my servants the prophets. But they did not listen or pay attention. They were stiff-necked and did more evil than their forefathers." (Jeremiah 7:25,26). We may call "Amen", nod in agreement with the prophetic word, smile benignly at the message, and walk away unchanged. The Lord, ever patient, keeps sending prophets to the people, yet day by day we neither listen, nor pay any attention. Their words will haunt us, they will testify against us on the last day.

3. It is possible to have the prophets come regularly, yet despise their message

"God... sent word to them through His messengers again and again, because He had pity on His people and on His dwelling place. But they mocked God's messengers, despised His words and scoffed at His prophets." (2 Chronicles 36:15,16). When we snigger at the concept of judgement, when we jest at the thought of justice, we are mocking God's message. When we murmur, "This message is for someone else," we despise the message. God in His unceasing grace, sends word to His people relentlessly. Yet, even in the abundance of His loving guidance, people mock the messenger and despise the message.

4. It is possible to hear the prophets and resist them.

"You are just like your fathers: You always resist the Holy Spirit! Was there ever a prophet your fathers did not persecute?.... you who have received the law... have not obeyed it." (Acts 7:51-53). Our complicit guilt in killing the prophets is proven when we become hearers of the word, and not doers of it also. Prophet killers spawn children who resist the Holy Spirit at every turn. By having the prophetic word and not obeying it, not practicing it, not living it, we say our, "Amen," to the actions of those who first killed the prophets.

WE KILL THE PROPHETS BY IMPLICATION

We have prophets, but do not hear them. We hear them but do not obey them. We despise their message or we simply resist the gravity of their message. Jesus said that in killing them, in silencing them, in failing to hear them, we remove the key of knowledge. Then what happens?

For Elisha, losing the key of knowledge would have meant a total loss of ministry. He could have turned aside at Bethel, his father would have departed unseen in a whirlwind, the end. But Elisha pursued his inheritance. For the Pharisees, it meant they would crucify their Saviour. What does it mean for us?

"Where there is no vision, the people perish, but happy is he who keeps the law." (Proverbs 29:18). People without prophetic vision perish, or wither on the vine. They slowly die without a vision of God before them. Another version of the text says, *"People without prophecy cast off restraint."* We walk away from living in the fear of God, and sin much.

"My people are held captive because they lack knowledge." (Isaiah 5:13). Without the prophetic warning, we are easily taken captive by the enemy. We are invaded. We are given over to rampant sin, having cast off restraint. We reap death, as the wages of our sin (more on this in chapter 27).

"They break all bounds... they stumble day and night, and the prophets stumble with them. So I will destroy your mother— my people are destroyed from lack of knowledge." (Hosea 4:2-6). Here again we see restraint cast off, we live in a society without boundaries, which approves all manner of sin. Such has happeneded in Cronulla, Sydney and Strasburg, France in 2005 with rioting, looting and destruction.

Without the prophets, we lose those who bring us the nourishment of being closely connected to God. It is like losing our mother. We are therefore destroyed, perishing for lack of nourishing prophetic knowledge.

It is imperative that we repent for killing, silencing, removing, shutting down or failing to listen to the voices of those who have been sent by the Lord to speak to us. They bring us a light for our path, a lamp to our feet. They bring fresh water to the roots of the plant, to suckle our tender shoots with nutrients. Their word watches over us, protecting us. They bring a vision for us to pursue, and warn us in advance of impending threat. Oh how we need the prophets!

I know of at least one church in Melbourne, and another in Sydney, that flourishes because of their constant embrace of the prophetic word. Prophets live in their midst, prophets are honoured and made welcome from abroad. When the word is spoken, they weigh and test it. Then the elders seek God for ways to implement it. Generation by generation the church thrives, spawning smaller fellowships, home groups, conferences and international affiliations. What a blessing, when people walk in the light of God's counsel. How they do prosper!

REFERENCES

Austin-Sparks, T. "Prophetic Ministry." Chapter 5. Republished 2000, Destiny Image.
Denten, Kerry. "Don't Kill the Prophets!" Audio message. Green Tree Prophetic School, 1998.

Chapter Nine
THE SWORD OF THE LORD

"[Elisha] picked up the mantle of Elijah that fell from him, and returned and stood by the bank of the Jordan... and struck the waters and said, "Where is the Lord, the God of Elijah?" (2 Kings 2:13,14).

Elisha picked up a mantle that he had never used, and called on his spiritual father's God. The word of Elijah now had to become the word of Elisha. They had spent years together, and after the years of training, this is the test. Has the word got in? Has the power transferred? Is the anointing with him as it was with Elijah? Did Elisha have a relationship with God, personal and unique to himself? Or was he relying on his father's reputation?

THE WORD OF GOD IN THE WOMB

Our prayers will not penetrate heaven until they first penetrate our own soul. Put another way, the Lord will not take our cry seriously unless it comes from our heart. We can't quote some famous preacher; we can't claim another man's anointing. Just ask the sons of Sceva![1] From the abundance of the heart the mouth speaks.[2] A friend of mine, Julia Mason says, "We prophesy from the environment in which we dwell." That is **so** true.

Do we struggle to see prayer answered, our prophecy to hold weight? What personal ownership do we take for the message we share, the prayer we pray, the prophecy we speak, and the sharing we give? Are we sharing from the heart, or are we being a pharisee?

---

1. Acts 19:14   2. Matthew 12:34

A pharisee is someone who fails to practise what they preach: *"You tried to look like upright people outwardly, but inside your hearts are filled with hypocrisy!"* (Mathew 23:28).

During a meeting in Oklahoma in 1999, there was a supernatural manifestation of the fire of God. I was flat on the floor with my face in the dust, the room was filled with searing heat. The preacher, Brian, was roasting us with a repentance message and I felt like its sole target. In the midst of this moment I had a vision of a cup. The Lord said, "You are clean on the outside, but let me cleanse you with hyssop, let me wash you with vinegar and you will be truly clean." It reminded me of the Lord's comments to the pharisees.

The searching gaze of the Lord penetrated areas of hidden darkness in me that night, and I repented of every one. Some time before this, the Lord had told Brian to clean his coffee pot. He had scrubbed and cleaned it till it shone. The next day the Lord instructed him to clean it again. This went on for three days until a "home help" show came on. They were cleaning coffee pots that day. They used vinegar and a mixture of acrid herbs. Brian tried it, and the results were startling – a beautifully clean pot. The Lord told him, 'It must be the same with your life." A clean word starts with a clean heart.

A SWORD FOR YOUR SOUL

"This child is destined to cause the falling and rising of many in Israel, and to be a sign that will be spoken against, so that the thoughts of many hearts will be revealed. And a sword will pierce your own soul too." (Luke 2:34,35). Simeon's prophecy to Mary told her that although she carried the Saviour of Mankind, the harbinger of trouble for many in the land – that same sword would pierce her soul too.

She could not simply be an onlooker, a spectator in the drama of saving the world. She would be profoundly influenced by her Son's life. As the mother of a prophet, He would have to choose His calling over family ties. She would face the humiliation and incredible pain of watching Him die on the cross like a common thief.[3]

Do our prayers bounce off the ceiling? Do we experience the heavens being like brass?[4] God uses this circumstance of unanswered prayer, of isolation from Him, to break down our stubborn pride and get us off our high horses, back on our faces before Him. If we are experiencing this phenomenon, there is no hiding it. David knew the problem – it was one of hypocrisy – of hiding sin in his life while trying to pray. He said, *"I cried out to Him with my mouth; His praise was on my tongue. If I had cherished sin in my heart, the Lord would not have listened; but God has surely listened and heard my voice in prayer."* (Psalm 66:16-20).

PIERCE MY SOUL GOD!

Throughout the Bible God made His servants possess their message. They could not escape being affected by their own prophecies, and they could not merely act as "mouth pieces". They had to get involved.

Consider Ezekiel. God warned the nation that He was bringing a sword upon them, and Ezekiel was told, *"Therefore groan, son of man! Groan before them with broken heart and bitter grief."* (Ezekiel 21:5,6). Another version of Scripture uses more graphic language. God says, *"Moan, groan and sigh with a ruptured soul."* He says, *"Cry out with pangs of despair!"*

---

3. John 19:26,27   4. Leviticus 26:17-19

Jeremiah seems to have experienced this too – though he seemed to take the message to heart more naturally. We regularly find him in agony over the state of his own life and for that of the nation. *"Oh, my anguish, my anguish! I writhe in pain. Oh, the agony of my heart! My heart pounds within me, I cannot keep silent."* (Jeremiah 4:19). One reading through Lamentations shows the depth to which the prophet was affected.

Christ stood before Jerusalem, knowing its destruction was soon at hand. We are told, *"As He came near and saw the city He wept over it."* (Luke 19:41).

A CALLOUSED HEART AND AN INOCULATION

Any one who has done a day's hard physical labour will know about callouses. They are hard protrusions of skin which our body produces in response to constant rubbing and friction. They protect the soft tissue underneath the skin from being damaged. If our heart rubs against the truth for long enough, we face the danger of getting a calloused heart.

Medical scientists have learned how to inoculate people against many viruses and infections. Doctors will take a suspension of sterilised bacteria or a dead virus vaccine and inject it into our body to provide immunity against infectious diseases. White blood corpuscles develop the right antibodies to fight any future infections from the same diseases. The effect of short bursts of man-altered-truth into our system can inoculate us against the truth. Some of the most difficult people to reach are the gospel hardened second and third generation Christians from the Bible belts. They have calloused hearts. How can we avoid this?

The word of God should pierce our soul, not rub against it. It should split our man-made intelligence asunder! *"The word of God is living and active. Sharper than any double-edged sword, it penetrates even to dividing soul and spirit, joints and marrow; it judges the thoughts and attitudes of the heart."* (Hebrews 4:12).

SPLITTING THE HEAVENS

Once the word of the Lord has pierced our soul, we are empowered to use that weapon in spiritual warfare. Thus, Paul told Timothy, *"This charge I commit to you, son Timothy, according to the prophecies previously made concerning you, that by them you may wage the good warfare, having faith and a good conscience."* (1 Timothy 1:18). Paul told Timothy that he needed to fight; he needed to rend the heavens, using the prophecies over his life.

In describing the spirtual equipment the Lord gives every believer, Paul uses the Roman armour and weapons as his guide. He describes a helmet, shield, breastplate, shoes, and belt. For offensive strikes, we are given, *"The sword of the Spirit, which is the word (rhema) of God."* (Ephesians 6:17). Not the written (*logos*) word of God, and not the seasonal (*kairos*) word of God. Paul says the rhema, the spoken now word of God, is our sword of the Spirit.

We need to be sure that we are armed for a fight. We need to know what the *rhema* word is for our life! I have taken care to transcribe the prophetic words over my life. They number more than 100 separate words from all over the world, and from every calibre of prophetic person.

I have condensed the salient elements of these words, and carry a typed copy of these wherever I go. I refer to them often, praying over them, seeking ways to obey the word of God in my life.

We are to use our prophecies, our personal relationship with God, the advice He has spoken to us directly, to wage war in the Spirit, but first, that word must pierce our own soul.

REFERENCES

Grewal, Brian. "Clean the Cup." Audio message, Marietta OK. June, 1999.
Denten, Kerry. "The Sword of the Spirit." Audio message, London, UK. Feb, 2002.

Chapter Ten
THE PROPHETIC CONTROL PANEL

"Did not my spirit go with you, when the man turned back his chariot to meet you?... therefore the leprosy of Naaman shall cling to you and your descendants." (2 Kings 5:26,27).

Elisha is sitting in his house. A powerful warrior, a foreign dignitary, has come to visit and he has not even gone out to meet him. Elisha is probably reading a book, feet up on the table, sipping coffee. He dispatches Gehazi to take the message out to Naaman. He does not say, "Go see who it is," for he already knows. "Go *tell* Naaman to dip in the river, seven times and he will be healed." Elisha knows who is coming, what he needs and what will heal him. All this has been gained through the prophetic gift. Once Naaman is healed, he comes back to pay homage to God, and Elisha refuses his gift – we cannot buy healing or prophecy. It's free.

Now, Elisha knows what is in Gehazi's heart, his legerdemain servant has the sparkle of money in his eyes. Elisha "goes out", in the spirit, and watches what transpires. He is aware of it all. This is a master, in command of his skill, who transcends all relevant technology. If he were a pilot, he could <u>really</u> fly that plane!

THE PROPHETIC PLANE

Imagine yourself sitting in the cockpit of an aircraft. Everything you need is at your fingertips. All the controls are within reach. In this space, from this one seat, you have the flying controls, indicators, dials, and instruments.

You can access information about the engine and aircraft conditions; aircraft position; location and state of play; and the environmental conditions. Imagine that all these controls are for your prophetic gift. The cockpit contains everything you need to govern this gift, starting with a smooth take-off and concluding with a safe landing. Your cargo is revelation: information that needs to be delivered safely.

Friends who have a pilot's license tell me that it takes a lot of skill, and hundreds of hours of training, to master the flight of any aircraft. The larger and more complex the plane, the more hours you must put in. It's exactly the same with developing the 1 Corinthians 12 gifts, unleashing the Romans 12 gifts or becoming a fully-fledged Ephesians 4 prophet. It's like moving from a Cessna 172 to a twin-engine Dash-8 to a Jet powered FA-18.

Although the basics are the same for all aircraft, our skill can always be improved. Prophetic risks are no less than with flying, and the rewards no less exhilarating. Let's assume we manage a successful take-off, and we're flying along happily. We look around the cockpit, and what do we see?

COMMUNICATIONS DEVICES

We're seeking God, we're flying with Him, and real communication is going on. Sitting squarely in front of us is the radio/transmission equipment. We have all sorts of information input. There is an AM/FM radio, CB radio, Short Wave Radio, Medium Wave Radio, DVD/VCD and a CD player. Through one or more of these instruments, we receive the word of God. We are scanning them, asking, "Is there a *rhema* word? Is the Scripture quickened to me as a *logos* word?"

The Prophetic Control Panel

Do we sense a seasonal *kairos* word? Is there bubbling *naba* word in our spirit; a dawning *nataph* word coming to mind; a visual *massa* or an auditory *neum* word coming in? Is there a vision, a dream or a revelation? What about a word of knowledge, a word of wisdom or a prophecy? OK we have it now, what do we do with it?

On our lap, strapped to our leg, is the pilot's log in which we journal all the communications. We make sure we write every part and piece down. We remember to separate revelation, interpretation, and application. More advanced models of aircraft have the black box flight recorder, to help us keep track of all communications.

Part of the communications equipment is also an Operator's manual. If we're flying along, and something just does not seem right, we need to check it in the manual. This is our gift of discernment operating. There is also the Maintenance manual, to check and see what certain things mean. Always go back to the Bible to confirm our revelation!

INTERNAL CHECK

To the left are a group of instruments that help determine the condition of the plane:

The Tachometer tells how fast we're running. Are we tired, awake or aware? How fast is our internal engine going? How long have we been active, is it time for a rest?

The Speedometer tells how fast we're travelling. What is our air speed? Don't approach the runway too fast, engage the audience at the right pace.

The Attitude Indicator. A plane's attitude is what angle of incline/ decline and rate of change it is undertaking. How is our attitude toward people?

The Accelerometer. This indicates the level of thrust, or rate of increase/ decrease in speed. How strong are we being with the person, do we need to back off, slow down? Are we loosing them?

The CAT indicator. This instrument identifies when we enter Clear Air Turbulence. What is our inner state? Are we at peace or in turmoil? This will come out in our word. What about the environment we're operating in? Is it full of turmoil or peace?

The Altimeter. This instrument tells how high we're flying. Is our revelation "over the top" or "over their heads"... do we need to come down to earth? What language are we using? Is it appropriate? Are our feet on the ground, or are we being a little too "sacred scary"?

Engine/ Oil Temperature Gauge. Are we running hot? Do we need to cool down, take a little more time before sharing this revelation? Maybe our emotions are getting involved... we may need to take time out.

Fuel Gauge. Can we go the distance? How many people are there left to minister to? Is the Holy Spirit still active, or do we need to land now? Don't give in to the need of men, respond to the fuel of the Holy Spirit left in the tank. What is the Father doing?

More advanced "aircraft" come equipped with a couple of other things like:

Long Range Fuel Tanks. People who have been in ministry for a longer period of time develop a certain kind of stamina, an ability to push through by faith.

Wing Light Switch. Powerful spotlights can be illuminated to light the runway when the landing strip is inadequately prepared for landing. Are these lights on? Can we see the field well enough to negotiate a landing on an unknown strip?

Lock On Warning. Fighter aircraft have a radar lock on indicator telling you if enemy aircraft have locked you into their missile guidance systems. Are we a target of the enemy right now?

After Burners. On fighter jet aircraft, power can be increased by engaging after-burners. The problem with increased power is that flames result from the rear of the aircraft. Try not to burn anyone!

Ejection Seat Activator. If trouble comes at high speed, the ejection button will propel us from the aircraft before it terminates the flight in a ball of flames! How often do we eject from a conversation before the person has received the revelation?

There are also the Registration details and manual for regular service and maintenance to ensure we are in good spiritual, emotional and physical condition.

External Check

To the right there are the external and environmental indicators. These help us check the environment through which we are travelling, and the state of the runway (the recipient of the revelation):

Aspiration Meter. Changing air pressure, temperature and moisture level requires an adjustment in the air/ fuel mixture for the engines. We need to be aware of the recipient's responses to our word, and adjust as we go.

Compass. What direction is the person heading right now as it relates to the "true north" for his or her life?

Bearing Measurement. What "heading" are they on, what are the flight plans and course corrections needed along the way because adverse wind conditions blow them off course?

Global Positioning System. What is their present location in relation to the will of God for their lives? Are they on course or off? Where are the nearest landmarks?

Transponder: What is the location of clear navigation markers, which emit radio signals, allowing aircraft to fly over and turn above them? What milestones does God want them to see?

Radar: Are there storms ahead? Are there any other aircraft or mountain ranges to be avoided? What are the upcoming events? Does the radar detect any long-range issues they need to be aware of?

Clock: What time is it in their life? What is the speed of events? Do we have a kairos or seasonal word for them? It is helpful to express some concept of timing to the recipient of the word. It is unhelpful to get too specific if the Lord has not given us the timing.

More advanced models also come equipped with things like:

Pitch and Yaw: This instrument gauges the wind velocity coming from behind, in front, or from the side, and we need to adjust the nose of the plane accordingly. We may be running into some resistance, which it putting us off course.

G-force Register: How much pressure is this creating for us, for the person and on the relationship? We can't go through too much of a "turn" in too short a space of time. It creates G force "black outs."

Happy flying, pilot!

References

"Microsoft Flight Simulator." Cessna 310 orientation manual, 2004.
"Microsoft Combat Flight Simulator." FA-18 by Janes Combat Simulators, 2001.

Chapter Eleven
PROPHESYING THE WILL OF GOD

"Elisha said [to Joash] 'Take a bow and arrows... open the window toward the east... shoot!' And he shot. And he said, 'The Lord's arrow of victory, even the arrow of victory over Aram; for you shall defeat the Arameans at Apek until you have destroyed them.' Then he said, 'Take the arrows... and strike the ground,' and he struck the ground three times and stopped. The man of God was angry with him and said, 'You should have struck five or six times, then you would have struck Aram until you would have destroyed it. But now you shall only strike them three times'." (2 Kings 13:15-19).

We all remember coming into class one day, and hearing the teacher say, "I hope you studied for the test today," only to realise we forgot the whole thing! We felt a sinking feeling in the pit of our stomach, and wanted to leave. Still, we had to stay, and sit through the agony of an exam we were not quite ready for! I suspect that's how Joash felt that day with Elisha.

Joash (also known as Jehoash), was the son of king Ahaziah. When Ahaziah died, his mother Athaliah went on a rampage. She slayed all the king's children so she could be queen mother. His aunt saved the life of Joash, and took care of him for six years.[1] He lived his early childhood, fatherless in the house of the Lord. He was an orphan son, afraid of the "monster" on the throne. Jehoiada the priest took care of the boy until he came of age.

---

1. 2 Kings 11:2

Once he assumed the throne, Joash was a righteous king. He tore down the idols of Baal, and restored covenant with God. He rebuilt the temple which was lying in ruins, and developed such a level of trust among the workers in the temple that they did not need to give an account of expenditure.[2] Obviously, there remained something in him, some timidity, some orphan tendency, which needed to be tested. Enter Elisha, lacking lenity, to bring the testing word of the Lord to bear on Joash's boldness.

REVELATION IS CONDITIONAL

For us, as for Joash, all revelation is contingent upon the response of the hearer. This occurs in two ways. Not only does all Biblical prophecy have an, "If you – then I," nature to it, but all personal prophecy requires a response from the hearer. The Lord is looking for an outcome that requires His sovereignty and our freewill to interplay. Calvin meets Armenius in prophecy. The prediction takes two partners: His will, and our obedience.

Prophecies gather dust unless they are acted upon. Prophecies are worthless without a faith-filled response. What's the filing system like? I am an avid filer. I keep all manner of things, referenced, cross-referenced, and filed away. I write down all revelation received, whether visions, dreams, words, or impressions in my diary.

We encourage the people in our fellowship to review the words they have received. The first thing we do is to sit down together and decide which ones are "bunk" (rubbish). Sometimes "words" are produced in a frenzy of prophetic activity at a conference; words which seem good, are actually relevant for someone else.

---

2. 2 Kings 12:15

Then there are the words that have simply not come to pass yet. They seem to be valid, but have yet to bear fruit. It is those words we need to look at more carefully. There are three other reasons a word may not yet have come to pass. Revelation is positional, it is possessive and it is progressive. To get a handle on that, we need to understand God's will for our lives, and how it plays out in real time.

1. Revelation is positional

God will speak to us based on where we are. He will speak to us in one city, and tell us to move to another. He will speak to us when we do not have children, and tell us of those we will have (one day). Our position – geographic, economic, emotional or otherwise, will determine the kind of revelation God gives us. Documenting insights we get from God can be really liberating and encouraging. Years later we read the file and find it fulfilled.

Our lives all have seasons. Very often we find the Lord speaking to us about the next season in our lives. The word seems to clash because it goes against our present circumstance – we are flying high and someone takes the wind out of our sails with a word about darkness coming. God is kind, shedding light on the pathways ahead of us so we may walk forward faithfully.

2. Revelation is possessive

Our response to a word has a profound effect on its outcome. Ninevah for example, turned the heart of God from a declared intention to destroy the city, to a repealing of that judgement. The people at Ninevah repented and averted disaster. After receiving a word, and having tested it, we should pursue God for it.

"Everything done without faith is sin." (Romans 14:23). If we fail to receive and act on a word, we are effectively in sin.

The inhabitants of Jerusalem had the prophetic word of Jesus to tell them the temple would one day be torn down, one stone from another (see Mathew 24:2). Jewish historian Josephus recorded that a star resembling a sword appeared in the night sky over Jerusalem for more than four weeks before it was besieged. In addition, many Christians had visions of chariots and soldiers running around among the clouds and in cities of Palestine.[3] Christians took this as a sign that the hand of God was against Jerusalem, and they fled to Petra. In 70AD the armies of Titus from Rome encamped about Jerusalem, and starved the people out. Eventually they set fire to the city, and burned much of it to the ground. Not one stone was left upon another in the temple. The words of Jesus were fulfilled.

Do we actually believe the words God has given to us? Is it time to act on them? Sometimes circumstance will prevail against us, and things will go the opposite way to the word. God said to Moses, "You will enter the promised land," but instead they crossed the Red Sea into the desert! The first place in the desert they came to was Marah or "bitter waters" and these circumstances sorely tested the hearts of the Israelites. As Graham Cooke says, "We either let circumstance test the word, or use the word to test our circumstance!"[4]

3. REVELATION IS PROGRESSIVE

Very often God does not tell us the full picture, or give us the end-game strategy. He only tells us the next move, and until we obey, we cannot receive the next piece of the puzzle.

---

3. Josephus. Book VI, Chapter 6, Section 3
4. "Majesty & Warfare conference" Audio tape 3.

Until we do all that we know, He will not give us more. *"It is the glory of God to conceal a matter, it is the glory of kings to find it out."* (Proverbs 25:2).

In the life of Abraham we see the way God leads progressively, unfolding His purposes and plans before us. Abraham's life is a superb example to us of the need to obey with only limited information. God's first instruction to the father of faith was "leave". Leave his country, his home Ur of the Chaldees,[5] his family and his house must be left behind. He is not told the destination, even for the first leg of the journey, let alone the final one!

Abraham journeyed to Moreh[6] and there God gave him His first promise, a land that God showed him, would one day be his. He built an altar there, and journeyed on, again without a specific destination. From Moreh, via Bethel and the Negev, he journeyed to Egypt. Drought drove him onward to Egypt.[7] Later, God would reveal that Abraham's children would one day be enslaved there.

From Egypt he journeyed to Canaan where he parted from his nephew, Lot. In Canaan he came to Mamre and received instruction to walk the land.[8] God told him that everywhere his feet trod, his children would one day live. From Mamre he journeyed to Shaveh[9] or the Kings Valley, and there, God gave him the promise of offspring. God had alluded to it twice before, but this was Abraham's first specific promise of children. He spent ten years in the region of Canaan, and whilst waiting for the promised child, his wife's maid Hagar conceived Ishmael.[10] The angels visited him again in Mamre and reminded him about the child of promise[11] who was still yet to come. Abraham was living now in the land God promised to him.

---

5. Genesis 12:1
6. Genesis 12:7
7. Genesis 12:10
8. Genesis 13:12-18
9. Genesis 14:17
10. Genesis 16:3
11. Genesis 18:1

He uprooted once again and journeyed to Gerar [12] where his wife finally conceived Isaac, the child of promise, and God prospered them greatly. The entire process was an unfolding, a discovering. What a glorious "king" Abraham made, as the father of faith! Though it is not said in the original text, the author of Hebrews looks back and says, *"Abraham when he was called, obeyed by going out to a place which he was to receive for an inheritance; and went out **not knowing** where he was going."* (Hebrews 11:8 emphasis mine). He did not know the entire plan up front, just one step at a time.

CONCLUSION

The revelation God gave Abraham depended on: his location (position), his possession (of the promises by faith), and his progression (through obedience). There is a tell-tale line in the story about his having to wait, and the unfolding progressive revelation he received. Sarah bore Isaac to him, *"At the set time of which God had spoken to him."* (Genesis 21:2). How many of us derail the process of God because we are unwilling to leave, or to travel, or to flee, or to keep walking until we see the payoff? Rest assured, God is not wringing His hands in despair because we will not rise to the occasion, He will simply find someone else. As Esther was told by Mordecai, *"If you remain completely silent at this time, relief and deliverance will arise for the Jews from another place, but you and your father's house will perish."* (Esther 4:14).

REFERENCES

Cooke, Graham. "Majesty & Warfare conference." Audio tape Grace Church, Sept 1999.
Katz, Arthur. "The Spirit of Prophecy." Ben Israel, 2000.

---

12. Genesis 20:1

PART TWO

PROPHECY AND THE CHURCH

In the second section of this book we will turn our attention to the first place a person's gift usually finds expression – the Church. We look at the prophetic gift from the point of view of the local church, the pastor/ leader; those administering the gift and include some helpful watch-outs. We start by looking at the pitfalls of the prophetic. Chapter 12 zeros in on the common mistakes and how to avoid them.

We then look at how one might construct an environment for this gift to work well – describing different levels of the prophetic, and developing a local prophetic policy for the Church. We'll look at how prophecy can positively team with intercession and worship.

Under the general heading of environmental issues, we examine the Ezekiel 14 trap and looking at rooting out idols in our heart. To complete the picture, we examine how the prophetic relates to leadership – which includes the priestly role of pastors and the leadership role of apostles.

We will examine discernment of spirits more closely, making friends with rejection (a prophetic person's best friend at times), and the error Balaam fell into. We close out this section with a look back at error in prophecy, and examine the false claim that prophecy has to be 100% accurate "or else"!

CHAPTER TWELVE
PITFALLS OF THE PROPHETIC

The people in one city said to Elisha: *"The situation of this city is pleasant... but the water is bad and the land is unfruitful. [Elisha] said, 'Bring me a new jar and put salt in it.' So they brought it to him. He went out to the spring of water and threw salt in it and said, "Thus says the Lord, 'I have purified these waters'."* (2 Kings 2:19-21).

Elisha's prophetic ministry began when he parted the waters of the Jordan. From that point on, he moved directly into being of benefit to the believers. He walked straight into the gathering (*ekklesia*) of the brethren in the city, who explained their need to the man of God. Elisha listened both to their need, and to the heart of God. Then he demonstrated the heart of the Father to them, by healing their waters.

The prophetic ministry stands in a constant tension between the need of men and the heart of God. Prophets stand at times in intercession (before God on behalf of men) and at times in the gift of prophecy (standing before men on behalf of God). One needs, at a moment's notice to reverse direction. But danger exists in preaching what you should pray, or praying what you should prophesy! We must be like a circuit, carrying alternating current (AC).

Our "polarity" switches from moment to moment. Reverse it in the wrong way, and one blows the circuit. Reverse the flow in the prophetic, and great harm can be done, when great blessing is meant.

OCCUPATIONAL HEALTH AND SAFETY

Every church that values spiritual gifts will have to cross the bridge of safe-guarding, and overseeing the prophetic gift amongst the people. Often this happens a little late – perhaps after people have been hurt by bad prophecy, or perhaps because people are over-exhilarated by the power of God. Either way, we can lay some secure foundations for dealing with the prophetic in a healthy, balanced way from the very beginning. When seeking to identify safe guards or safety nets for something powerful, it is helpful to think of worst-case scenarios and work back from that point. We can ensure the proper use of the prophetic, by ensuring proper administration in the place where it is most likely to happen.

Any gift can be abused, (think of teaching or administration, finances or pastoral care for example). But the possibility of damage can be minimised by careful teaching and sensible regulation. There is no need to extinguish the Spirit's fire, quench the Spirit or discourage the gift. I am talking about protecting against extremes. Rick Joyner has pointed out that, "We spend most of our time in one gutter or the other. Very little of our walk is on middle of the narrow road." [1]

PANDERING THE PROPHET

In the early 1980's there was a great deal of excess in the conference and speaking circuit. David Pytches was perhaps the first to note that everyone was, "running to the prophet", a pressure which produced false prophetic utterances in the Latter Rain Movement. [2] It was partly because of the amazing displays of power and sign gifts, partly because of the presence of God at the meetings, and partly to obtain a word from a real "prophet".

---

1. "The Call." Pg 37-39.
2. "Some Said it Thundered." Pg 12,13.

It is right and proper to honour one another, and it is good to honour our leaders and those in ministry, but don't let it turn into worship!

HAIL THE HERO!

People tend to honour others inappropriately – by worshiping the vessel God chooses to exhibit his power through. Some prophetic people have enjoyed the rush of stardom, others have shunned the limelight. But in too many cases the people have insisted on placing prophets on a pedestal – thereby setting them up for a fall. Members of the Body become immobilised when they wait for "the Lord's anointed ones" to do it. We fall into a realm where only "special" people are qualified for ministry and everyone else watches. Church becomes a spectator sport! That is never the way God intended!

PRIDE IN PERFORMANCE

Those being used in prophetic ministry often fall foul of pride. There is probably no uglier form of pride than thinking we have done something to deserve being given the gift of prophecy. Paul said, *"What do you have that you have not received? And if you have received it, why then do you boast about it as though it was not freely given?"* (1 Corinthians 4:7). This is especially true of spiritual gifts. We must be careful not to attribute merit to ourselves, just because we (or anyone else) can hear His voice.

RETAINING OUR REPUTATION

When we have ministered effectively for some time, we begin to develop a track record. In the early days we may have missed that mark a fair bit, but eventually our faith will harness the gift, and we will get it right a lot more often. Then comes the danger. People will develop an expectation of us to prophesy all the time. They will come in private, asking for guidance. They may expect us to prophesy at the drop of a hat. In the short term, this serves our ego well, as we feel wanted and needed, but it quickly becomes a trap. There is a reputation to uphold, a record to keep, and a demanding audience. If we go down that track too far, we can end up becoming a prophetic person performing for our audience, and receiving a sweet financial 'treat'.

RELIANCE ON REVELATION

There is a tendancy in the Body of Christ for people to rely too heavily upon prophecy for personal guidance. Prophetic words can be emotionally intoxicating but they can also benefit people greatly, helping them to see ahead in times of trouble. While we should be elated at accuracy, and encouraged when prophecy comes to pass, we should be careful of relying too heavily on it. God is first our Father, then our Guide. Christ is first our Lord and then our Brother. He never intended us to rely on the prophetic in every situation. As Michael Sullivant has pointed out, "God wants to transform us within, so that we catch his thoughts and feelings by becoming more like Him – having His attitudes and perspectives incorporated deeply into our being."[3] Having His heart more than hearing His voice.

NEGLECTING THE NORMAL

Hearing and speaking the word of God is amazing, but it is not a substitute for other aspects of the Christian life. Embracing the prophetic does give us license to neglect prayer, reading the Bible, study, loving your spouse, feeding the poor, missions, working, or caring for your children. It is very healthy to develop teams made up of a range of gifts. Sadly, prophetic cliques form where, "birds of a feather flock together." Their conversation becomes so narrow and their focus so inward.

---

3. "Prophetic Etiquette". Pg100

IDENTITY AND GIFTING

It is easy for gifted people to begin to allow their giftedness, or the fact that they hear from God, to become entwined with their self-esteem. We are not our gifts. We are not our achievements either. We must always distinguish between gifts and identity. We are first and foremost children of God, we are secondly servants, and we are ministers lastly. Paul announced himself as, "I Paul, an apostle," not, "The apostle Paul." We must also remember that we are given gifts to serve others, but those gifts are not essential to our relationship with God or men.

TAKING OURSEVES TOO SERIOUSLY

People who regularly speak for God can begin to develop an unhealthy opinion of their own importance. Just as an ambassador is not the country he represents, a prophetic person is not the Lord he speaks for. Speaking for God is a serious job, but it can also lead us into the deception of self-importance. Jerry Cook describes it well, "The Win/ Lose mentality is rampant in our society and in the Church. This way of looking at life produces a certain grimness I call the Busy/ Important/ Serious syndrome. Busy, important, and serious hang out together and they take over the lives of people constantly trying to win."[4]

Prophetic people are prone to taking themselves too seriously, walking around with the weight of the world on their shoulders. They often talk about the "burden of prayer" and the "weight of revelation." They begin to take responsibility for the fulfillment of the word they carry. True, we will be held accountable if we do not share a word, but implementing it is not our bag to carry.

---

4. "A Few Things I've Learned Since I Knew it All." Pg 17.

FEAR OF FAILURE

We can only prophesy according to our level of faith.[5] When people move out in faith and minister words to others, there is always the distinct possibility of failure. For the pastoral staff of a local church, error in prophecy can be very damaging. It can misrepresent the Lord, it can over extend a person's trust, it can lead to deception. There is not one spirit-filled believer who has learned to minister effectively, who has not made mistakes. Failure is a normal part of any growth curve.

Our embarrassment increases when we are claiming to speak for God and "He" seems to get it wrong! For this reason, even seasoned prophets avoid using phrases like, "For the Lord would say…" unless they are very confident about the word they are giving. In order to protect the sheep from abuse, church leaders often set tight, controlling rules over prophesy – but it would be better if they would provide a safe place to mess up. Protection is not guaranteed by forbidding prophecy, or in demanding 100% accuracy before going public. It is best provided by teaching people to weigh and test all revelation, and safety guards for prophetic people.

REFERENCES

Cook, Jerry. "A Few Things I've Learned Since I Knew it All." Peacemakers, 1990.
Joyner, Rick. "The Call." Morningstar Publications, 1999.
Pytches, David. "Some Said It Thundered." Thomas Nelson, 1991.
Sullivant, Michael. "Prophetic Etiquette." Creation House, 2000.

---

5. Romans 12:6

CHAPTER THIRTEEN
LEVELS OF PROPHETIC IN THE CHURCH

"Then the king talked with Gehazi, the servant of the man of God saying, 'Tell me all the great things Elisha has done.' Now it happened as he was telling the king... that there was the woman whose son he had restored to life, appealing to the king for her house and land." (2 Kings 8:4,5).

Fame has existed for a long time. A queen ventured half way across the world to hear of Solomon's wisdom and to gape and gaze at his wealth. A general travelled a great distance to receive healing from the desert-dwelling prophet. A king heard of the prophet's work in the earth.

Here is the king, asking Gehazi (the fallen servant of Elisha) to tell stories of God's miracles by the hand of his old master. At that very moment, the widow whose son was raised entered the courts of the king. She had lost her land during the drought, presumably to raiders, or nomad squatters. Because of Elisha's reputation, the widow received full restoration from the king. How did Elisha arrive at such a reputation? How did he rise through training and submission, exercise and faith? How did he gain fame enough to restore the fortunes of a widow?

COULD HE BE IN OUR CHURCH?

Is there anyone in your church who is known nationally or internationally? Can their name open doors – or close them? Can they restore lost land to the poor? If not – could someone like this be raised up in your church? Does your church have any sort of action plan to bring people to such a place? Sadly – very few do! And many who have the plan allow it to gather dust on the shelves of the church library. It's one of those things we could do, should do, but it seldom actually gets done.

It's time to get practical. Time to present a structured format that can be used in the church to help administer the prophetic. The "system" you are about to read through, the very thought of making stages may make some people feel uneasy. It appears too structured. However, it is not our intention that this matrix be used as a hoop-jumping exercise, nor as a rigid pass/fail system of promotion.

Rather, it stems from conversations I held with pastors and prophetic leaders around the world, who have needed to implement a structure for growth. All too often, a prophetic person "pitches" themselves higher than the pastoral leader, or the oversight in a church world. Very often we esteem ourselves more highly than we ought to. This matrix is meant to show some very practical outcomes, character, and conduct issues which should appear commensurate with the level of giftedness claimed.

A TRIP TO THE PROPHET'S CHURCH

I recall my first visit to Kansas City Metro, the "world famous" church that was at the forefront of restoring prophets to the Church in the eighties. John MacGirvin collected me at the airport. At the time he was assistant to Michael Sullivant – the administrator and prophets' pastor at the church. Between the airport and our lodging (some two hours) I received the standard "introduction to Kansas" lecture. It was all good natured, but I was told in no uncertain terms how things were done.

They had engineered a very structured approach to handling growth in the prophetic. Because of their leading role in restoring prophetic ministry to the Church at that time, they had two to four people a week ring up and say, "God told me to move to Kansas to join your church." And if someone quizzed the caller more carefully, they would be told that God had also instructed the caller to "Travel with Mike Bickle," or "Move in with Paul Cain," or "Start my world wide ministry!" It had to be every pastor's worst nightmare!

Not surprisingly, Kansas City Metro implemented a rather strict series of measures to restrain such "fervour", and contain the more delusional individuals attracted to the church. I'm not suggesting we need to go to that extent. Your church isn't Metro, and neither is mine. In fact according to recent studies, 90% of churches worldwide have less than 100 members. But we can learn from them.

A MEDIUM SIZED MODEL

Grace Christian Fellowship, based in Garema Place, Canberra is a medium sized church I love working with. During 2002 I was teaching there on the prophetic, the head of the prophetic "department" was Rex Jefferson-Taite. Rex had previously been the Principle of Unity (Bible) College. He had taken on the task of raising up prophetic ministry at Grace, and together we worked out a model prophetic policy for a medium sized church.

We tossed around various things we had seen – including the Metro model. What we wanted was an easily understood program, a path into which people could slot readily. The policy needed to take into account a person's maturity level, level of gifting, and the stage of development when they joined the team.

The following matrix is the result of our efforts. It is not perfect, because it reflects the path we walked to the place we minister from now. It provides a starting place for anyone who wishes to implement a working policy that will raise up the prophetic in a local church. Without apology, this model acknowledges that people can only grow to the level of their gift, and will plateau at some stage. The gifts and callings are distributed by God, without respect to persons. Some have ten talents, some have five talents and others one. This matrix also includes some practical steps that a person can take to grow beyond their present level.

We presuppose that the local church will implement a mentoring program (which we will cover in a chapter 19), and that someone will oversee the general development of people in the program. This may be very structured in a larger church, or more informal in a house church. Whoever "oversees" this function in the church needs to be a strong, mature Christian. They do not (as in the case of Metro) have to be a prophet. In fact it might be better not to appoint a prophet as the leader. In any case, that "point-person" needs to have delegated authority and a good relationship with the other leaders in the church. Those coming through the "ranks" will want to find expression in the life of the church, which necessitates interaction with a wide variety of other ministry areas.

LEVEL ONE. BASIC PROPHETIC WORD

Every person in the Church can and should learn to prophesy, regardless of maturity level. In terms of the gift, this person is an infant (*nepios*). The key Scripture for basic prophetic word is 1 Corinthians chapter 12. There is a need to grow in openness and readiness for the manifestation, the *energema* of the Spirit. There are three stages to growth in this level of ministry:

Levels of Prophetic in the Church

Stage 1: The person is dealing with personal/ family issues. They should go through some kind of healing or wholeness seminar like, "Cleansing Stream." The person may have received deliverance, and should be filled with the Spirit.

Stage 2: The person is showing an active/ servant interest in the local church. The person is getting involved, and is willing to serve and grow. They observe things prophetically, not just naturally and submit such observation to leaders in the congregation.

Stage 3: The person receives occasional words on a personal level. They makes insightful remarks during conversation. They have a developing prayer life. Dreaming is starting to happen, but they find interpretation difficult. 1 Corinthians 13:11 and Ephesians 4:14 are relevant.

LEVEL TWO. ADVANCED PROPHETIC WORD

People at this level are growing in the use of the prophetic gift (of 1 Corinthians 12). They demonstrate words of knowledge, words of wisdom and words of prophecy. They have some prophetic maturity (*padion*). They operate in the area of prophetic inspiration but the operation of the gift is sporadic and unreliable.

Stage 1: The person knows they have a gift and believe they are called. They have undertaken a "gifting" course such as "Discover Your Portfolio". They have documented the prophetic words over their life.

Stage 2: The person is seeking to be accountable. He or she will be developing a working relationship with the pastoral leader or oversight of the local church. They are being actively discipled, and having regular meetings with a mentor.

Stage 3: The person is receiving strong/ frequent words from the Lord. Dreaming is becoming stronger, with better insight and interpretation skills. They may have undertaken a dream interpretation course. Luke 7:32-35 is insturmental at this stage.

LEVEL THREE. PROPHETIC GIFTEDNESS

By now the person has discovered a level of Romans 12 giftedness. He or she is growing in the gift and mastering the technical skills (*teknon*), but their character is still in the process of development. They will make plenty of mistakes, so give them grace and understanding. Create a "space" for them to practise without hurting anyone!

Stage 1: The person is seeking to grow, and be mentored by Level Four ministries. They should undertake prophetic training such as "Prophetic Intensives" or a school, preferably one in which their mentor is involved in.

Stage 2: Other prophetic people are naturally gathering to this person. He or she may run a cell group, home group or Bible study which might form into a prophetic prayer or worship group. The prophetic will express itself in whatever area they operate in (worship, prayer, public service, work).

Stage 3: The person is receiving reliable/accurate words from the Lord. They are called upon regularly to communicate revelation. Ministry in services, use of word of knowledge and prophecy is opening up. Mathew. 10:19,20 and Romans 8:14 are relevant at this stage.

LEVEL FOUR. INTERMEDIATE PROPHETIC MINISTRY

By this time, prophetic people have grown in their Romans 12 gift and are strongly developed. They are growing in confidence and have sufficiently mature character to be relied upon in a range of circumstances. Spiritually speaking, they are teenagers (*neoterios*). They have gained the notice of visiting ministries, are on team with local staff and bring regular words.

Stage 1: The person undertakes a more advanced, "Prophetic Ministry" Course. We would expect them to be teaching basic prophetic courses and beginning to move around the various ministry expressions of the church.

Stage 2: The person is actively (and with permission) discipling more immature people. Mentored by a Level Five minister is taking place, (which might include others outside the local fellowship).

Stage 3: The person is speaking into leadership as a trusted, reliable adviser. He or she brings the prophetic word during worship or ministry times. Acts 2:17, 18 and 1 Timothy 4:12-14 are relevant at this stage.

LEVEL FIVE. PROPHETIC MINISTER

There is something of a glass ceiling here. Few people take the time, embrace the pain, mature their character to the point where they become a "high end" Romans 12 minister. In terms of the gift, they are fully mature (*huios*) and able to minister in their own right, but they are willingly submitted to other brethren and well able to work in team.

Stage 1: The person is starting to assist others in addressing major (fundamental) issues. He or she may sit in leadership circles, or have regular meetings with the pastoral staff. Raising up and releasing Level Four ministries is integral and natural to them.

Stage 2: The person is able to teach or preach at services, will probably be teaching more broadly and starting to travel (itinerate). The person will counsel others (prophetically).

Stage 3: They are able to deliver a word or teaching to Church government. They may need to seek a mentor with national or international standing, or relate to a larger program for the whole prophetic ministry. Mathew 3:15-17 and 2 Peter 1:17 are relevant to those at this stage.

Level Six. Intern to Prophet (Son of the Prophet)

To be recognised beyond Level Five, a person needs to be called, chosen and then commissioned as an Ephesians 4:11 ministry (*doma*). He or she will value taking the form of a servant (*doulos*). Even though mature, the person might still be apprenticed to someone more experienced in the gift.

Stage 1: The person may have become a deacon (servant) to a more senior prophet, to aid them and travel with their ministry. Personal ministry, deliverance and counselling have become part of normal life. Phillipians 2:22 is relevant to them.

Stage 2: The person is welcomed to speak, with authority, insight and wisdom into the measure (*metron*) of another (especially his/her mentor). 1 Timothy 1:18 and 1 Corinthians 4:17 are key for them. Trusted is given with the assets (ministry) of another.

Stage 3: The person will join their mentor, speaking into governmental issues. Many spheres (church, marketplace, political, trans-local) are opening and he/she may have the word of the Lord for the citywide Church and for regions. 1 Corinthians 4:15 has become a key verse.

Level Seven. Mantled Prophet

A person at this level is a fully commissioned prophet. He/she has become a father in the prophetic (*pater*). The person has an established track record, and have their own ministry and work. There are children in the faith, churches that receive them as father/leader and ministries who call on them for insight and oversight.

Stage 1: The person is a recognised minister, needing no other to testify on their behalf. Their ministry is widely accepted and the individual has a peer relationship with pastors, apostles, teachers and evangelists.

Stage 2: The person is fathering/overseeing churches, regions, movements and other ministers. They would also mentor Level Five and Six ministries. Acts 15:32 is their truth.

Stage 3: The person is received as a peer or advisor by leaders in other spheres like business, church, government. 1 Thessalonians 2:10-12 is true of them.

SOME PRACTICAL ADVICE

Churches wishing to see the prophetic grow in their midst can take many approaches. They can regularly invite external ministry in to speak to them, or they can raise the prophetic up from within.

In my experience, those who rely exclusively on external prophetic ministry, rarely see it grow from within. But those who try exclusively to raise it up within also produce inferior results. Their prophets become "company men" who speak the party line. Alternately, the people hungry for growth go seeking affirmation and development outside the congregation.

A balanced approach of internal support and external input is needed for good growth. If a group decide to raise the prophetic up from within, they can be structured, or informal about it. They can provide training, development and places for expression. Or they can just allow it to happen, as and where it will.

Once again my advice is to take the middle path. Do not over structure, and grip the life out of the prophetic – for by nature it is spontaneous and inspirational. Though at the same time, do not be so unstructured, that your people wander around listlessly, trying to find a place to grow.

THE RESOURCE SQUEEZE

Before a person builds a tower, he makes sure he has the resources to complete it. Implementing a program such as we suggest in this chapter will take time – planning, strategy, prayer, mentoring, followup time. We need to be sure that is time well spent. It will come at the expense of some other project we might wish to work on.

It will also take money – for resources, printing, recording, followup and (perhaps) external training. This creates a resource squeeze, because (if you are anything like the local churches I have belonged to), your expenses outstrip your income. We will need to be willing to divert finances away from some other worthy project.

Just as a mother and father long for children, count the cost and then embark on parenthood, so we should look forward to the results. Prophetic ministry brings wonderful results to every department, every expression of the church local and corporate.

REFERENCES

I am deeply indebted to Rex Jefferson-Taite for labouring on: "A Structure for Administering the Prophetic." GCF 2002. This has been trialled and implemented at GCF because of his hard work.

CHAPTER FOURTEEN
DEVELOPING A LOCAL PROPHETIC POLICY

"The king of Syria said, "Go now and I will send a letter to the king of Israel"... he brought the letter to the king of Israel... and when the king of Israel read the letter he tore his clothes and said, "Am I God, to kill and make alive?"... when Elisha heard that the king of Israel had torn his clothes, he sent [word] to the king." (2 Kings 5:5-7).

In the days of Elisha there were rules of engagement for battle, rules for legal negotiation, and rules about diplomatic exchange. Naaman entered the king's court and explained his need to the king of Syria. The king of Syria wrote a letter to the king of Israel. The king of Israel tore his clothes – indicating in the strongest possible way his distress at the request, and announced to God his heartfelt concern. Elisha heard about it, either directly from the Lord, or through an intermediary working in the king's court. We are seeing an intricate series of moves made silently, in accordance with the political etiquette of the day.

Most organisations today have policy and procedure manuals. These manuals themselves do not govern the behaviour of people in the organisation. Rather, they are a record of the culture, the etiquette of the group. The officers of the company enforce this procedure, and when necessary, interpret the policy backing it. The Church of Jesus Christ has such a manual, recorded for us in the gospels of the New Testament. From the key Kingdom principles espoused by our Leader, we can draft a policy that will safely guide our behaviour.

To do this, we must come to some agreement about what we want, and what the Kingdom demands of our prophetic ministers. Those issues will be as varied and diverse as the local expressions of "Church" in your city. The policy we draft will be peculiar to our environment. What are the things we need to consider when developing a local prophetic policy?

Most of us will naturally start to think of the prophetic as it relates to the local church. We will begin to fashion a policy which will govern Sunday morning prophecy, or home group prophecy. We have read enough of Elisha's life so far to clearly show that prophecy has applications in every facet of life. It happens in the community of believers, within the church, with visiting foreign dignitaries, in a prayer time for the nation and at home quite naturally. Prophecy reaches out and touches ordinary life. The policy needs to:

- Govern the person doing the ministry;
- Guard the recipient of prophecy against destructive outcomes;
- Encourage the prophetic to flourish without restriction.

These potentially conflicting requirements will guide us in developing the policy. In order to address these requirements, there are three overarching considerations:

- What CONTEXT will prophecy occur in? There will be environmental issues which govern the use of this gift. Will one policy fit all possible situations?
- What CONDUCT does prophecy take place through? The recipient of the word will need to be able to recognise that they are actually receiving a prophecy.
- What CONTENT does the prophecy contain? Is it harmless or does it contain directive elements? Is it short term or long term? How is the word packaged?

WHAT CONTEXT DOES PROPHECY OCCUR IN?

Until we get used to the idea of ministering in the marketplace, most prophecy will take place in a church setting. Even in this (rather predictable) environment, however, there are many areas of life and focus. Prophecy will differ on a weekend (Sunday) service, youth service, midweek service, Bible study/ cell group and a fellowship group. What about those delivered in a seminar/ conference setting?

Prophecy can also take place out in the world. Apart from the obvious language shift, how do we adjust to an un-churched audience? The Lord can speak in the workplace, on the sportsfield, on holiday, on the bus, in the taxi and at the shopping mall. Our policy needs to consider all these contexts too!

We are responsible to train people to hear God's voice in any context, and be able to frame what God says in such a way that it is of benefit to the audience, whoever they may be. The man seated next to us in the plane; the Jew in the marketplace; the Muslim store owner; someone at work; a close family member or a believer at church. Inclusiveness and flexibility will allow us to do this – rigidity and over-control will, of necessity, curtail the use of the gift.

WHAT CONDUCT WILL THE PROPHECY COME THROUGH?

Everyone of us fulfills a number of different roles in our lives. For example, I am a husband, a father, a pastor, an itinerant speaker, a worshipper, musician, prophet and a business consultant. In each of these roles, I impact different spheres of life, interact with different people, and I adopt a different posture toward each "audience". My role in relation to the recipient of a word of prophecy, needs to be considered in the delivery of that word or insight.

Consider these differing situations:

- A pastoral counselling situation   (pastor);
- A prayer meeting   (intercessor);
- A confrontation   (counsellor);
- A leadership forum   (leader);
- Street evangelism   (evangelist).

It is not difficult to see how different the "texture" of the word will be when it is delivered by a pastor, prayer leader, counsellor, leader, evangelist or businessman. What governs our conduct in each of these roles? In every society there are unspoken rules that govern our behaviour. We are expected to be silent in a movie theatre, we all face forward in an elevator, on an English train one does not look a person in the eye and in an American restaurant one does not wink at a waitress! Our conduct must be appropriate if our prophecy is to achieve maximum benefit.

One day in 2005 I was having lunch with some business people in Tasmania. The Holy Spirit gave me a word of knowledge for the waitress. She was pregnant (though not obviously so) and I sensed that the baby was in danger of miscarriage. I could not stop the meal, invite her forward for ministry, and make sure an MP3 recorder was on hand. When it came time for the bill to be paid, she naturally came back. I asked her if she was married. She said no. I asked her if her boyfriend and she were planning a family. She smiled and said yes. I told her I was a "man of God," and asked permission to bless her child. Naturally she engaged the opportunity. Lost as she was, we prayed for her child, and by way of prayer (with eyes open and facing her), I prophetically blessed the baby.

What policy could you write to cover such an event? Should this woman wish to complain, she would need my contact details for example. She also had several witnesses (my lunch companions) and an opportunity to reply to us after the prayer.

WHAT CONTENT WILL THE PROPHECY CONTAIN?

The content is the actual prophecy, along with its inherent risk (of error), which gives rise to the need for control. When there is increased risk – the word brought can be wrong – and that the error may create harm, there must be increased control. So content must be weighed according to the risk inherent in the particular form of content. Here is a suggested list of increasing risk, calling for increasing control over the utterance:

Lowest risk (low control needed)

The prophecy contains:	The effect is:
1. Love	Affection (e.g. restoration)
2. Edification	Building up
3. Exhortation	Stirring up
4. Comfort	Mercy, grace or compassion
5. Challenge	Repentance
6. Direction	An altered decision made (e.g. mates/ dates)
7. Prediction	Preparation for the future (e.g. investment)
8. Correction	Reproof or rebuke
9. Control	Apprehending destiny (e.g. healing)
10. Destruction/ judgement critcism	Speaking a judgement

Highest risk (most control needed)

IMPLEMENTING RELEVANT CONTROLS

Because of the differing kinds of revelation (*naba* bubbles up but *nataph* is slowly dawning) and the different kinds of context, content, and conduct, there is no "one-size-fits-all" solution. It is too simplistic to say, "All prophecy must be given to an elder before it is delivered," because there may not be an elder sitting next to us on the plane to London!

We need a series of appropriate controls that we can implement to assist the Church and the prophetic ministries in it. Whatever we do, we need to:

- Keep the policy simple (follow the K.I.S.S. principle);
- Communicate the policy regularly and publically;
- Plan ahead for many possible contingencies;
- Avoid engendering fear!

KINDS OF CONTROLS

Control can take two forms – internal and external control.

INTERNAL CONTROLS: are character, conduct and self control;
EXTERNAL CONTROLS: are policy and procedures.

The Church creates the environment in which character, self control and conduct are taught, caught or learned – not just in the context of prophetic ministry. Do we have a mentoring program? Do we have a training program? Do we do discipleship well? Are our prophetic people accountable to anyone? The Church should develop the policy and procedure "manual" for all of its conduct.

SHUT THE BACK DOOR!

When a mentoring program is put in place; the training program is formalised or a policy is put in place, there are some who will refuse to participate. Their reasons vary, but the effect is the same. They will want to be considered aside from any program. Some people (especially those budding into leadership, or developing into the mantle of prophet) will want special treatment.

We should steer clear of such "exceptions", because it undermines the very fabric of the community. It tears at the sense of right and wrong, and creates a double standard.

To avoid this, we should involve the whole fellowship in drafting our training programs, mentoring programs and policies. Participation removes the excuse that "we did not know", or that "we had no input to it". In addition, we should allow access by all people – regardless of education, race, gender or theological background. In this way, all excuse to avoid participation is removed.

This cannot be underscored strongly enough. Do not allow a backdoor for private prophecy. When you find people violating the principles you have all agreed on, it must be dealt with and not ignored. The policy applies equally to worship leaders speaking on the platform; counsellors in the back room; intercessors sharing a burden with leadership and businessmen in an administration meeting.

This material has been applied in many local churches. In Appendix One, you will find the draft policy for a church of 200 members. It is not intended as a "cut and paste," but rather as a model, or example for you to see how these principles can be applied in any local environment.

REFERENCES

Thanks to Len Rossow, Brett Lush and the team at Genesis Christian Ministries. The refinement of this work was largely due to workshops held at their church in Carrara, QLD. For an example policy see *Appendix One*.

Chapter Fifteen
PRAYER, PRAISE & PROPHECY

" 'Were it not for the presence of Jehoshaphat the king of Judah, I would not look at you nor see you. But now bring me a minstrel.' And it came about, when the minstrel played, that the hand of the Lord came upon him." (2 Kings 3:14b-15).

Elisha's address appears short handed, rude. He seems to be short on temper. He has parted the Jordan, healed the waters at Jericho, been mocked by young men (who got mauled by She-bears), had a prayer meeting up Mt Carmel and walked to Samaria. Now the kings of Edom, Judah and Israel are going out together to fight the Moabites... and they need a word from the Lord. Elisha is standing before three kings, two of whom he has no regard for. He only respects Jehoshaphat because of his father David.

So what does Elisha do? Will he, "Fake it till he makes it?" Will he reject their request and tell them to come back after he has prayed? No, he calls for a minstrel! In modern terms, a guitarist, a really hot player. Then he sits down in the presence of music and starts to pray... and what's the result? Prophecy!

Prayer (intercession, reflection, meditation); praise (dance, drama, worship, instrumental music) and prophecy (of all kinds) are kissing cousins (that means they're close!). We see this in the New Testament: *"When He had taken the **scroll**, the four living creatures and the twenty four elders fell down before the Lamb, each having a **harp**, and golden bowls full of incense, which are the **prayers** of the saints."* (Revelation 5:8 emphasis mine).

Here in heaven, we find a beautiful picture of the interaction between God and His creation; between heaven and earth; between prayer, praise, and prophecy. Here is the Lamb of God – Jesus Christ, with the four living creatures – heavenly, angelic beings with the elders – representatives of the Church on earth. Here is the Transcendent One, receiving worship from eternal celestial beings, enjoying the company of mortal men.

- The *scroll* of the Lamb is prophecy,
- The *bowls* full of incense is prayer,
- The *harps* of the saints are for praise.

COMPARING PRAYER AND PROPHECY

Prayer and prophecy are similar in some ways. Interceding, praying, and prophesying are things that every believer should be able and confident to do. They both use revelation and insight to accomplish their roles. Cindy Jacobs defines Spirit-led intercession as, "The ability to receive an immediate prayer request from God and pray about it in a divinely anointed utterance."[1] When interceding, we need to know what God's will and mind are on the matter – and this can only come by revelation. Likewise our revelation, rightly delivered, needs to come from God and not from our own mind and will.

THE DIFFERENCES

Intercession is standing before God on behalf of man,
The prophetic is standing before man on behalf of God.

The intercessor brings the needs of men before God,
The prophetic brings the heart of God to men.

---

1. "The Voice of God." Pg 39.

The intercessor is looking heavenward,
The prophet is looking earthward.

Paul outlines the burden of God-ward intercession in this way, *"We do not know what we ought to pray for, but the Spirit Himself intercedes for us with groans that words can not express. He who searches our hearts knows the mind of the Spirit, because the Spirit intercedes for the saints in accordance with God's will."* (Romans 8:26,27).

The Spirit within us searches the mind of God, to stir up a prayer from our hearts. It is directed at God, and we intercede in accordance with God's will.

In contrast, Paul describes prophetic ministry this way, *"Everyone who prophesies, speaks to men for their strengthening, encouragement and comfort. He who speaks in a tongue edifies himself, but he who prophesies edifies the Church."* (1 Corinthians 14:4,5).

The Spirit within us hears the word of God, and brings it to men. We are ministering to men on behalf of God.

Prayer has no "office" or mantle in the Bible. Every believer is commanded to pray. "Intercessor" is not a title given to any mortal man in the Bible. People erroneously use the word intercessor as a title or an office. There is only one Person mentioned in the Bible as an intercessor by office and His name is Jesus Christ. Intercessors may 'stand in the gap' but, *"There is one God, and one mediator also between God and men, Christ Jesus."* (1 Timothy 2:5). Still, Jesus **has** given mantled prophets to the Body.

COMPARING PRAISE AND THE PROPHETIC

The prophetic ministry and true worship both require the ability to be in the spirit, and not in the soul or flesh. Jesus said, *"The hour is coming, and is now here, when the true worshipers will worship the Father in spirit and truth, for the Father seeks such as these to worship him. God is spirit, and those who worship him must worship in spirit and truth."* (John 4:23,24). The combination of being in the spirit (and not the soul or flesh) and being honest (truthful) makes for true worship and also true prophetic ministry.

They both deal with, or are undermined by sin. Consider another statement made about worship, *"We know that God does not listen to sinners, but he does listen to one who worships him and obeys his will."* (John 9:31). Notice again the connection with honesty, obedience, humility, and worship.

THE DIFFERENCES

Worship ministry is directed heavenward,
Prophetic ministry is directed earthward.

Worshipful music takes technical proficiency and skill,
Prophetic ministry is not based on proficiency but grace.

Worship can tend toward routine and a practiced performance,
Prophecy tends toward spontaneity and stirring up.

Worship celebrates accomplishment of God's will and vision,
Prophecy imparts God's will and vision.

CONCLUSION

In the book of Revelation we see the scroll – prophecy, in the Hands of God, from the Heart of God, proceeding from the Mouth of God. There is the bowl – prayer in the hands of the saints, from the needs of the saints, proceeding from the mouth of the saints.

There are the harps – praise, ushered in by man, resonating throughout all creation, adjoined to the voice of angels. There are three beautiful elements in harmony, a symphony. The Greek word for that is *sumphoneo*. This composite word is made from *sum:* with; and *phoneo:* to call, to sound, to harmonise. To harmonise together!

"If two of you agree on earth about anything that they may ask, it shall be done for them by my Father who is in heaven." (Matthew 18:19). With prayer, praise, and prophecy there are three voices in harmony. There is symphony, agreement, and beauty. That happened in another place... in the upper room, when 120 people were praying. They were in on accord, in agreement, composing a *sumphoneo* and the Lord joined in... and there was wind and fire! (Acts 2:1,2).

Watch out Church, when we learn to work together, lifting our voices together, in unity and harmony. Watch out devil, when the Lord, His Church, and the angels work together.

REFERENCES

Hughes, Ray. "Sound of Heaven, Symphony of Earth." MorningStar, 2000.
Jacobs, Cindy. "The Voice of God." Generals of Intercession, 1997.

CHAPTER SIXTEEN
THE EZEKIEL FOURTEEN TRAP!

"Any of those of the house of Israel, or of the aliens who reside in Israel, who separate themselves from me, taking their idols into their hearts and placing their iniquity as a stumbling block before them, and yet come to a prophet to inquire of me by him, I the LORD will answer them myself. I will set my face against them; I will make them a sign and a byword and cut them off from the midst of my people; and you shall know that I am the LORD. If a prophet is deceived and speaks a word, I, the LORD, have deceived that prophet, and I will stretch out my hand against him, and will destroy him from the midst of my people Israel. And they shall bear their punishment—the punishment of the inquirer and the punishment of the prophet shall be the same." (Ezekiel 14:7-11).

We take a moment out here to learn a lesson from another respected prophet in the Old Testament. In the midst of talking about the prophetic gift and the Church, we need to examine the interaction between a minister and those receiving ministry. Ezekiel was a contemporary of Daniel, and lived some three hundred years after Elisha.

Some leaders in Israel approached Ezekiel. It was the custom for leaders to consult the Lord's anointed in regards to their decisions. In this instance, Ezekiel had sought the Lord about these leaders, for he said of them as they approached, *"Shall I let them inquire of me at all?"* (14:3). He asked this because he had seen the hidden secrets of their hearts.

According to the testimony of God, these leaders had idols in their hearts, which amounted to, "A stumbling block of iniquity before their faces". It was a good thing Ezekiel inquired of God before he answered, for in the Scripture quoted above, the prophet would have found himself in some serious hot water! We have to ask, what is their idolatry? What is this "stumbling block of iniquity" that we should beware of? We **must** understand idolatry if we are to practise effective prophetic ministry.

IDOLATRY

I define an idol as, "A person, object or thing that becomes the object of excessive devotion", or "An image of deity which is worshiped." H. H. Rowley makes this pertinent comment, "Idolatry becomes evident when a people possessing pure worship of God, become seduced by various ways, and move away from Him."[1]

One day I was ministering in a church in St Louis, Missouri. Before the service, the angel of the Lord had come and told me, "I am here to take people's excess baggage." After the message, a hundred or so people came forward for prayer. We had made it clear that the ministry line was initially for the purpose of helping with "excess baggage."

If people had other needs they should wait until the end. In the line, I found a couple of sincere believers who were sick, and wanted healing. They were sent back to wait until the Lord had dealt with "excess baggage," and then they were invited to come back up for prayer. A memory of one lady stands out to me, all these years later. When I laid hands on her, there was **no** unction to pray. There was silence for a moment and I asked her, "Why are you here?"

---

1. "The Faith of Israel," Pg 74.

She said, "I am burdened about a very important decision to make on Monday and I need a word." Though she couched her "decision" as excess baggage, I was troubled. I explained to her the reason people were in the line, but she persisted. I tried to explain, "Your need does not seem reason enough to come up," and then in a flash the Lord showed me that she wanted to know what colour she should choose for her car, which would be delivered on Monday! I confirmed that this was what she was asking for, and then I felt the anger of the Lord burning against her. She had violated the instruction of the angel, and my counsel on who was to receive ministry, she had manufactured a "need" and absolutely trivialised the prophetic function. That's idolatry!

THE BOOK OF JUDGES

The book of Judges, chapters 17-19 provide a chilling description of the end results of idolatry. It shows the effect on society, family, or a person who allows the stumbling block of iniquity to remain before their consciences. It is a candid story of a perverse and degraded society which walked the road of religious corruption (17:1-13), allowed social unrest and general lawlessness to become entrenched (18:1-31) and ended in complete moral declension (19:1-20).

Both Old and New Testament polemics against idolatry recognise that the idol itself is nothing[2] but behind the idol lies a sinister, active spiritual force. Idolatry is a spiritual menace, an agent of decline, and a major cause of backsliding. It is not a passive or harmless pastime.[3] Idolatry is anything whatsoever which usurps the rightful place of Christ on the throne of our hearts. At its core, idolatry is a grave sin that constitutes spiritual adultery.[4]

---

2. Isaiah 2:8, Psalm 115:4-7, 1 Corinthians 8:4   3. Isaiah 44:18-20
4. Deuteronomy 31:16, Judges 2:17

The apostle John underscored the fullness of revelation we have in our relationship with Christ, then goes on to warn that any deviation is idolatry. [5] An idol claims loyalty that rightly belongs to God alone. [6]

Let's come back to Ezekiel. Were these elders men who sacrificed to idols on the altars of Baal? Do we think they assembled beside the Asherah poles, or sacrificed their children to Molech? It is highly unlikely! They were elders in Israel, respectable men. In the same way, we will not find people bowing down to poles or stones in the Church today. Are we not just as guilty of idolatry?

They had made peace with secret sins in their lives, and sacrificed their peace with God. They had allowed something else to take the place of their devotion to the Lord alone. They, like many believers today tolerated sin. They probably knew what the sin was, yet their consciences were deadened.

David Orton suggests that, "Deep within the walls of the temple, in a dark and secret room, the elders worshiped false images. The KJV describes the room as, 'the chambers of his own imagery,' (Ezekiel 8:12)... inside the room Ezekiel saw images covering the walls of 'crawling things, detestable animals, and all the idols of Israel.' [7] (Ezekiel 8:10). These images were in the secret place, hidden inside the temple. Today, we are the temple and the secret place is in our hearts.

For post modern Christians, living in the post-christendom era, the warning resounds against bitterness, envy, strife, faction, fight or sectarianism. [8] These are listed right alongside idolatry as acts of the flesh. Paul says greed is idolatry.

---

5. 1 John 5:19-21   6. Isaiah 42:8
7. "Snakes in the Temple." Pg 68   8. Galatians 5:20

He says: *"Put to death, therefore, whatever in you is earthly: fornication, impurity, passion, evil desire, and greed (which is idolatry). On account of these the wrath of God is coming on those who are disobedient."* (Colossians 3:5 c.f.) (Ephesians 5:5). In this, he agrees wholeheartedly with Ezekiel. Paul states that we, as Christians, should not eat with people who practise idolatry, nor be partners with them in any way. [9]

THE EFFECTS OF HIDDEN SIN

Whenever we make peace with sin, and allow a stumbling block of iniquity to take root in our lives, we suffer the consequences. The very first symptom is that our passion for Jesus cools. Immediately following that, we cease hearing the true voice of God. Idolatry stopped Saul hearing from God, and it distressed him sorely. This idolatrous, envious, proud, angry king inquired again and again of the Lord. But He refused to answer. Saul despaired, and finally resorted to asking a witch what the will of God would be! Saul cried, *"I am in great distress, for the Philistines are warring against me, and God has turned away from me and answers me no more, either by prophets or by dreams; so I have summoned you to tell me what I should do."* (1 Samuel 28:15).

In the book of Judges, the tribe of Ephraim wandered from the Lord and strayed into idolatry. They eventually repented and came back into the counsel of God. [10] David knew about the effects of hiding sin too. He clearly states, *"If I had cherished iniquity in my heart the Lord would not have heard my cry."* (Psalm 66:8). If we persist in our sins, the loving Lord, whom we serve, and whose name we have taken upon us, **will** answer us.

---

9. Ephesians 5:7, 1 Corinthians 5:11   10. Jeremiah 31:19

He will answer, but not according to what He wants us to hear. Scripture tells us that He will answer according to our sin, according to our idols. This was shown to Ezekiel, *"Any of those of the house of Israel who... place their iniquity as a stumbling block before them, and yet come to the prophet—I the LORD will answer those who come according to their great idolatry, in order that I may take hold of the hearts of the house of Israel."* (Ezekiel 14:4 KJV).

ACCORDING TO THEIR IDOLATRY

When God answers us according to our idolatry He speaks to us according to the will of the idol that sits upon the throne of our hearts. He misleads us so as to bring our hearts back to Him.

Balaam, that greedy and perverted prophet from Midian, had agreed to prophesy against Israel for the king of Moab. Balak had offered him gold and silver for the work. Balaam was sorely troubled by the offer and thought to ask God himself. Scripture testifies that God answered him all right, *"That night God came to Balaam and said to him, 'If the men have come to summon you, get up and go with them; but do only what I tell you to do'."* Balaam got up the next morning to go out to Balak and God's anger was kindled against him. The Lord immediately sent the angel to oppose him.[11] God answered his idol.

Ahab was perhaps the most idolatrous and evil king Israel had ever known. He and his wife Jezebel single-handedly perverted the entire nation except for a few thousand faithful. When Ahab wanted to go to war at Ramoth-Gilead he asked the prophets of Israel to tell him the mind of the Lord on the matter.

---

11. Numbers 22:20-22

The Ezekiel Fourteen Trap!

The prophets confirmed his desire to go up, and he was killed in battle the very next day. [12] God answered his idol.

The thankless generation of Israelites, who God miraculously delivered from slavery in Egypt, wandered in the desert. They complained against God because they did not have meat to eat (one would have thought that the supernatural supply of manna would have taught them the fear of God?). He answered their prayers wonderfully, by providing quail. They munched merrily upon the birds' flesh thinking, "God is with us, for surely he has heard our cry," and while the flesh was still between their teeth... the anger of the Lord was kindled against them and he struck them with a plague! [13] God answered their idol.

BEWARE OF ADVISING SUCH PEOPLE

So it is with us, God Himself will answer us according to our idolatry and our hidden sin, if we have made peace with it, and cling to it in our hearts. Remember Ahab asking the advice of the prophets? We know from the passage in Ezekiel that, *"If a prophet is deceived and speaks a word, I, the LORD, have deceived that prophet."* (Ezekiel 14:9). God sent a lying spirit to deceive the prophets and confirm His judgement against Ahab. [14] These prophets were not careful about the one they ministered to. Unlike Ezekiel, who inquired after the state of the leadership's heart, Ahab's prophets stuck to the party line, and became deceived.

We dare not be drawn into prophesying to people whose hearts are under the control of sinful idols. We should always first ask the Lord about the state of an inquirers heart. If we are drawn to prophesy to an idolatrous person, we will be deceived.

---

12. 1 Kings 22:37   13. Numbers 11:33
14. 1 Kings 22:20-22

We will prophesy a lie to them, confirming them in their judgement and thus bringing ourselves under the very same judgement. As Ezekiel was warned, *"I will stretch out my hand against him, and will destroy him from the midst of my people Israel. And they shall bear their punishment—the punishment of the inquirer and the punishment of the prophet shall be the same."* (Ezekiel 14:10).

This is also a New Testament concept, as Paul warned the Thessalonians, *"The coming of the lawless one is apparent in the working of Satan, who uses all power, signs, lying wonders, and every kind of wicked deception for those who are perishing, because they refused to love the truth and so be saved. For this reason God sends them a powerful delusion, leading them to believe what is false, so that all who have not believed the truth but took pleasure in unrighteousness will be condemned"* (2 Thessalonians 2:9-11).

The prophet Agabus from Jerusalem, who had received such a clear prophetic word about drought in Israel,[15] then stumbled into error in his prophecy to Paul. He stated, *"Thus says the Holy Spirit, 'This is the way the Jews in Jerusalem will bind the man who owns this belt and will hand him over to the Gentiles'."* (Acts 21:11).

According to Luke (who writes his account for us in Acts chapter 25), it was not the Jews, but the Romans who bound Paul. Yes, the High Preist from Jerusalem accused Paul, but he did so in Caesarea. It was the Gentiles who saved Paul from the Jews! Who knows what was in the heart of Agabus? He and many other believers clearly thought it would be bad for Paul to go to Jerusalem. Paul says many had tried to dissuade him from going.[16]

---

15. Acts 11:28   16. Acts 21:13

OUR RESPONSIBILITY

Paul had heard clearly from the Lord himself. He said, *"The Holy Spirit testifies to me in every city that imprisonment and persecutions are waiting for me."* (Acts 20:23). He knew what was coming, and was not prepared to put the will of men in place of the witness of the Holy Spirit. It is the prerogative of all who minister prophetically, to inquire of God as to the state of a man's heart – starting with their own! This is after all, one aspect of the prophetic ministry. Paul told the Corinthians that should an unbeliever enter a meeting when people are prophesying, *"The secrets of the unbeliever's heart will be disclosed, that person will bow down before God and worship him."* (1 Corinthians 14:25).

We should never go along with, endorse or support those who are persisting in sin, don't prophesy to them! There is only one measure of communication the Lord will enter into with such people, and that is judgement. He will answer according to their idolatry. A prophetic minister may be used of God to pronounce judgement against them. Jeremiah rebuked king Zedekiah, who inquired of him three times about the Lord's will. In each case the answer was judgement.[17] This king did what was evil in the Lord's sight, he persisted in evil, became proud, arrogant, hardhearted, and rebellious.

MERCY TRIUMPHS OVER JUDGEMENT

God's judgement arises from the righteous aspect of His character. It is balanced by His mercy and kindness. Incredibly, His mercy always triumphs over judgement.[18] The prophet Shemaiah brought word of God's retributive justice against the idolatrous king Rehoboam.

---

17. 2 Chronicles 36:12, Jeremiah 37:12   18. James 2:13

Upon hearing the word, Rehoboam was very distressed. He and all his men repented wholeheartedly, and the Lord diverted His judgement against them.[19]

Likewise, king Manasseh made his son pass through fire in the valley of the son of Hinnom (an act specifically denounced by God); practised soothsaying, augury, sorcery; dealt with mediums and did incredible evil, provoking God to anger. Yet, when the Lord rebuked him, he repented wholeheartedly and was restored![20] Thank God it is written, so we know that if we honestly repent we will be restored.

CONCLUSION

Idolatry is an insidious and debilitating disease of the soul that brings God's judgement against the idolater. Idolatry exists when we allow anything to usurp the place of Christ on the throne of our hearts. It includes such evils as greed, envy, bitterness, strife, or sectarianism. It is also characterised by making peace with our sin (whatever it may be), so that our consciences become deadened.

The effect of failing to repent of this secret sin is threefold; firstly our passion for Jesus cools; then we become deaf to the voice of God. We may hear "confirmation" to continue in our course of action; it will result in our destruction. The third thing which happens is that we suffer judgement. This judgement is aimed at bringing us to repentance and a turning around toward Him, because He is merciful and just.

People who minister prophetically must be wise like Ezekiel. We need to ask the Lord about the state of the inquirer's heart before answering them.

---

19. 2 Chronicles 12:6-8   20. 2 Chronicles 33:13

If we answer an idolater, then we will come under the same judgement as them. Ask God, and He will indeed show us, or make known the secrets of the heart.

Will we be able to deliver a true word to people who are unrepentant and living in peace with their sin? Yes, but it will be a word of judgement. We can expect God to ask us to speak to the idolater directly, as He has throughout the ages.

Guard yourselves. As the people of God, we must beware of making peace with our own sin. Let us seek God earnestly for anything that may have become an object of excessive devotion to us, lest having spoken the word to others we ourselves should be cast away. [21]

REFERENCES

Lods, Allmen and Pederson, "The Illustrated Bible Dictionary." Volume two, article "Idolatry"
Orton, David. "Snakes in the Temple." Sovereign World, 2004.
Rowley, H.H. "Faith of Israel." 1956.
Wilkerson, D. "The Stumbling Block of Iniquity." Times Square Pulpit Series. Feb, 1997.

---

21. 1 Corinthians 9:27

Chapter Seventeen
BALANCED LEADERSHIP

[Elisha said]: *"God will give the Moabites into your hand... you shall strike every fortified city."* (2 Kings 3:18,19).

Elisha has just interacted with the *nawgan* (the minstrel). He now gives the kings a sign by which they will know his word is true, the valley will fill with water. It is going to well up and rain down. Here we find Elisha the prophet serving in a team environment. Around him are generals and captains from the army, administrators and engineers from the civil service, the king and his advisors, along with the scribes and priests ready to make sacrifice.

The government of Israel was balanced because it relied upon the prophets as counsellors and the priests as its moral compass. When one became corrupted, the other two were supposed to bring them back into order.

The New Testament Church also has threefold leadership: the apostle, the prophet, and the teacher. Once again these three hold one another in the balance, and provide safe leadership for the Church.[1]

Consider these leaders as being the three points of a balanced propeller, on an aeroplane. If one is out of order, the whole is out of balance and endangers the passengers.

---

1. 1 Corinthians 12:28. Some would argue that it is a five fold leadership. However, at its simplest, there are three. Teacher can be considered part of the priestly/ pastor role and evangelist as part of the apostolic or church planting mandate. Acts 13:1-3 illustrates the role of prophet and teacher in setting apart the apostle for further church growth.

To understand the gift of prophecy and the role of prophet in the Church, we must place them in a team environment. No prophet is an island; no minister a law unto himself.

In practice, if we remove a blade from the propeller, the balance shifts toward its opposite. Scripture has a lot to say about these three vital roles, and how they function together. Here are six illustrative examples:

1. 1 Peter 2:9

Peter describes the position or status of all believers. We are a royal (kingly) priesthood (godly) and a holy (prophetic) nation. The opposite, which manifests when we are lacking some element, is a common (disordered), godless (carnal) and an unholy (sinful) nation.

2. 1 Corinthians 12:28

Paul describes the positional (not hierarchical) state of leadership in the Church. God appointed first apostles (fathers), second prophets (revelators) and third teachers (truth bringers). The opposite, which manifests when we are lacking one of these leaders, is false apostles (controllers), false prophets (speaking from vain imagination) and false teachers (breeding deception).

3. Jude 11

Jude, the brother of Jesus, warned us about those who blaspheme and speak against things they do not understand. He presents us with three false leaders as warnings to our faith. First, their opposites: humble leadership (represented in Moses), faithful prophecy (in Phineas) and sacrificial worship (by Abel). Jude warns us not to walk in rebellion (like Korah), in error (taught by Balaam), or in works (of Cain).

4. Micah 3:11
Micah addresses leadership and corruption in this chapter. We are seeking righteous judgement (from an impartial perspective), godly counsel (correct insight), and uninhibited teaching (unfettered by love of men or money). Micah, then, lashes out against leaders who judge for a bribe (showing partiality), divine for money (a form of witchcraft), and teach for payment (bribery).

5. Ezekiel 7:26
Ezekiel highlighted the corruption of leadership in this chapter. He looked for protective eldership (who brought helpful counsel), invigorating prophets (who gave vision), and educating priests (who built knowledge into the people). In his day, corrupted leaders were in power. False elders isolated themselves (brought bad judgement), false prophets obfuscated the truth (which led to the people perishing), and corrupt priests spread ignorance (which resulted in destruction).

6. Revelation 3:18
John the apostle was shown this three-fold leadership as necessary for life, godliness, and freedom. He spoke to the church at Laodicea, and he counselled them to buy gold (wealth owned by the kings and commerce); get eye salve (insight that they might see); and a white garment (of purity). The opposite is to be in bondage to slavery (losing the gold), be blind (from infected eyes), and have a soiled garment (impure lifestyle).

IN ALL SPHERES OF GOVERNANCE

These forms of leadership should find their expression at every level of life – in the home, the Church, the marketplace, military, police force, political world, and so forth. The Bible presents us with three forms of government: the institution of marriage, the institution of the Church, and the institution of secular government. God has placed the rod of discipline in the hands of parents. He has placed the shepherds staff in the hands of the church, and the sword of justice in the hands of government. Each of these three divinely appointed institutions was designed to achieve different outcomes for the establishment of the Kingdom of God. I present a more thorough treatment of this in my book, "The Spirit of Elijah" (chapter 16).

The home
Home is the place of nurturing, of discipline and correction, the place of love, education, and provision. Parents raise the children in godly fear, loving nurture and prepare their character and gifts. *"Train up a child in the way he should go, even when he is old he will not depart from it."* (Proverbs 22:6).

The Church
The Church is called to shepherd, disciple and train. It is the place of healing and restoration, the place of worship and devotion. Shepherds humbly raise the sheep in the ways of God, modelling respect, and honour to all: *"Make disciples of all nations."* (Mathew 28:19).

Secular government
The government is to hold the sword of justice, correction and administration. It brings law, order, defense, research, and community development. Governors are guardians of peace and truth. *"Government does not bear the sword for nothing; for it is a minister of God, an avenger who brings wrath on the one who does evil."* (Romans 13:4).

When a nation has moved away from God, these institutions become corrupt, and the effect is felt by all the inhabitants of the land. Ezekiel gives an example in chapter 7:23, where he said the cities were filled with violence and bloodshed; the homes were over-run by Gentiles, and the whole place had become defiled.

EXPANDING THE PICTURE

All things are in Christ; He is our pattern, He is our all, and our gifts come from Him. From Him extends this three-fold leadership pattern we have described: prophet, priest, and king. Each of these is an outworking of His nature.

Ephesians chapter 4 describes these extending outward to five: apostle, prophet, evangelist, pastor, and teacher. The Book of Romans chapter 12 describes seven separate gifts from the Spirit: prophecy (insight), ministry (service), teaching (training), exhortation (encouragement), giving (hospitality), leading (administration), and mercy (love).

Each person has a different way of viewing the world, of imposing meaning on events. Consider a car crash. Each person has a perspective; the driver, the bystander, the policeman and the insurance agent all bring different views.

MENTAL EXERCISE

Let's do an exercise together, to paint this picture. Imagine we are at the birthday party of a seven year old child. There is a table piled high with presents, and another with food of all kinds. On the edge of a second table is a birthday cake, ready for the candles to be lit. In runs an excited boy, and as he passes by the table his sleeve catches the cake, and knocks it onto the floor, ruining it. Disaster!

- How do you feel about this incident?
- To whom do you speak about it?

- What do you say?
- What do you want to see done about it?

Stop reading for a moment, and write down your answers to those four questions before you read the next section. Go on, no cheating! Then come back and read on!

CONCLUSION

We have tabled the results of this exercise many times, and the results are fairly consistent across cultures, times, and seasons. There are many responses to a crisis, each providing a relevant solution. In this case there are about seven, based on the gifting in Romans 12:

The Prophet
The Seer has insight. "I knew it. How could we have avoided this? Can we correct it?"
The Exhorter has encouragement. "It will be alright. Is the child OK? It's good that nobody got hurt."

The Priest
The Server does ministry. "I'll clean it up. Let's get all the children to move outside."
The Teacher wants to train. "How did this happen? What can we learn from this?"
The Compassionate person shows love. "Don't feel bad. It was only an accident. Kiss and make up."

The King
The Giver shows hospitality. "I'll go buy another cake. Let's get some ice cream!"
The Leader will administrate. "OK team, arrange a game for the kids. Someone clean it up."

If all these characters are present, there will be a balanced solution to the situation! The birthday boy is consoled, the running child is reprimanded, the mess is cleaned up, the other partygoers are entertained, a new cake is bought, and all is well. We learn from the mistake and move on.

"Each of you has a gift and each one can minister for the profit of all." (1 Corinthians 12:7). *"Submit to one another in the fear of God."* (Ephesians 5:21).

The prophet's view is only one of seven possible, legitimate views. Humility enables us to accept that others will see it differently. We will empathise with them. As prophetic people we bring **one** point of view to the team, and we need to value the rest of the team equally.

REFERENCES

Fortune, Don & Katie. "Discover Your God Given Gifts." Peacemakers, 1994.
Holmes, Robert. "The Spirit of Elijah." Storm Harvest Inc., 2005. Chapter 16 & 17.

Chapter Eighteen
DISCERNING OF SPIRITS

"Now the sons of the prophets were sitting before [Elisha]; and he said to his servant, 'Put on the large pot and boil stew for the sons of the prophets.' So one went out into the field to gather herbs and found a wild vine and gathered from it a lap full of wild gourds, and came and sliced them into the pot of stew... now it happened that whilst they were eating the stew that they cried, 'Man of God there is death in the pot!' and they could not eat it." (2 Kings 4:38b-40).

There is a guest, a dignitary, a leader coming over for dinner. To prepare the meal, we buy the ingredients and they all look good. Once we have made the dinner, though, we discover that the ingredients are past their "use-by date". No matter, the dish seems to smell fine. When the meal is served, however, we discover that the whole meal is off! The cook is mortally embarrassed! If only they had prepared more carefully.

In the same way, we need to approach what we eat spiritually with care. The gift of discernment helps those eating to make sense of what they are eating! It also helps the "cook" pick the ingredients with care, so that his meal is not poisonous!

What would we do if an apparition purporting to be an angel appeared before us with a "message from the Lord"? Or what if we had a vision a saint, long dead? Should we seek advice from the angel, the saint, or only from the Lord? Where does a fascination with the supernatural communication of God lead us anyway? Can we expect God Almighty to use angels to speak with us, and bring us messages?

THE BASICS OF DISCERNMENT

"All who obey His commandments abide in Him, and He abides in them. And by this we know that He abides in us, by the Spirit that He has given us. Beloved, do not believe every spirit, but test the spirits to see whether they are from God; for many false prophets have gone out into the world." (1 John 3:24-4:3). The Holy Spirit is the One who gives us experiential knowledge of Christ living in us... we can know if a spirit is from God by whether or not it acknowledges that Christ has come in the flesh. There will be an internal witness, a peace.

If the spirit at work within the messenger is the Holy Spirit, He will recognise and acknowledge that Jesus lives in us. If the spirit does not recognise Christ in our flesh, then it must be false. Imperfect humans, however, can operate out of different spirits at different times. Christ blessed Peter for manifesting revelatory knowledge from the Father, and then in the next passage rebuked him for speaking out of the spirit of satan (Mathew 16:23). We can know by the inner witness of the Spirit whether a messenger is from God or not – but we can never base our discernment on our own understanding.

Discerning of spirits is therefore not only about telling the difference between angels and demons; or whether a message is from God or the pit of hell; it is also about discerning the human spirit. *"This I pray, that your love may abound still more and more in knowledge and all discernment."* (Phillipians 1:9). This was Paul's desire for the Church. Discernment is a gift we desperately need today. Particularly when coupled with the prophetic. Insight without wisdom is a bit like a gold ring in a pig's snout. It is interesting, but useless.

TWO "GIFTS" OF DISCERNMENT

There are two kinds of discernment, one natural and the other spiritual. The natural gift is described in Hebrews: *"Solid food belongs to those of full age, that is, those who by reason of use have their senses exercised to discern both good and evil."* (Hebrews 5:14). This gift is gained by exercise – by practice. The spiritual gift of discernment is mentioned by Paul: *"But the manifestation of the Spirit is given to each one for the profit of all... to another discerning of spirits."* (1 Corinthians 12:7,10).

This gift is an outworking of grace given when natural wisdom alone will not suffice. We employ both natural and spiritual discernment to tell one thing from the other: a demon from an angel, or to discern a person's spirit. For example, how would you know what kind of spirit glided past Job;[1] which spirits Micaiah saw gathered before God;[2] or which spirit from God troubled Saul?[3]

THREE REALMS OF DISCERNMENT

Let us look a little more closely at three realms: discerning in the demonic realm, discerning in the heavenly realm, and discerning in the earthly realm. Or to put it another way, discerning between kinds of demonic oppression, discerning between kinds of angelic encounters, and discerning the human spirit.

In Hebrew culture, and therefore in the language of the Bible, a name defines a nature. Names told the hearer (or reader) something about that person, place, or object. For example Jacob was a deceiver (his name means supplanter), until he became Israel (he will rule as God does).

---

1. Job 4:15   2. 2 Chronicles 18:20
3. 1 Samuel 16:14

Abram (high father) became Abraham (father of many nations). Similarly, the Gadarene demoniac identified his demon as "Legion" for they were many. The destroying angel in Revelation is called "Abaddon" meaning destruction etc.

THE DEMONIC REALM

Several words are used to describe the demonic realm. The generic term for them in the New Testament is "unclean spirits," meaning they are fallen, and unclean before God because of their rebellion. There are seven words in the Greek for demonic entities in the New Testament:

- *Daimon*: demon (minor follower); [4]
- *Daimonion*: unclean spirit (demon behind idols); [5]
- *Therion*: brute beast (defiling and deceiving spirits); [6]
- *Exousia*: power (freedom fighter, potentate, strong man); [7]
- *Arche*: principality (power, chief ruler, first); [8]
- *Kosmokrator*: world ruler (controller, prince of darkness); [9]
- *Diabolos*: The devil (satan). [10]

When we engage forces of evil, whether in deliverance or spiritual warfare, it is important to discern what kind of entity we are dealing with. People often say, "The devil is giving me a hard time today." Do they honestly believe the entity called *diabolos*, the devil personified in satan, has the time to come and hassle **them**? Does he even know their name? Probably not. We attribute skills and abilities to demons that they do not possess. They do not have vast knowledge, or the ability to be in several places at once.

---

4. Luke 8:29, Revelation 16:14
5. Mathew. 7:22, 1 Corinthians 10:20
6. Revelation 11:7, 14:9-11
7. Ephesians 6:12, Collosians 2:14,15
8. Romans 8:38, Collosians 2:15, Jude 6
9. John 12:28-32, Daniel 10:2
10. Mathew 4:1, Mathew 25:41

Most of the time we are working against entities that are ignorant of us, and our specific weaknesses. What they do possess is an intimate working knowledge of the human frame, or disposition. Some have agrued that there is a distinction to be made between demons and fallen angels. Dr Brian Bailey does and excellent job in his book, "Angels Good & Bad". This split may have implications for deliverance and prayer ministries.

THE HEAVENLY REALM

Often in Scripture we find the word "angel" appended to a descriptive word, or compounded with them. The list is endless, but here is a selection from Greek (Gk.), Hebrew (Heb.) and Chaldean (Chal.) languages of the Bible, outlining the kinds of angels:

- *Aggelos* (Gk.): angel (ministering spirit, messenger); [11]
- *Aggelos ekklesia* (Gk.): angel of the church (assigned to a city); [12]
- *Mal'ak* (Heb.): guardian angel; [13]
- *Iyr* (Chal.): watcher, (Hebrew: *uwr*, meaning awake); [14]
- *Doxa-aggelos* (Gk.): celestial being; [15]
- *Cherubim* (Heb.): cherub (wings of the wind); [16]
- *Seraphim* (Heb.): seraph (flame of fire); [17]
- *Ischuros-aggelos* (Gk.): mighty angel; [18]
- *Arche* (Gk.): authority (chief angel); [19]
- *Arch-aggelos* (Gk.): arch angel (prince); [20]
- *Exousia* (Gk.): Ruler (godly principalities); [21]

---

11. Hebrews 1:14
12. Revelation 2 & 3
13. Psalm 92:11, Mathew. 18:10
14. Daniel 4:13, 17
15. 2 Peter 2:10, Jude 8
16. Genesis 3:24, Exodus 25:18-22
17. Isaiah 6, Ezekiel 10:21
18. Revelation 5:2, 10:1, 18:21
19. Ephesians 3:10
20. Daniel 8:16, Daniel 10:13, Jude 9, 1 Thessalonians 4:16
21. Ephesians 3:10

When we worship, seek the Father in meditation of the Scriptures, or listen in the Spirit realm, it is important to know what we are dealing with. If our service is attended by an angelic being, or a minister claims to have heard from an angel, it is important to be able to discern these phenomena. Angels are clean and carry with them a sense of holiness, awe, and love. They are never frivolous, never unkind, never disrespectful, and are usually quite businesslike.

Angels which come from the presence of God carry a message, an anointing, a blessing, or strengthening for the saints. They do not waste time, they do not argue over points of doctrine. Other angels camp about the saints, attend and protect meetings, minister with the prophets, and there is some argument to be made for guardian angels.

THE EARTHLY REALM

Jesus discerned people. He knew where they were at, understood their character and how they were going to respond to Him. He told Nathaniel, *"I knew you from under the tree."* (John 1:48). He knew what was in the heart of every man [22] and often in crowds could discern what men were thinking. [23] We have authority to use the gift of discernment in all of these ways.

This gift is desperately needed in the prophetic today. One example springs to mind, of a prophet ministering in California. She was prophesying over the young, male pastor of the church. The church was a cutting edge, pumping place. She proclaimed, "This man is a prototype, exactly the kind of leader God is raising up in this nation, a man to be followed and copied". To her chagrin, three weeks later his homosexual lifestyle was uncovered by the local newspaper. He had been intimate with many of the male staff in his church. How tragic, but avoidable, if discernment had been exhibited!

---

22. John 2:25   23. Mark 2:8

JUDGING PEOPLE

There is a fine line between discerning and judging. When we use discernment, we aim to tell where a person is coming from, what is going on inside them, rather than what motivated them, or the reason they acted the way they did. Discernment becomes fraught with danger as soon as we assign motives.

Consider, for example, observing a woman in your audience crossing her arms, then crossing her legs. You conclude, "She crossed her arms, she crossed her legs… she might be cold… no she is closed to my ideas and statements." That is discernment. To go on and say, "She is closed because she does not believe in… she is closed because of what her pastor said to her…," would be judging and the Bible warns us not to judge another person. Below is a non-exhaustive list of the state of person's spirit. People can have a:

- Sleeping spirit (spirit of stupor) – Romans 11:8;
- Lying spirit – 1 Kings 22:23;
- Spirit of prostitution – Hosea 5:4;
- Broken spirit – Psalm 51:17;
- Haughty spirit – Proverbs 16:18;
- Timid spirit – 2 Timothy 1:7;
- Sullen spirit – 1 Kings 21:1-5;
- Willing spirit – Psalm 51:12;
- Faithful spirit – Proverbs 11:13;
- Spirit of power – 2 Timothy 1:7;
- Quiet and gentle spirit – 1 Peter 3:4;
- Spirit of judgment(alism) – Isaiah 4:4;
- Spirit of justice – Isaiah 28:6;
- Renewed spirit – Ezekiel 18:31;
- Spirit of grace and supplication – Zechariah. 12:10;
- Spirit of sonship – Romans 8:15 or a;
- Spirit of unity – Romans 15:5.

THE CROSS-OVER LINE

Many people ask me in prophetic schools and spiritual warfare seminars, "Where is the line between the prophetic and the occult? What is the difference between discernment and soul or mind reading? How can I tell if I am crossing over?" These are fair questions, albeit sometimes driven by fear of failure or fear of sin.

The gift of discernment is a God-given, God-activated matter. Though our eyes are on a person, we are asking God for His perspective. We are "reading" them spiritually, rather than trying to peer into their soul. It is like the difference between reading body language, and being a peeping Tom. Soul reading, or mind reading as some call it, is a much more intrusive affair. Whoever does this is seeking to probe, to find out, to discover information hidden from them. Their eyes are on the people (as Saul's were), their attention is on gaining information and there is no reference to Jesus Christ.

Of Jesus it is said, *"His delight shall be in the fear of the LORD. He shall not judge by what His eyes see, or decide by what His ears hear."* (Isaiah 11:3). Jesus gave us a living demonstration of how to walk with God, using discernment. We can judge by the Spirit – and sense what is true and real. We observe during ordinary conversation, we are alert to key words they keep using, we check our internal reaction to see if we feel well about what they say, we are listening to our "inner man".

There is a key contained in the book of Ezekiel, who distinguishes between those who minister to men in the outer court, and those who minister to God in the Holy place. Those who are undertaking ministry unto the Lord are told, *"They shall not sweat."* (Ezekiel 44:18). Their ministry is not based on labour; they are not trying to force the matter. They are clothed carefully, and their conduct is pure. Those who are sweating, labouring, trying, working hard, must check their conduct and pull back.

CONCLUSION

The gift of discernment gives us the ability to discern all three spheres or realms – the heavenly, the demonic, and the realm of human nature. It encompasses the realm of behaviour, performance, motivation, instinct, and outcomes. A discerning person can tell right away what a person is like, gauge the atmosphere of a church, business, or street situation immediately. It is like the ability to smell if food is off, or if wine is excellent. It is to stand beside a person and know what the person is like – with no specific detail, nor even cognitive rationale to support our "gut instinct".

Author Malcolm Gladwell describes this as the ability to "thin slice" life.[24] It is being able to make a compelling decision on the basis of a very small amount of information, or from a very small sample of someone's life. It happens every day. The nurse in E.R., the policeman under fire, the soldier in battle, the counsellor listening to marriage troubles, the doctor diagnosing sickness on the basis of a fifteen minute conversation. People can all thin-slice, or make decisions based on a small sample. Consider the axiom that, "A man's mind is like his sock drawer", or that "A woman's emotions are like their living room". We are saying that just by looking at a small portion of a person's living space, we can fairly accurately discern what they are like.

---

24. "Blink" Pg 23, 43-47.

For those who lack spiritual discernment, there is a natural, learned variety. The good news is that, *"If any of you is lacking in wisdom, ask God, who gives to all generously and ungrudgingly, and it will be given you."* (James 1:5). There's hope for us yet! No more eating poisoned soup. Amen.

REFERENCES

Bailey, Brian. "Angels Good and Bad." Zion Christian Publishers, 2002.
Gladwell, Malcolm. "Blink." 2005. Little, Brown & Co, 2005.
Graham, Billy. "Angels, God's Secret Agents." Hodder Christian Paperbacks, 1975, 1986.
Vine, W.E. "Vine's Expository Dictionary." Thomas Nelson, 1997.

Chapter Nineteen
MENTORING THE PROPHETIC

"Gird up your loins [Gehazi] and take my staff in your hand, and go your way; if you meet any man, do not salute him and if anyone salutes you, do not answer him; and lay my staff on the lad's face." (2 Kings 4:29).

Elisha, who learned all he knew about the prophetic from his spiritual father Elijah, was taking the opportunity to train another, just as Jesus would do in His ministry. Gehazi had been with him for years, watching, seeing, hearing, and absorbing. The son of the widow had died, and Elisha knew in his spirit that the lad could be raised. He handed his staff to Gehazi and gave him clear instructions. All Gehazi needed to do was apply his faith.

I made many faux pas as a young person whose prophetic gift was beginning to emerge. I had a propensity to stick my foot into other people's mouths! I recall my first word of knowledge, within seven days of being saved, delivered, and filled with the Spirit. There was a healing line at the front of our Anglican Church, and they were praying for a girl named Meagan. She had a sore foot, swollen so much she could not walk. While the team were rebuking the devil, binding the swelling, speaking to the tendons, and rubbing it with oil. In my spirit I could hear Meagan being yelled at by her father. I saw a picture of her sitting in her room, angry with him. Out of my mouth came, "Why are you so angry at your dad?" Everything stopped, and she stared at me, "How did you know?" she asked. I really did not know how, I just knew... and spoke a little to quickly for the rest of the team.

The elders and deacons promptly took me to the back of the room to explain prophetic etiquette to me, Meagan's ankle was healed. In those days it seemed as though I was in trouble more than I was out of it. I couldn't understand what I was doing wrong. I made all the mistakes that young prophetic people make: poor timing of prophecy, harshness, pride in being the one "hearing from God," and that old faithful – rejection. What I really needed was a mentor.

THE ORIGIN OF MENTOR

In the ancient Greek Poem, "The Odyssey," written by Homer, there are several characters. The central warrior was Laertes, King of Ithaca. He was away at war for over thirty years, and left his son Odysseus (Ulysses) in the care of his chief servant Mentor. Mentor raised Ulysses in-stead (that is, in the place of) his father. He did not draw the son's heart to himself, but raised him just as his father would. He raised Ulysses in the way of a king, not a chief steward.

In "The Voice of God," there is an excellent working definition of mentoring: "Mentoring refers to the process where a person with a serving, giving, encouraging attitude [the mentor], sees leadership potential in a still-to-be developed person [the protégé], and is able to promote or otherwise significantly influence the protégé along in the realisation of potential."[1]

BEING A MENTOR

We do not have to be prophetic to mentor prophetic people, but it certainly helps. Mentoring prophetic people can be intimidating. They have a spectacular gift, which can awe and impress unwise leaders. Their gift mis-fires from time to time, and they need to be coached through the reasons why error creeps into their words.

---

1. "The Voice of God," quotes Robert Clinton's definition. Pg 114.

They may be struggling with character issues like pride, overconfidence, super spirituality, and impatience. These struggles are compounded by the environment in which they must minister, which is often very pastoral. They are afraid of making a mistake, desire to impress and be praised, and work hard not to step over the line.

Prophetic people – particularly those with developing gifts – find it really hard to pace themselves. Tyro prophets (learners) tend to have one speed: fast forward! Everything they hear from God has an intangible immediacy about it. Many have typical "Type A" personalities [hard driving, task oriented] who want everything to happen NOW! They are seeing life through a set of binoculars. Everything appears closer than it actually is. Most prophetic types would burn themselves out (and the rest of us with them) long before maturity if they were not given some help by a competent mentor.

Mentoring must be viewed as a long term process. We are not in a rush to create perfect prophets. God takes time with us. To quote two dear friends of mine: Mario Liu says, "Slow change makes good and lasting change." Kerry Denten says, "God will keep raising an issue until it is dealt with to His satisfaction, not ours," (or the protégé's). This can be very frustrating for the person being discipled, because it feels like the mentor is hammering on the same issues over and over again. He or she can become disheartened, or threatened that we might withdraw our love.

God makes us go around the mountain one more time until we learn, and some of us dig a big furrow from the endless walking! We go through pain the first time by mistake, we go through it a second time because of stubbornness, but by the third time, it is just plain pride. A mentor's job is to assist the mentoree out of this endless circling of the mountain.

WAITING

Freshly felled trees are hewn, then laid aside to dry off. Waiting will season the timber, improving its strength and durability. One of God's favourite ways to season us is through the fiery furnace of waiting. During this time we are training, learning, doing a work-out. Paul loved this comparison, saying we needed to train consistently like athletes for the big race.[2] Waiting tempers and trains us. The mentor stands by the mentoree during this time, and may be instrumental in making them wait.

Jeremiah was told a similar thing: *"If you have run with the footmen, and they have wearied you, then how can you contend with horses? And if in the land of peace, in which you trusted, they wearied you, then how will you do in the floodplain of the Jordan?"* (Jeremiah 12:5). We have to be good at walking before we can succeed at running! We need to be a good servant before trying to lead!

SERVING

One of the best ways to develop character is through serving. It tests a person's willingness to submit to authority, and thereby exercise authority. It tests our humility, and therefore our fitness for promotion. We have already seen that Elisha was known as the servant of Elijah – doing the menial women's labour of pouring water on the hands. Joshua went through the same kind of training. Joshua was known in Israel as, "The servant of Moses." He was not called, "The servant of Jehovah," until the book of Joshua. *"Moses and his servant Joshua,"* (Exodus 24:13) went everywhere together. The word servant (*sharath*) used here means: "to minister, to serve, to wait upon."

---

2. 1 Corinthians 9:27

The same word was used throughout the Old Testament for one who attended as a menial labourer. The equivalent New Testament Greek word *diakonea* meaning a menial servant or deacon. Joshua was willing to serve Moses and be known as Moses' deacon. Joshua, Elisha and Timothy illustrate a key leadership principle to us. A true leader will first be faithful to others as a servant. Afterward, this ministry will realise its full potential in direct service to God.

A Practical note on mentoring

Mentoring – by its very nature – will be a long-term relationship if it is to bear good fruit. So, mentors and mentorees should take time to carefully consider what they are embarking upon, before committing themselves to what can become an extremely intense relationship. Make sure there is good communication. Discuss expectations of each other. Draft an agreement, a schedule of expectations, before beginning.

Try to sketch out the length of time the relationship might last. Some mentoring relationships will last for the duration of one project. Others will last for a short season, and some will last for a lifetime. Consider how different the relationships of Ruth and Naomi, Esther and Mordecai, Jesus and Peter, or Paul and Silas were.

Often the mentoree will be fairly confident, but at the same time is personally unsure with the mentor. The more mature trainee may be over confident, and may struggle with being told what to do by a "youngster". They may resort to using put-downs, or "out-clauses" such as, "When I was your age" or "I am 45 years old now." They might be looking for more than we can give, or they do not know how much they don't know! They are not aware of the sort of things the mentor can provide. That help is often very practical, for example:

- Timely advice that encourages the protégé;
- Risking our reputation by backing the protégé;
- Providing necessary resources;
- Setting expectations that challenge the protégé;
- Writing letters, email and making phone calls;
- Giving financially, sometimes sacrificially;
- Co-ministering to increase their credibility and status.

Develop a folder full of exercises covering a wide range of topics, issues and problems. This might include discovering spiritual gifts, personality types, leadership weaknesses, time management, goal setting, core identity, understanding authority, handling revelation, problem solving, brain storming, memory exercises, body language, learning styles, communication skills, listening skills, perception and practical exercises. We can use these with the protégé; setting aside regular time together. With the help of modern technology it is also possible to mentor a person in another country, but nothing beats time together.

Draw up a list of "must read" books, videos, and CD's. Ask the protégé to go through the material and provide some kind of report, response, and evaluation or develop a message from it. It is good to let them use material we have developed. It will show them how to develop their own.

Initially, their personal style may start to mold itself after ours. Two things can happen during this time, which need to be watched out for. Firstly, they may (in the short term) become co-dependant on us. They may see us, "as the Lord". This period should pass. If it does not, then we must work on getting them to connect more directly with the Lord. This may involve some withdrawal. As we become more transparent, they will see the Lord more clearly.

Secondly, they may borrow or copy our words and take them as their own. This may offend you at first. One artist has said, "Copying is the highest form of praise." But our desire is to bring them through to full reliance on the Lord Himself. It is also offensive to the Lord for a prophet to borrow (steal) words from others. *"See, therefore, I am against the prophets, says the LORD, who steal my words from one another."* (Jeremiah 23:30). The tyro needs to be encouraged to hear God for themselves.

This tension, between them developing their own ministry, and using ours as a way forward, will change over time. There will be change in the relationship, growth and development. There will even be a time of letting go. One day you are not going to be there.

GRACE

Mentoring takes grace; it takes God given patience. Sadly, many gifted people do not make good mentors! We must be sure God has given us the gift (of patience) before we set out along the path. Paul could say to the Ephesian church, *"You have heard of the dispensation of the grace of God, which was given to me for you."* (Ephesians 3:2 NKJV). The word translated "dispensation" is from the Greek *oikonomia,* meaning administration, management, or stewardship. Paul had been equipped by God, with grace to manage, administer, or steward the growth of the Ephesian church.

Mentoring does not just mean teaching or discipleship. It takes a personal touch, allowing access by the protégé to a higher level than perhaps we allow others. We allow the protégé to see us in action, in ministry, at home, during study, under stress, on the road, and they learn how we handle matters. We impart the heart, not just knowledge.

A GRADUATION

Some years ago, a fiery young man asked me to mentor him. He had been saved for quite some time, so spiritually speaking, he was mature. He had only just become excited about the prophetic, so his gift was largely unexplored. He had been mentored before, and it was unpleasant, so we set about to debrief about why that went wrong. We drew up an Memorandum Of Understanding (M.O.U.), agreed on the basics of the relationship, then off we went!

We spent time together, doing events and travelling. I was able to give him mentoring exercises to do, observe him during conferences, give feedback, meet for coffee and debrief. We took full advantage of email and internet technology. He subscribed to the online list, and utilised many of my training CD's, mentoring powerpoints etc. He also attended every intensive we put on. After just five years, he developed fully, growing into maturity. Finally, our relationship went to the next level, he "graduated" if you like. We became peers, and he went on to do his own thing.

I think such relationships should be a two-way street. Paul said to the Roman church, *"I long to see you so that I may impart some spiritual gift to you, that you may be established; ... that I may be encouraged together with you while I am among you, **each of us** by the other's faith."* (Romans 1:11,12 emphasis mine). Paul was the "father", overseer or advisor, yet his heart was open to learn, be blessed, receive from them and be inspired by their faith.

REFERENCES

Homer, "The Odyssey."
Jacobs, Cindy. "The Voice of God." Regal Books, 1995.

Chapter Twenty
MAKING FRIENDS WITH REJECTION

"Behold, my master has spared this Naaman the Aramean by not receiving from his hand what he brought. As the Lord lives, I will run after him and take something from him." (2 Kings 5:20).

Betrayal begins so softly. The turn of phrase a friend uses with us. We overhear a conversation, and instead of referring to us as friend, they call us something else. Gehazi calls Elisha "master", in Gehazi's mind Elisha is not his mentor, friend or father... but a master. As soon as Gehazi assigns motives to Elisha, mistrust becomes fully blown accusation. Gehazi believes that Elisha, his erstwhile teacher, was wrong to refuse Naaman's gift. The final thrust comes when lust gives birth to sin; the final frontier of judgement and death is close at hand.[1]

Elisha must now deal with betrayal and sin in the man he was raising up into ministry. Rejection, the shadowy enemy of the prophetic soul, hides behind betrayal and sin. How does Elisha feel, being betrayed like that? How will he react? Will he go on? Can he find another person he can trust?

"Let us cleanse ourselves from all filthiness [defilement] of the flesh and spirit, perfecting holiness in the fear of God." (2 Corinthians 7:1).

As an adolescent, I was a victim of ruthless teenage antics. I don't believe my journey was particularly unique, but it was peculiarly painful.

---
1. James 1:15

At the age of fourteen I lost every friend I had because of gossip and slander. Groundless accusations were made against me over a girl, and "the gang" fled from me; every last person. Not being one to give in easily, I made a new batch of friends at school. They were the "in" crowd, the cool guys, but history was about to repeat itself. The "party" finally arrived at my house one fateful weekend, and trashed the place. On Monday morning I went to school and at fifteen years of age found myself friendless once again. I regrouped a third time, forming a whole new batch of friends. Then at the age of sixteen and nine months, I discovered Christ. One more time, almost to a person, the group left me. At least this time it was because of my faith in Christ!

By now my self-esteem was sorely bruised; my core identity largely shattered. I recall asking God, "What's wrong with me?" Repeated rejection had dealt a strong blow to my self-confidence, but worse than that, they had marked my soul with rejection. I started facing, what John Paul Jackson calls, the 'use me/ I feel used' syndrome. I wanted to be used of God, but got offended when people "used" me to hear from God!

A DEFINING MOMENT

As a young man, beginning to minister in the Church, I found acceptance for my musical skills and prophetic strength. Performance provided some "reward" through recognition, but very early on, I became labelled as a rebel. Chris Simon, my first pastor, said I was, "an angry young man." He was right! Nevertheless, he tried to foster my gifts. We moved to Sydney and I was embraced by another congregation. By now, I was flourishing in the prophetic, but the rejection I had previously suffered had not been dealt with. One day it reared its ugly head, and changed my life.

The prophetic utterances I brought, developed something of a track record. Predicting major events six to twelve months in advance can be a little breath taking. One day, in 1993 the Lord showed me that the drought my nation was suffering at that time, would be broken in the Diamantina River district of Queensland. God said He would cause a flood to wash down and fill Lake Eyre, (an arid inland desert sea basin). As was my practice, I gave this word to my friend Paul, who tested it for me. He came back the next day and said these immortal words... "Rob, given your track record, and given what I know of your integrity, there is no reason why I should doubt this word. But everything within me wants to reject it!"

His words caused an explosion of the past experience of rejection in me, and triggered a six-month process of investigation, which laid the foundation for restoration in my life. I needed to wash out the stains on my soul, to remove the defilement that rejection had left behind. I explored the whole issue with my pastor, John Davies and submitted to counselling. We delved into the wounds my youth had left in me. By exploring the forms of rejection found in the Bible, we can discover how to rid ourselves of it.

FORMS OF REJECTION

1. Rejected because of physical appearance.

Paul wrote gladly to the Galatians, thanking them for not rejecting him when he visited them.[2] Paul was apparently sick, and his illness must have marred his skin or made him appear ugly in some way, but the Galatian church looked beyond this disfigurement. This kind of rejection (*ekptuo*) means to stay away from, consider cursed, loathe. Lepers knew exactly what this rejection felt like, as Talmudic law required them to walk the streets crying, "Unclean. Unclean. Stay out of my way, I am an object of God's wrath".

---

2. Galatians 4:14

2. Rejection because of lifestyle choices.

A second form of rejection comes when people disapproved of us, or our decisions. Our parents may not approve of our choice of clothes, hairstyle, or spouse. Our friends may not approve of our career, living quarters, or vehicle. This kind of rejection (*apodokimazo*) is what Jesus felt from the elders of Israel,[3] who did not approve of Him. In fact, Jesus felt the disapproval of an entire generation.[4] No wonder He was a man of sorrows!

3. Rejection because of failure

A third form of rejection is to feel the shame of failing a test. I once had to sit a knowledge test to renew my motorbike licence. I failed the test first time through. We experience a 'hope no one sees me here' kind of feeling. This rejection (*adokimos*) is how we treat a timber joist or beam if it cannot hold the load. Land that bears thorns and thistles fails the test for productivity.[5] Paul wished to avoid being rejected by God in this way.[6]

4. Rejection as an individual

A fourth form of rejection is to be cast off, or thrown away (*apobletos*). We eat the chocolate and throw away the wrapper. We eat the banana and throw away the skin. We are made in the likeness and image of God, no person should have to suffer this kind of rejection. Paul told Timothy, *"Everything created by God is good, nothing is to be rejected."* (1 Timothy 4:4). To be rejected for what we stand for or believe in is tolerable. To be despised for who and what we are, cuts to the very core.

5. Rejection on the basis of perception

The fifth form of rejection is to be considered as if we were without value. People are told, "You'll never amount to anything!"

---

3. Mark 8:31
5. Hebrews 6:8
4. Luke 17:25
6. 1 Corinthians 9:27

To experience this kind of rejection (*atheteo*) is to be considered worthless, or to have our contribution discounted to zero. Jesus Christ experienced this at the hands of the Scribes, Pharisees, and Priests. [7] We are told that at the cross, all of Christ's disciples fled him. They did not understand a suffering Messiah, and rejected the message of the cross.

OUR REACTION

Rejection may come from fellow Christians or unbelievers. Sadly, it is often triggered by defilement in our spirit. Our body language, our mannerism, our conduct, our character gives a signal to others that prompts them to reject us. They may not cognitively ask why? Some people experience rejection as a result of defilement over and over again, never stopping to question why it is happening – and the result is untold personal damage. Few prophetic schools and fewer churches, take the time to address the issue of rejection – they simply reject the rejected as if that were an answer to the problem! Unless we learn to address rejection for ourselves the chances are good that it will severely inhibit our progress.

Christ went through every form of suffering and rejection we have listed, and yet remained without sin. How did He avoid suffering a wounded spirit? He was a man acquainted with our sufferings yet without the stain on His soul! The answer lies in the story of two old-time prophets, men who God called into a ministry situation doomed to fail, called to preach a gospel no-one would hear, suffering rejection at the hands of their brethren at every turn.

---

7. Luke 9:22

JEREMIAH AND EZEKIEL

God called Jeremiah and Ezekiel to speak to a hardhearted generation. God instructed Jeremiah, *"Gird up your loins! Arise and tell them all that I command you. Do not be dismayed and do not break down at the sight of their faces, lest I confound you before them and permit you to be overcome."* (Jeremiah 1:17 AMP). In the conversation following, the prophet is told that he must have a disposition of steel, a will of iron. God promises, *"I will give you a divine strength which no hostile power can overcome."* [8]

There is something here for us to apprehend. God sent Jeremiah to fight the unwinable war and warned him not to give up. "Gird up your loins." To some extent His advice was, "Prepare yourself for defeat and expect a fight. Know ahead of time they will not receive you or your message, and do not let yourself be broken down by it. Do not let the hurt in Jeremiah, because if you cry, I will break you before them." Mercifully, God does not leave him with this apparently harsh instruction. He promises to impart a divine strength to overcome the rejection.

Ezekiel was sent to speak his message to deaf ears; to hammer the hardest of hearts. It was the "mission impossible" of his day. Ezekiel was similarly advised, *"The house of Israel will not listen to you and obey you, since they will not listen to me and obey me... I have made your face strong and hard... like adamant stone, harder than flint or a diamond point have I made [you]. Fear them not, neither be dismayed at their looks, for they are a rebellious house."* (Ezekiel 3:7-9 AMP). Here too, Ezekiel is told in advance that they would reject him and his message.

---

8. Jeremiah 1:18

What does the eternal Counsel say to us? Do we imagine Jeremiah and Ezekiel wandering around hurt, wounded, pouting? Do we imagine they were suffering rejection, and causing the issue of hard-heartedness? Probably not! Then how did they manage?

I believe part of the solution lies in this: they were able to differentiate between the message and the messenger. For them, the message came from them, but rejection of it did not amount to rejection of them. Samuel was told by God, *"They have not rejected you, they have rejected Me."* (1 Samuel 8:7).

The second part of the answer lies in the calling itself. The very call of the prophetic contains grace to cope with rejection. God's grace is sufficient. He will make us strong. We will be equal to the task, if we reside, or live in the grace of our call. Rejection need not overcome us. Rejection does not even have to find a place in us!

FILTHINESS OF SPIRIT

I have been involved in deliverance ministry (the removal of oppression and demonisation) since the beginning of my walk with God. Since starting a local congregation, I have also been heavily involved in counselling and inner healing. I have noticed something important, however, when it comes to the issue of rejection. You can cast all the demons out, and heal all the wounds, and bring Christ into every memory, but still be plagued by rejection. Is it the incurable disease? Is it the unremovable stain, or do we have a spiritual cleanser which can remove it?

Paul reminded the Corinthian Christians that God promised, *" 'I will be your father, and you shall be my sons and daughters'... Since we have these promises, beloved, let us cleanse ourselves from every defilement of body and of spirit, making holiness perfect in the fear of God."* (2 Cor 6:18 – 7:1).

The first, and most powerful revelation is that we are sons and daughters of the Most High. He loves us, He made us, He ordained us to this work. His eye is on us. No matter what people say, no matter what we suffer, there is a God in heaven who accepts us. In that knowledge, Paul urges us to cleanse ourselves from all filthiness of spirit. We have the power to to that – in the fear of God. If we keep Him at the centre of our attention, we will progress in holiness.

We ask God to forgive us for letting the dismay, pain, and wounding go inward when we should have let it wash over us. God strengthen us and help us overcome the rejecting that must surely come, for Christ Himself suffered this and more, yet, He was not undone.

References

Gibson, Noel & Phyl. "Excuse Me, Your Rejection is Showing." Sovereign World, 1992.
Jackson, JP. "Rejection." Streams of Shiloh. Vol 2, Iss 8, 1994.

Chapter Twenty-One
THE ERROR OF BALAAM

"These men revile things they do not understand, and things which they know by instinct...woe to them, for they have gone the way of Cain and for pay, they have rushed headlong into the error of Balaam and perished in the rebellion of Korah." (Jude 10,11).

Balaam was a prophet in Samaria, next to Israel. He lived several hundred years before Elisha, but his lesson is an eternal warning to us all. The things Balaam got wrong recurred in the life of Elisha's servant Gehazi. The way of Balaam is to prostitute our gift for financial reward. Money and prophecy do not mix. *"The elders of Moab took with them a fee for **divination** and they came to Balaam and told them what Balak had requested."* (Numbers 22:7 emphasis mine). Balaam sold his prophetic insight for cash. Sadly, that is happening today too.

A brief survey of prophetic web sites, web-rings, on-line communities promoting prophetic services and churches advertising prophetic conferences, reveals a chilling trend. The topic of prophecy and money were interlinked closely in more than 50% of cases. Some of the more glaring examples include:

- "Every registered delegate will receive a prophetic word..." The conference fee was $395.00 (USD).
- "Prophetic presbytery available by bookings only. 15 minute segments only." Presbytery was available once a $90.00 (USD) booking fee was paid.
- "Come for a word. Just $15." (AUD). This team would "prophesy" onto audio cassettes, take payment, and ask the seeker to take the tape on the top of the pile.

That used to be called soothsaying! The dictionary definition of soothsaying is, "The practice of divination for money." I appreciate that ministers need money to run their ministry. There are overheads, travel costs, advertising, and all manner of other things. I also appreciate the fact that, *"The labourer is worthy of his hire."* (1 Corinthians 9:10). No-one questions the prophetic minister's claim to be paid in some way, *"For those who minister at the altar receive from the offerings at the altar."* (1 Corinthians 9:13). Paul even states that a minister has the right to earn a living from the gospel (vs 14).

Is it wise, though, to so closely connect money and prophetic utterance? Ministers should be careful to promote the freedom of giving and avoid creating the impression that they can be paid to bring God's word. To the casual onlooker, the connection between money and prophecy would seem quite strong on the prophetic circuit today.

THE TEACHING OF BALAAM

Jesus said, "A good tree brings forth good fruit." (Mathew 7:17). This is certainly so amongst prophetic ministries. We dare not look at prophetic accuracy, anointing, presence of God (manifest or otherwise) and use this to determine a person's integrity in ministry. Sadly for Balaam, he accepted money to prophesy, and the revelation was flowing thick and fast. Ninety percent of the things he said came to pass, but God does not weigh a prophet by his accuracy alone. He weighs the prophet by character, and who the people end up worshipping.

Balaam's lifestyle (of connecting money and prophecy) leads to sin. *"I have a few things against you, because you have there some who hold the teaching of Balaam, who kept teaching Balak to put a stumbling block before the sons of Israel, to eat things offered to idols and to commit acts of immorality."* (Revelation 2:14).

The Error of Balaam

To bring down the people of Israel, Balaam resorted to teaching error. He trained the enemy how to bring the people of God down, by employing God against the people. God was bound, by His own word, to curse the people if they intermarried, or if they offered worship to idols. So it was in the New Testament when the people brought themselves out from under the blood of Christ, and back under the Law. By trying to fulfil even one aspect of it, they were condemned to fulfil the whole lot.[1]

I am staggered at the amount of prophecy available today. There are dozens of prophetic lists pouring out a constant stream of revelation. Most Charismatic and Pentecostal churches endorse the prophetic, and one can walk into most churches of that ilk and find some level of utterance on any given Sunday.

Let us consider the Church today! The rate of divorce (35% of first marriages and 75% of second marriages) among Christians matches the world. Christians regularly move in together before they marry, and even when they do withhold from intercourse, they play with fire.

High school students at a prestigious and expensive Christian school were recently interviewed about their sexual practises. The researchers found that there was a common belief among students that "Christian" (oral) sex was OK. When we ran the story on our internet list, many people concurred that the story was true where they lived also. Balaam is alive and well.

Money and prophetic leadership do not mix. I believe we live in the days spoken of prophetically by Micah, *"Your heads judge for a bribe, your priests teach for pay and your prophets divine for money."* (Micah 3:11).

---

1. James 2:10

In Peter's day, a man called Simon had carved out for himself quite a ministry. He was wowing the crowds with his display of spiritual power and astonishing feats. He was not operating by divine power; it was magic, occult power.[2] Simon the sorcerer is our New Testament example of a man so enamoured with the power of the Holy Spirit, that he sought to buy it at the peril of his own soul. Even if we eschew monetary reward (as Peter did that day), the payment can come in other ways. Sexual gratification, admiration, self-glorification, honour, respect and many other forms of reward can come to us.

RESTRAINED MADNESS

"These... never cease from sin, enticing unstable souls, having a heart trained in greed, accursed children; forsaking the right way, they have gone astray, having followed **the way** *of Balaam, the son of Beor, who loved the wages of unrighteousness; but received a rebuke for his own transgression, for a mute donkey, speaking with a voice of a man, restrained the madness of the prophet."* (2 Peter 2:14-16).

The way of Balaam is to mix business and pleasure – the business of making money with the pleasure of being the Lord's holy servant. Balaam loved the wages of unrighteousness, and led Israel into sin. Both of these charges are laid at the feet of New Testament believers (through the authors Peter, Jude, and John).

This kind of behaviour leads to unrestrained madness. Balaam needed to be rebuked by an animal! Why a simple donkey? Was there no one else to restrain the man? No. Balaam had isolated himself. There was no companion to correct him. He lived in isolation; he was a law unto himself. He received no correction; he had no team. That made him implicitly unsafe.

The New Testament model is clear – prophets run in teams, either with other prophets,[3] or with teachers,[4] or with apostles.[5] Teamwork is the safest possible context for the prophetic gift, if we choose our team members with care.

We should note that "team" is not a fix-all answer either. Balaam was approached by Balak to join a team. This satanic union was based on favouritism and finances. Balaam had all the wrong reasons for participating in Balak's "team ministry". He would have been far safer in relationship with his contemporaries: Moses, Joshua, and the people of Israel.

Let us purify our motives, address our conduct, and be careful not to mix these two issues. No-one denies our need to put food on the table – but the Heavenly Father is our source and provider. No-one denies valid needs exist, and even the right to earn a wage from the Gospel. Be careful not to do so by selling out your gift for cash. Let us not be among those who, *"are peddlers of God's word like so many."* (2 Corinthians 2:17 NRSV).

BALAAM REPENTS

All of us have, at one time or another, been tempted by financial reward. For some, that temptation seems to be a long awaited answer to prayer; for others an answer to serious need. Some sully their anointing, by pursuing money greedily; others simply sell out for quick gain. Some have handed in the anointing and gone out into the world, corrupting themselves, whilst other have held on bravely, only to give in at the last moment. Whatever our reason, we must be assured that God's grace can still reach us, even there.

---

2. Acts 8:11,12
4. Acts 13:1
3. Acts 11:27
5. Acts 15:40

*"Now Balaam saw that it pleased the LORD to bless Israel, so he **did not go**, as at other times, to look for omens, but set his face toward the wilderness. Balaam looked up and saw Israel camping tribe by tribe. Then the spirit of God came upon him."* (Numbers 24:1,2 emphasis mine).

Balaam had given in again and again to Balak's demands. Then, there came a time that his eyes were opened, and He saw the Lord pleased. He chose not to go out "as at other times." He changed his ways, he changed his pattern. He attempted to move back from the edge of the precipice. He looked at the people of God, and no longer saw them as sheep to be fleeced, but as a nation camped tribe by tribe. He saw people as people, not as opportunities to get an offering!

The good news for us, is that after repentance, "The Spirit of God came upon him"! He was restored, instantly. We too can be restored, no matter how far we might have fallen, or how dirty our hands may be. Repentance brings us back into the Father's glory.

REFERENCES

Katz, Art. "The Prophetic." E-book, 2002. Chapter 12.
Pfanstiel, Kurt. "It's a New Day." Audio message, The Gathering, 2005. Storm Harvest Inc.
Ravenhill, David. "The Jesus Letters." Destiny Image, 2004.

Chapter Twenty-Two
ERROR IN PROPHECY

"Elisha said to him, 'Go say to your master you shall surely recover, however the Lord has shown me that he will really die.' Then [Hazael] set his countenance in a stare until he was ashamed, and the man of God wept." (1 Kings 8:10,11).

This passage is a particularly difficult one for those who say there can be no error in prophetic utterance, or who pontificate that prophets must be stoned to death for mistake or deceit. Here, Elisha instructs Hazael to bring a false prophecy to Ben Hadad, the king. Hazael, the heir apparent to the throne, has to stare Elisha down in disbelief, until the prophet breaks down and weeps. Did God tell Elisha to lie? I think not. Was Elisha responsible for his conduct? Absolutely!

Many prophetic people speak a word believing that we are only responsible to ensure that it lines up with the Scriptures. Some require that prophets, (why we single them out is beyond me), must get it right 100% of the time. If we carry that line of reasoning one step further, what about the tone we use in our voice; our choice of words; or the emotion we portray in prophecy?

How much flexibility does the prophetic minister have in presenting a prophetic word? How much should we, the recipients, be attributing to "God?" To ask the same question in another way: is anointing causal – the prophecy is anointed because it is correct – or could it be anointed and yet not be 100% correct? Can one speak error while under the anointing? Can one be in error and speak a true word from God?

Colouring the Word

Just how much of the message is supposed to be from God? On one hand, we can believe that a person delivering a prophetic word is just a mouthpiece for God. In that case, they are not responsible for anything but getting the words right. They act like a channeller or an automaton. At the other end of the spectrum is the belief that the prophetic person is only responsible for getting the gist of the word correct. These two points of view may each be valid (reasonable), but are either of them true?

Some argue that an Old Testament prophet was merely God's mouthpiece. One only needs to read the prophets one after another to see that their personality left an impression, a watermark on their prophetic declarations! Compare the zeal of Daniel with the tears of Jeremiah, or the strength of Isaiah and the compassion of Moses. The person moulds the message even as the cask naturally flavours the wine.

To take the other point of view, that we must simply get the gist of it right, is to dilute the responsibility we have before God. Peter says prophetic utterance is like an oracle of God,[1] it carries weight and measure.

> "We are not expected to accept every word spoken through the gift of utterance as being from God... but only what is quickened to us by the Holy Spirit and is in agreement with the Bible." Dennis Bennett.[2]

---

1. 1 Peter 4:11   2. "The Holy Spirit & You", Pg 146

Error in Prophecy

"It seems very difficult for some people to recognise any source of utterance except divine and satanic. They refuse to see the profound importance of the place of the human spirit in molding and affecting each utterance."
Donald Gee.[3]

"Prophecy can be impure – our own thoughts or ideas getting mixed into the message we receive, whether we get them directly or only a sense of them – the risk is very real."
Bruce Yocum.[4]

I am inclined to take a middle road. A road that says, "We must take this task seriously, with the proper respect and weight it demands." At the same time we must recognise that our utterance may (and probably does) contain error. If not error, then a palpable element of humanity in it.

SOME EXAMPLES FROM THE BIBLE

Those who argue the infallibility of prophetic utterance recorded in the Bible would do well to review some of the more pertinent examples of 'words' delivered in the stories of the Bible. I am not here speaking of the Biblical prophecies of the end times, or the Messiah – but of the words of advice and prophecy offered by a prophet to someone else. Here are some examples of colouring:

1. The prophet who said "go"!
Micaiah knew clearly that war with Syria was off God's agenda. But when intimidated by three kings, told them to go anyway. He was pressed for the truth, and he swore by the Lord, then lied! *"As the LORD lives, whatever the LORD says to me, that I will speak... then he answered him, 'Go up and triumph; the LORD will give it into the hand of the king'."* (1 Kings 22:14-15).

---
3. "Spiritual Gifts in the Work of Ministry Today." Pg 48,49
4. "Prophecy." Pg 79

Had the king not questioned him further it would have been left at that! But Jehoshaphat pressed him for more. Micaiah finally relented and told them the truth. If they went to war, Israel would be scattered, and the King of Israel would be killed.

2. The prophet who advised "build"

Late one night David had been fantasising about a big new temple for God. He asked Nathan what God thought of this plan and Nathan's first advice was, *"Do all that you have in mind, for God is with you."* That same night the word of the LORD came to Nathan, saying: *"Go and tell my servant David: Thus says the LORD: You shall not build me a house to live in."* (1 Chronicles 17:2, 3). Whoops, sorry David, Nathan got it 100% wrong the first time.

3. The prophet who said "stay"

What do we make of perhaps the most perplexing story in the Old Testament, captured in 1 Kings chapter 13? A nameless prophet of God leads a young prophet into rebellion against God's command – and then declares his destruction for that rebellion!

*"'I also am a prophet as you are, and an angel spoke to me by the word of the LORD: Bring him back with you into your house so that he may eat food and drink water.' But he was **deceiving** him... As they were sitting at the table, the word of the LORD came to the prophet who had brought him back... 'Because you have disobeyed the word of the LORD... your body shall not come to your ancestral tomb'."* (1 Kings 13:18-22).

A lion kills the young man and the Lord fulfils the deceptive prophet's words! The sly old prophet deceived him, yet the 'word of the Lord' came to him.

MIXTURE IN THE MESSAGE

Can one be in error, and speak a true word from God? The short answer is yes! Where does error or colouring enter into our 'word'? It comes from the one delivering the word. Whilst God may indeed speak through a donkey, and even the rocks may cry out before Him, He ordinarily uses people to get the message across. Every person has sin – if we say we have none, we deceive ourselves and the truth is not in us.[5] All have sinned and fallen short of the Glory of God.[6] Sin affects what we say and do because out of the abundance of the heart the mouth speaks. We know that the human heart is corrupt, *"The heart is devious above all else; it is perverse—who can understand it?"* (Jeremiah 17:9).

God has two choices when looking for a spokesperson – He can use a sinner, or He can use a sinner. Either way He has a broken vessel that is going to add 'colour' to the message in some way. If sin, or the presence of sin, debarred us from speaking for God, then we would all be silent! Imagine if the reverse were true – if we were unable or not allowed to prophesy as sinners. God would have to disqualify everybody! Or at the very least, He would be restrained from using anyone in a Church with error. He could not use any person with errant doctrine, and we would have a lot more talking donkeys!

If our messages were not coloured by us then Paul's command would be nonsensical – why otherwise would he say, *"Don't restrain the Holy Spirit, don't despise inspired messages."* (1 Thessalonians 5:19 GNB) and then immediately advise, *"Do not despise the words of prophets, but test everything; hold fast to what is good."* (1 Thessalonians 5:20-21 NRSV). Why would we have to test it if there wasn't some mixture?

---

5. 1 John 1:8   6. Romans 3:23

How about 100%?

We **can** get prophecy 100% right. How can I say this? Think of the Scriptures and how they came to be written. Orthodox understanding on the Bible says that it is inerrant – without fault (though it contains accounts of men with faults). God managed to write a perfect book through human agency. If we take a look at Bible prophecy and it's exacting fulfillment in history we know that we are, with God's help, able to hit the mark.

In practise, it is possible to hit the mark all the time. Think of the testimony given of Samuel – *"As Samuel grew up, the LORD was with him and let none of his words fall to the ground. And all Israel from Dan to Beersheba knew that Samuel was a trustworthy prophet of the LORD."* (1 Samuel 3:20). He let **none** of his words fall to the ground, not one.

There are at least two men that got it right all the time in recent history. One was Smith Wigglesworth. Everyone Smith prayed for was healed! That is because he did not pray for anyone who God had not shown him would be healed. Similarly, it was said that in the first 20 years of William Branham's ministry, "Of all the thousands of such 'words of knowledge' that he gave, none was ever known to be wrong or inaccurate. His gift was reportedly, exactly 100%." May it be so with us! If we aim at 100 fold, we shall never have to be content with the 30 or 60 fold!

References

Bennett, Dennis, "The Holy Spirit and You." Kingsway, 1971
Gee, Donald. "Spiritual Gifts in the Work of Ministry Today", Gospel, 1963.
Weaver, C. Douglas. "The Prophet Healer." Mercer, 1987.
Yocum, Bruce. "Prophecy." Servant Publications, 1993.

PART THREE

PROPHETS IN THE REAL WORLD

In this final section it is time to get really practical. From the dawn of the prophetic ministry, the prophet has performed eminently practical tasks. Moses confronted his step-brother and leader; Daniel served Nebuchadnezzar as an administrator; Joseph saved and governed Egypt with Pharaoh; Paul and Silas made tents in the marketplace; and Agabus predicted a drought, helping the believers prepare.

We will explore prophecy in the marketplace, the business realm and the streets. It can stand on its own (away from religious trappings, away from the safe harbour of the church service). We examine dream interpretation for the lost, (try doing this in your workplace or play group) and thus come into a broader understanding of how the Kingdom of God was designed to work.

We look back at the story of Elisha, seeing into the planning room of an enemy king, and bring it up-to-date with stories from this century. It gives us cause to pause and consider the role of the seer, and seeing "technology" in general, as well as the role of understanding signs and seasons.

We close out our treatment of the prophetic ministry by going back to the church, and examining four issues of the last days church: prophets serving an apostolic Church; apostolic/ prophetic partnerships; the sons of the prophets; and last gaze into the future. Enjoy!

Chapter Twenty-Three
PROPHECY IN BUSINESS

"Now a certain woman, among the wives of the sons of the prophets cried out to Elisha, 'Your servant, my husband is dead... your maidservant has nothing in the house except a jar of oil.' Then he said, 'Go borrow vessels at large from all of your neighbours, even empty vessels; do not get a few'... her sons brought the vessels to her and she poured [oil into them].

When the vessels were full she said to her son, 'Bring me another vessel.' And he said to her, 'There is not one vessel more.' And the oil stopped. Then she came and told the man of God, and he said, 'Go and sell the oil and pay your debt, and you and your sons can live on the rest'." (2 Kings 4:1-7).

Prophecy is supposed to be this practical, and of such earthy value. It is supposed to enable a king decide whether to enter battle, guide a general plan his strategy, help the stock market broker be aware of shifts in value, assist a widow make enough money to live on and empower Church leaders to build and grow the Kingdom of God.

It is at this precise place most of the "prophetic ministries" disappear! When the rubber meets the road, when a decision of financial or governmental importance arises and the word of the Lord is needed, the weak of heart lose faith. Oh that the prophetic ministry of the Church would rise up, and take the gift into the marketplace! Here is Elisha, presented with the legitimate needs of a woman in his community, and he prays. God gives him a word of knowledge about the state of her larder, and about the resources at her disposal. Then he brings her a practical answer to her debt, and a way to pay it off.

TAKING IT OUT THERE

Strip away all the religious trappings, the uniform dress code of denomination, the business cards announcing title and office, and what do we have? When we strip away the Christian jargon and the Biblical language and get prophecy right down to the ground where an ordinary person can understand it, what's left? These twin truths:

Our past brought us to our present.
Our present affects our future.

So we can use the prophetic gift in business to help:

> Overcome the past,
> Build in the present,
> and succeed in the future.

If business people follow the guidelines of Scripture (integrity, honesty, righteousness), and do business by the Book they will be blessed. But there is also a greater blessing available to those who embrace the prophetic at work. The truth is wrapped up in the prophet, priest, and king model of leadership we were discussing earlier. The king (in business) needs a social conscience (priestly view) and to hear the voice of God (prophetic function) to keep him in balance and help him grow. Just as the kings or Israel were told:

"Believe in the Lord and you shall be established, believe his prophets and you shall prosper." (2 Chronicles 20:20). **Prosper** is a word business people can relate to. The word for prosper is *tsalach* in Hebrew, which means to advance, move forward, become successful, prosper, thrive, and be victorious. This passage is about Jehoshaphat speaking, standing at the head of an army, prepared for battle, assembled according to the word of a prophet – Jahaziel.

They have put the singers forward, which doesn't make any sense to the gathered military men, but God is right there to fulfill His word.

My Experience

I once had a business friend ring me and say, "I have some money I need to invest, and I have prayerfully sought God about my investment. I intend to give some of the proceeds to charity, but I don't want to make a bad choice. Can you help?" I asked him about what research he had done, because he was the expert at investment. "I have narrowed my choice down to gold, oil or foreign exchange, a market I know very little about." I took it to the Lord and almost immediately He replied, "The Australian to US dollar exchange rate will fall to 55 cents in the dollar."

Now I am not a foreign exchange investor, nor have I ever seen the Lord do this before or since, but that's what I heard. I rang my friend back, and told him the information. "That's impossible," he replied. "It has been sitting at near 75 cents in the dollar for over a year, and is rising." Nevertheless, what I heard indicated a strong shift in the opposite direction. Sadly, my friend did not heed the advice, and sure enough, within the year the rate had fallen to 56 cents in the dollar.

"The elders of the Jews built and prospered through the prophesying of Haggai the prophet and of Zechariah, they built and they finished." (Ezra 6:14). The book of Ezra is an eminently practical book. It's about a construction project, and apparently the prophets were involved from the ground up. *"The prophets were with them, helping them."* (Ezra 5:2). They were down in the trenches, sleeves rolled up, helping them. Once again we are told they prospered, the Hebrew word *tselach* means they enjoyed success.

Everything went their way. This prosperity resulted "through the prophesying" of two key members of their team. Just imagine a boardroom that included prophets. Business decisions based on economics, statistics, strategic planning, sound business principles, and prophetic word! Imagine a department in your state political office, where the word of the Lord is sought for the decision makers and prayer ascends for the vote being taken.

OLD TESTAMENT EXAMPLES

Throughout the Old Testament we find prophets operating in the sphere of business, the marketplace, and politics:

- Daniel served Nebuchadnezzar, interpreted his dreams and worked in the administration of the kingdom of Babylon.
- Joseph served Pharaoh, interpreted his dreams and administrated in the kingdom of Egypt in its hardest trials.
- Isaiah was a friend of King Uzziah, and also prophetically determined the line of succession from Hezekiah to Eliakim.
- Elisha counselled the king of Israel on battle strategy, and helped him avoid traps and ambushes of the enemy.
- Agabus helped the Church and businesses in Jerusalem prepare for a drought that affected the entire region.

WHAT A PROPHET PROVIDES

The prophet is not in the marketplace because he can praise (unless he is in the music industry as a minstrel). He is not in the marketplace because he can pray (unless a business has hired him on as a pray-er). He is not in the marketplace because he can plan (though he might have financial or business skills). Nor is he in the marketplace because of his human resource skills (though he has good discernment and can read people well).

He is not there to be rewarded financially for his gift (thanks Balaam). He is there because he is a spiritual master of communication. He has a strong relationship with God, and can hear His Voice! What does that function look like in a business setting?

- Hindsight: Reviewing where we've been;
- Insight: Analysing where we're at;
- Foresight: Predicting where we're going.

THE BUSINESS PROPHET

I was trained in business consulting by the *Business Enterprise Centres of NSW*, and then in coaching by *Beyond Success*. This group base their enterprise on helping people achieve their personal best. They are a motivational group, who believes the best of individuals and brings out the best in companies. They would send a facilitator into a business to serve them, and bring them to a new level of prosperity.

Coming into companies as a consultant, my only job was to assist them to do better. I found that I could quickly employ prophetic insight. I used hindsight to review where they had been, gaining information through discussion with staff and management. I used insight into what they were doing now, gained with a 360-degree review of their business practices. I used foresight, gained by looking at their budgeting, forecasting, business planning. During the entire process, however, I was asking the Lord, "What else is here; what am I missing?" I often addressed sin issues in their life, challenged them to holiness, and even did marriage counselling! It has been a blast. Invariably, the Lord brought to light helpful issues which strengthened and prospered them.

I know prophetic people who work in the auditing and accounting departments of their company. They review statistical data, plough through accounting information, and provide the managers great review (hindsight) of where they have been. I know prophetic people who consult the board of companies. Whilst they never get up and say, "Thus saith the Lord," they certainly provide wisdom (insight) that no one else has thought of. Especially, as it comes to looking at the way people are behaving, and the communication/ interactions that take place. One man I know, worked for a very large firm, and they called him "The Trouble Shooter". If there was a flaw in the system, he could find it.

I know prophetic people who sit in the planning meetings of military forecasting groups, and who advise national leaders. They bring valuable prophetic information about geo-political situations: war, terrorism, and economic situations. This goes into the mix of information sources the strategists use for decision making.

I know Christian policemen in MI6 in the UK, who are opening the way for prophetic people to speak into investigations. The police force in London has been using clairvoyants for over 20 years, to help detect or locate cadavers (the bodies of murder victims). Why should the enemy corner the market on helping our community? We are currently exploring ways to assist police in Australia too.

I have worked on the board of management for community organisations and community development groups. In both these situations I am a local businessman, a concerned local citizen, but I employ the prophetic gift gainfully to assist them to move ahead. What about you? You might not be a prophet, but certainly the prophetic gift works in your life. Can you work in these three areas assisting people?

Chapter Twenty-Four
PROPHECY IN THE MARKETPLACE

Elisha said to his hostess, *"You have been careful for us with all this care; what can I do for you? Would you be spoken for to the king or to the captain of the army?"* (2 Kings 4:13).

Elisha often passed through the town of Shunem, where a wealthy couple lived. They perceived he was a man of God, and built a guest room for him. Elisha stayed there regularly, with thankfulness in his heart. One day he asked her, "What can I do for you?" He had access to the king and the captain of the guard, and offered to speak to them on her behalf. It wasn't access to business or politics she needed…

It was something far more practical than that. She needed, wanted a son. After prayer, the couple conceived and the child grew and developed. He went out to harvest time one day with his father, and complained of having a sore head. They took him home, and he died in his mother's lap. Great joy is turned to great tragedy. She called for Elisha to come, and he entered the house,[1] paced about, laid himself upon the lad and prayed. The boy was raised from the dead, sneezed seven times, and opened his eyes.

Here is a prophet, in the face of great tragedy, in the face of opposition, against all odds, calling upon his God. There is no good reason why our gifts cannot function in the marketplace, against the same odds. If we can pray down a line after the Sunday night service, then we **can** function in the shopping mall!

---

1. 2 Kings 4:35

If we have prophetic insight into dreams, and can sit in a seminar and interpret someone else's dreams, then we can do the same for the lady having coffee with us at morning tea break. If we have the gift of insight, and inspiration so as to give directive words to the Church leadership on where they are headed, then we are qualified to bring God given wisdom to boardroom planning sessions. If we have the gift of word of knowledge, and by the Spirit know what people were doing yesterday, then that same gift can enable us to audit the accounts of a business, and find errors or misappropriations, by the Spirit.

I have a friend, Susanna, who does evangelism in the marketplace in Canberra. She will walk up to inquisitive strangers, and say to them, "Are you interested in spiritual things?" If they say "yes" she says, "Can I give you a reading?" Most often the people are eager. Taking their hand she will say something like, "Oh your hand is too dirty, let me look at you instead." Then gazing into their eyes (can you see the twinkle in hers?) she says, "The Spirit of the Lord has something to say about you." Why not?

A WORD OF WARNING BEFORE WE PROCEED

There are three basic institutions in the world: the Marriage (home), the Church (kingdom), and the Government (world). It is unlikely that we will be financially rewarded for being prophetic in the home. We might be able to profit a little from the Church. Using the gifts in the world, under the direction of the Spirit, is a totally valid expression of our gift. But the marketplace is fraught with financial tags and dangers. Beware of franchising the gift. Business people are not necessarily bound by Christian morals or beliefs – so when using prophecy in the marketplace we dare not present our gift as something to be bought, traded, or used for gain – don't allow business to put a price tag on prophecy!

Find the line between services rendered, or bought for money (sometimes called the time for money swap) and "freely you have received, freely give."

One day a friend of mine was cleaning the apartment of a New Age lady. This lady was cold and shivering in the kitchen. When asked what was wrong the lady replied, "The energy in the room is all wrong, it is negative, can't you feel it?" Sensing it was demonic oppression, this friend said to her, "Why yes. Do you chant, and call?" The lady brightened up and said, "Yes, what spirit shall we call upon?" The friend said, "I know a very powerful spirit, the most powerful. Shall we call upon El-elyown [God Most High]? He also goes by the name of Ruarch [Breath of God, Holy Spirit]. Let's call upon Him now, if you don't mind I will speak in another language – it helps that way."

The outcome could not have been more profound – my friend began to pray in tongues, calling upon the name of the Most High God. The room warmed noticeably, and the lady felt great peace flood in upon her soul. The work, she was paid for (cleaning); the ministry and healing was free! Her conscience was clean, she was not being paid to be prophetic.

THE ANOINTING OF THE CRAFTSMEN

To understand more broadly the role of the Christian in the marketplace, we need to go to an Old Testament prophet, Zechariah. Zechariah, in the opening chapter of his lengthy vision, sees four horns terrifying Israel, attacking them, and making war. He then sees this: *"The Lord showed me four craftsmen... the craftsmen have come to terrify the horns and to throw them down."* (Zechariah 1:20,21).

In Scripture, horns represent earthly powers. Four craftsmen, one per horn, were sent to terrify the horns and overcome them. Here we see an allegory of the authority given to the craftsmen – those who manufacture, skilled smiths, engravers, plowmen, and artisans. Not only the 'spiritually' gifted, but also the very 'naturally' gifted are anointed by God to bring down demonic oppression. God anoints workers to do the ministry.

When we use the word 'ministry', images come to mind of Church, clergy, full-time work 'for the Lord', sacred not secular. It comes as a rude shock to find that God's anointing was first given to those who worked with their hands. His Spirit equipped 'workers' to act as sentry for the Kingdom of God in that place and deliver the nation. The first man in Scripture mentioned as being filled with the Spirit was Bezalel. Bezalel was a craftsman. His job was to lead teams in designing and constructing the Tabernacle and all its accoutrements.

"The Lord has chosen Bezalel... and filled him with the Spirit, with skill and ability and knowledge in all kinds of crafts... to make." (Exodus 35:30). His anointing was to be used for building, working, and manufacturing – it poured itself out in his sweat and tears, not in supplication and priestly ministry.

The Israelites had just come from Egypt, from 440 years of slavery. Does it not strike you as odd that they should even have craftsmen? In spite of what the Dreamworks, "Prince of Egypt" movie portrays, not all of them made bricks and carried stone for Pharaoh. That much is clear, from the gathering of craftsmen available for the construction of the Tabernacle. They learned all manner of "worldly" technical skills in Egypt, which God used for good.

At this time, there were a number of classes developing:

- The priest class: scribes, teachers, and priests.
- The seer class: visionaries, miracle workers, and prophets.
- The warrior class: scouts, fighters, and mercenaries.
- The pastoral class: farmers, hunters, and shepherds.
- The leader class: elders, captains, leaders, and judges.
- The craftsmen class: potters, carpenters, jewellers, and perfumers.

Though they did not form "rank and file", as we imagine a caste system would work, there were still prestigious callings, and more pedestrian callings. The craftsmen were at the top end of the "blue collar" workers of the day. These were the guys God chose to anoint!

GOD IS INVOLVED IN BUSINESS

Businessmen and politicians need the prophetic just as badly as leaders of the Church. We should see God's anointing on the craftsmen, and His desire is to lead, guide, and assist them in their work. They have been armed to go up against the "horns" of authority in our day, and fight for justice. That is a prophetic destiny. This battle is played out day by day in the workplaces in a thousand cities across the globe.

One thing is for sure: we need to drop the religious language in the workplace. There is an entirely separate Christian verbiage, a vocabulary we use in Church that is not appropriate outside the Church. We must present the prophetic in language that anyone can understand. We need to communicate what God is saying in a very ordinary, practical way.

REFERENCES

Marshall, Rich. "God @ Work." Destiny Image, 2000
Oliver, David. "Work, Prison or Place of Destiny?" Authentic Publishing, 1999.
"Prince of Egypt", Dreamworks Pictures, 1999.
Silvoso, Ed. "Anointed For Business." Regal Books, 2002
Woelk, Mike. Private conversation on craftsmen, July 2001.

Chapter Twenty Five
DREAM INTERPRETATION FOR THE LOST

"A man came from Baal-Shalishah, bringing food from the first fruits to the man of God: twenty loaves of barley and fresh ears of grain in his sack. Elisha said, 'Give it to the people and let them eat.' But his servant said, 'How can I set this before a hundred people?' So he repeated, 'Give it to the people and let them eat,' for thus says the LORD, 'They shall eat and have some left.' He set it before them, they ate, and had some left, according to the word of the LORD." (2 Kings 4:42-44).

Taking what we have, and sharing it with our loved ones, is exciting, but taking what we have, blessing it, and sharing it with the entire village – that's a whole new level of exciting! There were people in this town that were not even "saved", people who didn't love or serve the Lord. How rewarding it was to bring the food, physical and spiritual to the people.

I know of a church in Nashville, who hold a huge celebration every Christmas. They have, several times, seen creative miracles in feeding the poor. They hold a massive banquet, and give presents to every child. Baskets of food are given away, and those serving say the effort is all worth it. It is the same with the prophetic gift.

I was once invited to a wedding in Cagayan de Oro city, Mindanao (in the Philippines). I did not know the couple being married, but my friend Bing Gadian was officiating the wedding. The bridal couple was saved, but none of their family members were. Yet, there in the midst of strangers, the prophetic gift stirred in me.

I felt I had a word for them. The wedding proceeded to a point, and I was fussing about how I might share the word (especially given the language barrier). Just then, Bing called me over, and asked me to pray for the couple. I began to pray/prophesy into the detail of their past, their present hopes, and their future plans. The parents of were stunned. Bing interpreted the word, given by a stranger, to their children, and this gave him the leverage to preach a powerful sermon on how much God loves us. Seven people gave their lives to Jesus! What a blessing.

Taking the gift out into the world can be an invigorating process. It can be scary and fraught with danger too, but I love it. We can't fool unsaved people with hype, fraud, and pretence. Your gift has to be honed and ready, the faith levels run high. Some friends of mine, Phil and Lorellee Colley, have taken teams into Psychic Fair. They set up a table, and minister free of charge, use word of knowledge, prophecy, and gifts of healing. The lines that form in front of their table are long, and people wait to see them.

Julia Mason and I have taken teams down to the main commercial district of Honolulu, Hawaii. We worked with a local church, trained them in using the gift on the street, and off we went. Some went to the beach, some went to the mall, and others to the coffee shop. What joy we had that day, sharing the good news and prophesying over open hearted residents. Whilst, Julia took off for the Occult Bookshops. One of the bookstore owners gave her life to Jesus, and closed the shop, all because of the boldness of some Christians willing to go into enemy territory.

CANDLES, CARDS, AND DREAM INTERPRETATION

One of my favourite experiments was going with Alison Papenfus and David Newby to Hillfox markets in Johannesburg.

Right there among the food stalls, candlestick holders, clothing, musical instruments, and card sellers, we opened a booth and offered dream interpretation. How rich and rewarding it was for us to interpret the dreams of the Buddhist clothes seller next door to us, and see him open his heart about the personal troubles he had, and how they expressed themselves in his dreams.

It is fair to say that the process of dream interpretation is fraught with danger, simply because it is so personal. There are symbols that have meaning to the dreamer, but are meaningless to the interpreter. We need the Holy Spirit, who represents the Father – the one who bestowed or gave the dream in the first place. For this reason, we need transparency from the dreamer about what the symbols mean. There needs to be dialogue about the dream, a discussion encompassing the theme, context, elements, and the reason it was given.

God chooses many different ways to speak to people. Just one of these ways is through dreams. *"He causes His sun to rise on the evil and the good and sends rain on the righteous and the unrighteous."* (Mathew 5:45). Everyone dreams at night, and most of those make sense, if we would just write them down.

DREAMS IN THE BIBLE

Job well understood the voice of God in dreams, for he said, *"God speaks in one way, and in two, though man does not perceive it. In a dream, in a vision of the night, when deep sleep falls on mortals... he opens their ears."* (Job 33:14-18).

God chooses to use dreams and speak in a kind of double-speak to force us to pursue Him for the interpretation. It keeps us going after Him. God speaks to us when we are asleep because during the night our conscious minds, which so often get in the way of revelation and spiritual understanding, don't interfere with the dream received when we are asleep. He "opens our ears," to hear a message from Him.

I recall one day, when I was working in the offices of a large corporation, I overheard some of the accountants talking about dreams. The girls in the accounts department were discussing one particularly troublesome dream. The elder girl said she had read a book on the subject, but this dream did not make much sense to her. Then the three of them said, "Hey, Rob is a Christian, maybe he knows what it means." They very naturally made the connection between their dream, and the God of the Christians having the key to what it meant. It was such a natural opportunity to testify of God.

Pharaoh called for Joseph, known to be a man who could understand all visions and dreams. Nebuchadnezzar called for Daniel, who understood the need to wait upon God for the understanding. Daniel pressed in at times and asked the angelic host for help, *"I approached one of the attendants to ask him the truth concerning all this. So he said that he would disclose to me the interpretation of the matter."* (Daniel 7:16). The attendant here is a strange Chaldean word meaning "watcher" or angel.

GENERAL PRINCIPLES ABOUT DREAMS

There are a huge number of dreams in the Bible. In each case God used them to reveal His will, impart His gifts, warn of the future, guide the course of history, and impact the lives of ordinary men and women. If dreams were removed from the Bible, over one third of its content would be lost, as would most of its critical turning points! So what general principles of interpretation can we glean from these dreams and how the servants of God handled them?

- It is possible to control the outcome of our dreams at times, and converse with the Lord in them – see King Abimelech in Genesis 20.
- Dreams can be given to guide, give wisdom, or instruction. If we listen to them and gain understanding about their meaning, we can walk closer to God's will – see Jacob in Genesis 28 and Laban in Genesis 31.
- Numbers often have a significant meaning in dreams. See Joseph dreaming of his brothers in Genesis 37.
- Dreams can be God's way of revealing the future circumstances in a person's life – see the butler and the baker in Genesis 41:1-5.
- If a dream is repeated twice or more, (with similar metaphors or images), on the same night or over several nights, the matter is fixed and will come to pass – see Pharaoh in Genesis 41:25.
- Dreams are often given to encourage or lift the vision of a person beyond their present circumstances into God's understanding of the situation – see Gideon in Judges 7.
- Dreams can be the medium through which God imparts a calling, commissioning, or gifting – see Samuel in 1 Samuel 3:2-21 or Solomon in 1 Kings 3:5.
- Dreams can be used to reveal the secret intentions and thoughts of our hearts – see Nebuchadnezzar in Daniel 2:30 or Job's comment in Job 33:18.
- Some dreams are the product of what we have eaten, or failed to eat. As Isaiah pointed out, *"A hungry person dreams of eating and wakes up still hungry, a thirsty person dreams of drinking."* (Isaiah 29:8).

Dreams may result from, or be affected by, medication we are taking. They may also be affected by the mental state we are in at the time of dreaming. People who are deeply distressed, or taking mood altering medication should be careful not to place too much reliance on dreams as a form of guidance.

NON BELIEVERS

There are many significant examples of dreams given to unbelievers in the Bible. In many instances the dreamer understood them perfectly. Pilate's wife was troubled with dreams about Jesus. Abraham lied to king Abimelech about his wife being a sister, and God warned the king in a dream.

There are also instances where God sent an agent to assist with the dream – such as Daniel in Babylon, Joseph in the jail. The moment at which an unbeliever receives a perplexing dream, is the moment of our opportunity. John Paul Jackson recently took teams of dream interpreters out into the marketplace. They went into secular bookstores, ran dream interpretation classes, offering to help people understand their dreams. By all accounts, it proved very successful.

"But as for me, this mystery has not been revealed to me because of any wisdom that I have more than any other living being, but in order that the interpretation may be known to the king and that you may understand the thoughts of your mind." (Daniel 2:30).

SOME PRINCIPLES TO FOLLOW

"[Do not] let your heart be quick to utter a word before God, for God is in heaven, and you are upon earth; therefore let your words be few. For dreams come with many cares, and a fool's voice with many words... With many dreams come vanities and a multitude of words; but fear God." (Eccesiates 5:2,3,7).

Dreams must be taken on balance with the rest of ordinary life. We must not over focus on them, but rather use them as a normal part of our lives. If in doubt, ask God! He will give wisdom to those who cry out for it: *"If you indeed cry out for insight, and raise your voice for understanding; if you seek it like silver, and search for it as for hidden treasures—then you will understand the fear of the LORD and find the knowledge of God."* (Proverbs 2:3-5).

Make it clear to those you are working with (especially the lost) that you are not working on your own, but with the Holy Spirit. *"Now we have received not the spirit of the world, but the Spirit that is from God, so that we may understand the gifts bestowed on us by God."* (1 Corinthians 2:12).

The following notes have been adapted from a very helpful tool developed by John Paul Jackson on dream interpretation, which I often use as an introduction to the subject with people.

1. The source of the dream
It is helpful to determine the source of the dream because then we may understand why God would allow the person to have it and what it might mean. We must determine if it is a dark dream, one from the enemy, or one revealing revelation from the second heaven. Some distinguishing dark dream characteristics:

- Distinctive lack of colour (black and white, grey or sepia)
- Foreboding sense of terror throughout
- Unwarranted violence or murder in cold blood (rather than battle).

2. The theme of the dream
It is then useful to reduce the dream to its most essential elements. Who is the central character? What is the main thrust of the story? What remains constant throughout each scene (if there are several)?

Most of the meaning of the dream will center on this central issue/character. Write out the dream more simply with this in mind.

3. Determine the context

In order to unravel the meaning of the dream, we examine the context in which the dream occurred. Some helpful questions might include:

- Were you part of the action in the dream, or only an observer?
- If you were part of the action, were you part of the main theme or not?
- Did the story or action of the dream address personal emotional or mental issues – or was it descriptive of some events or actions?
- Did the dream appear to be driven by energy within yourself or from outside of yourself?
- Were the actions that occurred deserved or unwarranted?

4. Element interpretation

It is tempting to look for a rule of thumb or a book on interpreting the elements of dreams. Just as words have no meaning without context in a sentence, elements in a dream have no innate meaning either. The elements of any given dream must be taken in context, and with reference to the central issue or character.

We must rely on a vocabulary unique to the dreamer – experiences they have had in their life, images, people, references that will be part of life for them. Of course, there are universally understood symbols, and the Bible uses certain pictures and images regularly enough to be a guide for us. Nevertheless, avoid excessive reliance on numerology or other allegorical methods. God uses dreams to encourage us to seek Him, rather than rushing off to a library full of books on symbols and signs.

5. Why did you have this dream?

God gives dreams to men for a number of reasons. When thinking about how to apply the dream to life, ask why God gave this dream. What was happening in life, what was going on before the dream?

END NOTE

According to medical research, every person dreams. The statistics show that most nights we dream, but most mornings we find it difficult to remember them. Every work place is ripe with conversational opportunity. A simple question like, "Do you dream much?" or "Did you dream last night" can open wide a gate into a person's life.

If they do not remember something today, they will certainly come to you when they do have a dream. That's how it worked for Joseph. The prisoners had heard of his interpretation for others. One of them recalled years later, when Pharaoh had a dream and it opened a door for him.

Do not be afraid to say, "I don't know what it means." But set your face to pray and ask God about it. The simple offer to try and help a person demonstrates your love.

REFERENCES

Jackson, John Paul. "Your Dream Journal." Streams 2002.
Milligan, Ira. "Understanding the Dreams You Dream." Destiny Image, 1997.
Riffel, Herman. "Dreams: Wisdom Within." Destiny Image, 1990.
Ryle, James. "A Dream Come True." Harper Collins, 1995.

WORKSHEET FOR DREAM INTERPRETATION

Type of Revelation

Source of the dream (General tone)

Central Character (Theme)

Outline of the main story (Summarised)

Context for the dream

Element Interpretation

Why did God allow me to have this dream?

What am I going to do about it? (Action required):

Chapter Twenty-Six
THE KINGDOM OF GOD

"Naaman... was a great man with his master, and highly respected because by him the Lord had given victory to Aram. The man was also a valiant warrior, but he was a leper." (2 Kings 5:1).

Great, respected, victorious, valiant, warrior, and leper... They just don't go together do they? Naaman was captain of the Aramaen army, and a man keen in the skills of war. Notice who gave him victory; it was the LORD of Israel. This man was a secular power, a captain, and a military genius. It was God who gave him victory. Truly, all good gifts come down from heaven, bestowed by the Father of lights,[1] but Naaman had a problem. He had leprosy, an incurable disease that would eventually kill him.

God's kingdom affects everyone on earth. It will reach out and touch the most distant parts of the earth, because His heart is toward even the most depraved killer. How can the Kingdom touch every life, every land, and every kingdom on earth? In Naaman's case, he had a servant girl, captured in Israel. The kingdom of God had come down and touched Abraham, who had sired Isaac, who had raised Jacob, who became Israel. The kingdom of God had touched this girl's life, and through her it was about to touch Naaman's life too.

She knew of the prophet Elisha, who was in Israel, and urged Naaman to pay him a visit. We know the end of this story... Naaman goes, dips in the muddy waters of the Jordan seven times, and is healed.

---

1. James 1:17

The Kingdom touches his life and changes it forever. He even takes some of the soil home with him, "So I may forever worship the God of Israel." God uses a prophet of Israel to touch the leader of a foreign nation which does not worship Him.

SEQUENTIAL CIRCLES OF THE KINGDOM

The Kingdom is still reaching out today, through the Church and its leaders – apostles, prophets, evangelists, and pastor/teachers. It is not easily, or well understood. The first souls to hear about the Kingdom sure struggled. The risen Christ returned to His Church and, *"For forty days He spoke to them about things pertaining to the Kingdom of God."* (Acts 1:3). Yet after all that (and how much was said?), they still asked, "Lord will you at this time restore the Kingdom to Israel?

The Kingdom of God is "already" and "not yet"; not fully, but really. It is macro and micro, both at once. Michael Sullivant has said, "The Kingdom of God was concealed in the Old Testament; revealed in the New Testament; delegated in the Church age; consummated in the age to come."[2]

Imagine a series of circles in a row, overlapping a little at the edge. The first circle represents the spirit and heart of a person. The second circle overlapping it slightly represents the person's soul and body. The next circle over is our home and family, then synagogue or Church, community and business, society and region, culture and nation, the world or planet earth, and the last circle represents all of creation and the universe.

Scripture speaks to the influence of the Kingdom at all these levels. It moves out from one sphere to the next.

---

2. "The Kingdom". Audio message 2, May 2005.

1. The spirit and our heart

To be received at all, the Kingdom must be received inwardly. The Kingdom comes by words, by proclamation, entering in like seed to soil, and bearing fruit.[3] It is received inwardly through repentance, and belief springs up in the heart.[4] The devil tries from the very sowing to pluck up the seed, and spoil it. If the seed of the gospel penetrates a heart, the next battle ground is...

2. The body and our soul

The kingdom grows within us, and seeks to cleanse, heal and restore our body and soul. Very often evil spirits are challenged, and a demon is cast out of a person. Jesus said, when this happened, the Kingdom of God has come to them.[5] The physical needs of a person are met, because they seek first the Kingdom of God.[6] This is the Kingdom working its way from the inside out. The devil tries at this level to oppress and re-inhabit a person, taking advantage of their sinful behaviour. When the Kingdom advances to this level, it's next target of transformation is...

3. The home and our family

A house divided against itself cannot stand. The Kingdom in a home brings unity between the family members, and expels darkness.[7] The Kingdom of heaven belongs to children, and those who trust with a childlike faith.[8] So, the devil tries to divide the family and home. He tempts children into rebellion, and rewards the parents who abandon their children. This is perhaps the most contended area of life in the 21st century, in the aftermath of post modern, industrialised, liberated, commercialised, secular, success oriented, morality free society. Once He has the family unit, the Lord aims for...

---

3. Mathew 13:20   4. Mark 1:14,15
5. Mathew 12:28   6. Mathew 6:33
7. Mark 3:24   8. Mathew 19:14

4. The synagogue or the Church

Religious communities are made up of familes. The Church is the next frontier for the Kingdom because it is the expression of the Kingdom that brings shade and rest to the community. [9] Jesus said that every scribe brings out of his treasure, things old and new, concerning the Kingdom. [10] He has a redemptive purpose for synagogues and Jewish communities too! It is found in the established ways, and the new wineskin. The old shadows and prefigures the new, leading us to it. The devil at this level tries to get us to swap the traditions of men (religion) for the word of God (life in relationships). Once the Church has understood her position as a frontier outpost for the Kindgom of God, she will naturally focus on...

5. The community including business

Because Christians are present in every street and business, the Kingdom is present everywhere in our community. Every Christian person is like leaven hidden in the dough. We make the whole batch (society) rise. [11] David knew this, and for that reason appointed men to be in charge of, *"The businesses of the Kingdom."* (1 Chronicles 26:30). Kingdom business, and marketplace ministry has certainly become a focus of Church life today. The devil, therefore, tries to cause a sacred/secular split in the minds of Christians; bringing compromise, temptation and trouble to Christian businesses and at a community level brings strife. Once business is won for the Kingdom, and economies are affected, the Kingdom naturally moves up to...

6. The society and regional issues

The Kingdom is present in society, the wheat and the tares growing together until the time of the harvest. [12] God affects the entire

---

9. Mathew 13:52
11. Luke 13:20,21
10. Mark 4:30
12. Mathew 13:24-30

society, casting the dragnet wide and bringing in all manner of fish. Eventually, they will be sorted out one from another. [13] Christian leaders and businessmen naturally begin to think of local government, regional economies and citywide gatherings. The devil at this level tries to bring premature "sorting", judgemental attitudes, pride, tribalism, competition, civil disobedience and eventually (if he can achieve it) anarchy. If a region or society accepts Kingdom change, it will start to affect...

7. The culture and each nation

Entire nations can embrace (and be affected by) the Kingdom, or they can reject it (as Israel did in the time of Christ). [14] This Kingdom and its King are taking over every other kingdom, one by one. [15] In nations like Fiji, Solomon Islands, and Argentina, the Kingdom has taken over the country. The devil at a national level, trying to affect government policy, rallying them against the Lord and His anointed. [16] He tries to engender a spirit of lawlessness among political leaders, incite genocide between tribes and move through legislature to bring national sin (such as abortion, gambling or euthanasia). Once the Kingdom of God has affected a nation, it will naturally move out into...

8. The world and into all of creation

God wants His Kingdom to come, and His will to be done on the entire earth, as it is being done right now in heaven. [17] Daniel saw this end-time take over and said the Kingdom shall break into pieces and consume all other kingdoms on earth. [18] Paul said it this way, *"For all of creation waits with eager longing for the revealing of the children of God; that the creation itself will be set free from its bondage to decay and will obtain the freedom of the glory of the children of God."* (Romans 8:19, 21).

---

13. Mathew 13:47
15. Revelation 11:15
17. Mathew 6:10
14. Mathew 21:43
16. Psalm 2:1,2
18. Daniel 2:44

As the sons and daughters of the Kingdom rise up and change their communities and nations, all of creation is affected. According to observer George Otis Jr, the city of Almolonga, Guatemala experienced significant impact in it's produce production as a result of revival.[19] Yield from fields, size of produce and rainfall were all affected.

According to observer David Newby, the nation of Fiji in the Pacific was deeply affected by transforming revival. The village of Sabeto experienced regeneration of mangroves, crabs, reef fish species and soil productivity.[20] The village of Nuku experienced healing of the stream (long poisonous), water supply and the restoration of the land.[21]

The devil has only this frontier left! He will try to increase the level of judgement the world will suffer through its disobedience to the King.

Our job is to seek first the Kingdom of God, and His righteousness. Our task is to receive the Kingdom into our heart, express it in our home, advance it through our business, fan the flames in our community, proclaim it to our culture, underwrite our legislature with its principles, and manifest it to all creation!

---

19. Transformations I video, section 4.   20 "Fiji: Healing the Land". Pg 30
21. Ibid, Pg 40

GRAPH 1: FROM THE SPIRIT OF A PERSON TO THEIR BODY

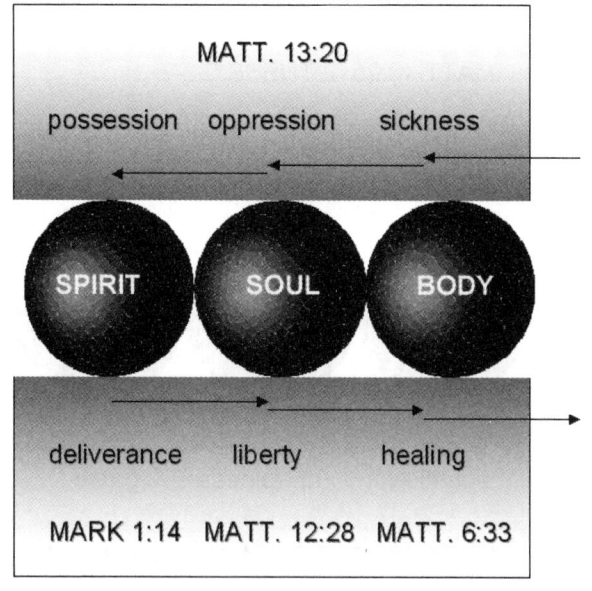

MATT. 13:20

possession   oppression   sickness

SPIRIT   SOUL   BODY

deliverance   liberty   healing

MARK 1:14   MATT. 12:28   MATT. 6:33

GRAPH 2: FROM THE FAMILY INTO THE WORKPLACE

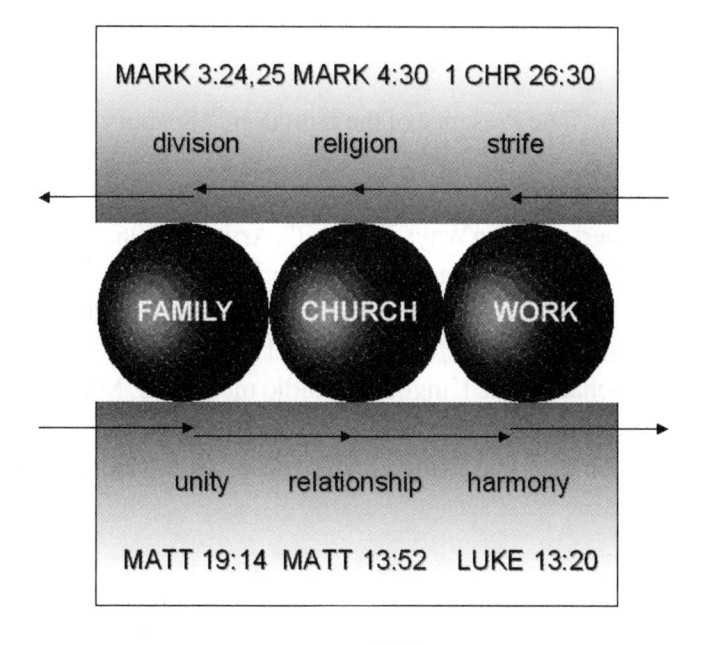

MARK 3:24,25   MARK 4:30   1 CHR 26:30

division   religion   strife

FAMILY   CHURCH   WORK

unity   relationship   harmony

MATT 19:14   MATT 13:52   LUKE 13:20

Graph 3: From Society Into The World

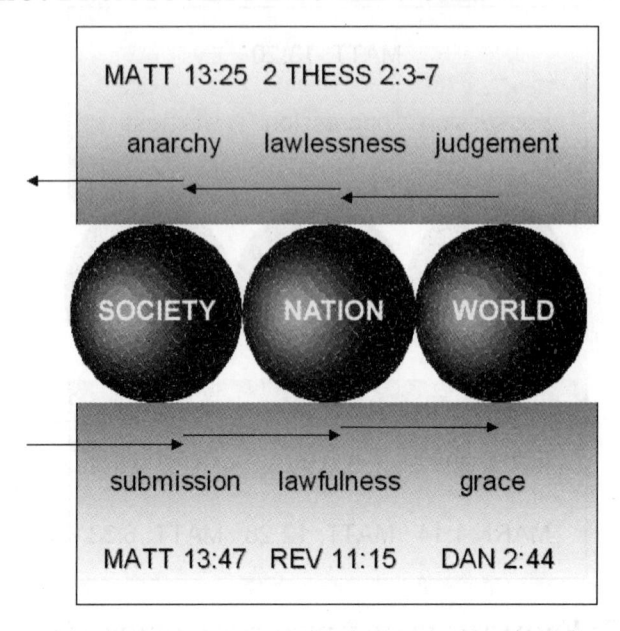

```
MATT 13:25  2 THESS 2:3-7

anarchy   lawlessness   judgement

[SOCIETY]  [NATION]  [WORLD]

submission   lawfulness   grace

MATT 13:47   REV 11:15   DAN 2:44
```

References

Ellul, Jacques. "The Presence of the Kingdom." Seabury Press, 1967
Hollingworth, Peter. "Kingdom Come!" AIO, 1991.
Holmes, Robert. "Seven Ways To Meet". Article, 2006.
Meyer, FB. "Inherit the Kingdom." Victor Books, 1904.
Newby, David. "Fiji: Healing the Land". Team Ministry, 2005.
Sentinel Group, the. "Transformations I". 1999.
Sullivant, Michael. "The Kingdom". Audio message2, May 2005. Storm Harvest Inc.
Sullivant, Michael. "Your Kingdom Come." Creation House, 2004.

Chapter Twenty-Seven
THE PLANNING CHAMBER

"The man of God had told [the king]; thus he warned him so that he guarded himself there more than once or twice... now the heart of the king of Aram was enraged over this thing; and he called his servants and said to them, 'Will you tell me which one of us is for the king of Israel?' One of the servants said, 'No, my Lord O king; but Elisha the prophet who is in Israel tells the king of Israel the words that you speak in your bedroom chamber'." (2 Kings 6: 8-12).

Here is another example of how the Kingdom of God reaches out and touches the lives of people inside Israel (the Church) and outside in Syria (the world). Only this time, the effect is not positive, as it was for Namaan, it is negative – adversely affecting those opposing the Kingdom. Syria is making war against Israel. The Syrian king is making plans with his generals and captains in his bedchamber – his war room or planning chamber. Unfortunately for him, God is showing Elisha, the prophet in Israel, all his plans. Not once or twice, but many times, the enemy's plans are thwarted because the king of Israel is forewarned.

At first, the king of Aram suspected a spy in their midst. After discovering the power of the prophetic, however, he sought to destroy the prophet. One sunny morning Elisha's servant opened the curtains to find an army encamped around the city preparing to destroy them! In spite of superior fire power, the outcome was total defeat for the Syrians, who were blinded by God and led away by Elisha! This story contains the now famous "look up and see" episode, where the angels of the Lord were gathered in fiery chariots.

In ancient times many cities were walled. The outer wall enclosed a village, and inside that was a fort. Inside the fort was a tower, and the king's chambers were located in the tower – the most securely protected place. At the top of the tower was a viewing platform for the watchmen, and below that was the king's bed chamber. It was usually a circular room with curtains and private meeting areas. This was called the war room or planning chamber where the king would meet with his counsellors.

Our modern day equivalent would be the Pentagon in Washington, or the head offices of ASIO in Canberra. Imagine a ministry in the Church that could listen to the conversations of our top military planners. Imagine a ministry that could see into the Caucus room of Parliament. Such is the power God wants to release to His Church and its prophetic servants. You don't have to imagine, because this ministry really exists, today.

Three Levels of Insight

There were three levels of prophetic insight operating in this story. Firstly, Elisha had revelation of the plans of the enemy. Secondly, he then saw beyond that into the spirit realm and saw the plans and work of the Lord. He saw the angels in chariots of fire. Lastly, his servant saw in the realm of the natural, all the armies of Syria.

The servant had a first heaven revelation – he could only see the natural. Above that was the realm of the celestial bodies – referred to as the second heaven. Elisha saw into this realm when he perceived the enemy's plans. Above that was the third heaven, what we would really call "heaven" today. It was the 'basement' of God's dwelling place. This was the realm Elisha saw into when he saw the chariots of fire.

Above the third heaven, the celestial dwelling place, rose to the seventh or "highest heaven".

EXAMPLES OF SEEING IN THE SPIRIT

There are several occasions in Scripture when a minister sees in the spirit realm, events and circumstances happening at great distance from their physical location.

Paul was with the churches in Colosse and Corinth, even whilst he was in prison. He said, "I am with you in spirit," both to bless and to judge.[1] Elisha "went with" Gehazi whilst he stole from the soldier who had been healed. "Did not my spirit go with you?" asked Elisha.[2]

John, whilst languishing on an island, wrote to the church in Smyrna, informing them that certain of their members belonged to the local coven of satan worshippers.[3] He told the church in Pergamum they lived where the throne of satan was placed – and as a result one of their number had been killed.[4] He warned the church in Thyatira not to tolerate the manipulative control of Jezebel in their midst, and also told them she had led some to worship idols and commit fornication.[5] All of this he saw by the Spirit.

In 1990, Paul Cain had met with the then president of the U.S.A. and was asked to provide prophetic insight concerning Middle East, the imminent Gulf War and any other events that might unfold in the region. After the meeting Paul was to ring the President with any further feedback. Paul foresaw the war, and the movements of Saddam Hussein, but had lost or misplaced the number to call. So he tried the general listed number of the White House.

---

1. Colossians 2:5, 1 Corinthians 5:3
2. 2 Kings 5:25,26
3. Revelation 2:9
4. Revelation 2:13
5. Revelation 2:20

After three unsuccessful attempts to connect via the switchboard he prayed, asking God for the phone number. When he received it, he called direct and gave his input. The very next day agents (we are told) from the FBI, CIA, and NSA were all over his office asking, "Who told you the number, who is the spy?"

A WARNING

The kind of spiritual insight offered by the prophetic, especially as it relates to this function, is very valuable. One does not need to stress how Israel profited from not being ambushed many times as Elisha warned them. The Churches of the Asia rim profited greatly from John's insight, given in his letters from Patmos. This insight is not mere knowledge, or even a "word of knowledge," but strategic insight. The Hebrews called this *da'ath* – being aware, cunning, planning, or foresight. Without this knowledge, understanding, perceptive insight, Scripture is clear:

"My people will go into exile for lack of understanding; their men of rank will die of hunger and their masses will be parched with thirst." (Isaiah 5:13).

"My people are destroyed from lack of knowledge. Because you have rejected knowledge, I also reject you." (Hosea 4:6).

Solomon took this thought a little further, indicating that without vision, without prophetic foresight, we would perish (die on the vine). The Hebrews called this *chazown* – oracle, vision, or a revelation:

"People without vision perish." (Proverbs 29:18).

David lamented that, *"We do not see our signs, there is no longer any prophet, nor is there anyone among us who knows how long."* (Psalm 74:9 NKJV).

A PROPHETIC EARLY WARNING SYSTEM

Back in 1996, there was a movie in the box office called "Twister". This movie was an education to me, not because of the content (though spectacular), but because of what the Lord taught me about the eyes and ears of the Body. In one scene a town was destroyed by a tornado. A woman was talking to her 'twister chasing' niece and she remarked, "Jo, we just didn't have any warning. No broadcast, no phone call, nothing! The sirens went off and seconds later we were hit... you've got to do something to give us more time!"

In the Church, our early warning system is the ministry of the eyes and ears. The prophetic is defined in several places in the word as being a watchman ministry. I wept openly in the auditorium, ashamed of the damage being done to the Body of Christ because its watchmen were not providing enough warning to the Church of danger. So many fall under spiritual attack, and even under the judgments of God, because they are not prepared.

God lamented so long ago to his servant that, *"I sought for anyone among them who would repair the wall and stand in the breach before me on behalf of the land, so that I would not destroy it; but I found no one. Therefore I have poured out my indignation upon them; I have consumed them with the fire of my wrath; I have returned their conduct upon their heads, says the Lord God."* (Ezekiel 22:30,31). Is it still not true today?

The Lord is earnest in His desire to restore the eyes and ears to the Church, to set up a 'prophetic' early warning system in the Church, to raise up prophets and intercessors who will stand on the battlements and watch. These men and women, in a local context, should be giving early warning of impending judgement from the

Lord, as well as impending attack from the enemy. The Lord told Ezekiel, *"If I bring the sword upon a land, and the people of the land take one of their number as their sentinel; and if the sentinel sees the sword coming upon the land and blows the trumpet and warns the people; then if any who hear the sound of the trumpet do not take warning, and the sword comes and takes them away, their blood shall be upon their own heads.... if they had taken [or been given] warning, they would have saved their lives. But if the sentinel sees the sword coming and does not blow the trumpet, so that the people are not warned, and the sword comes and takes any of them, they are taken away in their iniquity."* (Ezekiel 33:2-6). The same is true in our day also.

THINGS WHICH HINDER AN EARLY WARNING SYSTEM

There are several things that stand in the way of a local church setting up a spiritual early warning system. Many people do not even know their calling in life. When asked in meeting after meeting, people generally respond that they believe they have a gift, but do not know what it is. If they do know what it is, they do not know how to exercise it. They are either not trained to understand what they are seeing (discernment and interpretation), or do not have enough experience in discernment. Even those who do understand what they are seeing may face problems with local leadership.

1. The onus on leadership

'Upcoming' watchmen may not have authority with the leadership. That is, they are not given a place on the wall to watch, or they are not allowed to report what they see to the leaders. The Scripture above clearly places the requirement on the people of God to rouse the watchmen and to take note of their report. Note it says, "and the people of the land take one of their number as their sentinel". Sadly, many churches have not done this.

In other cases, the sentinel appoints himself. Small wonder they are not listened to by leadership. Other leaders ignore the constant warnings given them by the messengers, or redefine the messages they are given, to make it sound better than it is. Or worse, the leaders may gather about them those who only bring good news! In some cases they may persecute or destroy prophetic people in their midst, and this is truly tragic. In the account of Jeremiah we read of a report he brings from the watch-tower to the elders of his city, *"Blow the trumpet through the land; shout aloud and say, 'Gather together, and let us go into the fortified cities!' Raise a standard toward Zion, flee for safety, do not delay, for I am bringing evil from the north, and a great destruction."* (Jeremiah 4:5,6).

Sadly, the leaders of Israel at the time took Jeremiah's report rather poorly. One has a picture of young Jeremiah, standing on the battlements, prophetically seeing a brown cloud rising in the northern quarter. He is given insight that this cloud has, under its cloak, a great army from Babylon. He runs to the elders and tells them.

He is rebuffed, the elders prefer the report of those who tickle their ears, and tell them what they want to hear. There are other watchmen evidently, who see the same cloud rising, but take it merely to be a storm cloud, or a wind squall– a sand storm in the desert. They tell the elders, *"You shall not see the sword, nor shall you have famine, but I will give you true peace in this place."* (Jeremiah 14:13). The leaders choose to listen to these false prophets.

We'll look at the danger of prophesying falsely later. Both Ezekiel and Jeremiah faced a problem with local leadership. Their reports were sometimes not well received, because the leaders did not want to hear bad news. The judgement would then move from the prophet to the leader, because the prophet had discharged his duty.

Now the leaders were responsible to act on what they heard, to protect the people God had placed in their care.

2. Mistreated watchmen

Jeremiah gave a true warning to the leaders, but *"Pashur struck the prophet...and put him in stocks."* (Jeremiah 20:2). To the warning of danger, they retorted, *"You shall die! Why have you prophesied like this?"* (Jeremiah 26:9).As the enemy army rolled closer and closer Jeremiah grew distressed. He earnestly wanted his city to be prepared, but they continued in their unbelief.

Armed men gathered on the plains below Jerusalem, yet still the elders refused to listen. Finally, they besieged the city, and in disbelief, the leaders cried out for advice, (too late I'm afraid). Jeremiah sought the Lord, and the advice from the heavenly throne was, *"Serve the king of Babylon and live."* (Jeremiah 27:17). This advice was still not what they wanted to hear. They threw him into court, and from there they threw him in jail for treason against the state.[6] From his cell, Jeremiah still cried, *"Submit to the Babylonians or you shall die,"* (Jeremiah 38:1-4), which only served to infuriate the elders more! They took him bodily and threw him in a cistern to die.[7]

As leaders we must keep a soft heart toward the prophetic. The report they bring to us may not always be a good report. Still, we should not stone the messenger for the message they bring. We should take careful note, get further confirmation, and then take action. Sadly, many of our watchmen are sick and tired of being abused. They are weary in their jails, or lonely outcasts wandering in the wilderness. Meanwhile, the Body wanders blind and deaf into the attacks of the enemy and the judgements of God. It is time to make our peace with the watchmen, and bring them home.

---

6. Jeremiah 37:21   7. Jeremiah 38:6

3. The watchmen should look out

There are other reasons for why the early warning system is not working. These have more to do with the 'eyes' themselves rather than the leadership, or the rest of the Body. The watchmen may be too timid, or may not 'get up' on the battlements and stand in the breach. God declared to Ezekiel, *"You have not gone up into the breaches, or repaired the wall for the house of Israel, so that it might stand in the day of battle."* (Ezekiel 13:5).

Spiritually speaking, today's watchmen are supposed to edify the body of Christ, by repairing the walls of faith damaged by sin, and the stumbling blocks so many have tripped over. Some of today's servants also are not going up in to the breaches to repair them for the day of battle.

4. Seduction – the love of men

Another danger is being seduced into speaking what we know the leadership wants to hear. We covered this aspect in the Ezekiel 14 Trap. The need for respectability, for recognition, for a place or position, can sometimes be overwhelming. The need to be seen to have a word can lure the immature into prophesying the 'party line'.

Judgement falls upon the watchmen who speaks lies, or who misunderstand the signs and give false hope to the people. As the Lord reiterated to Jeremiah, *"The prophets are prophesying lies in my name; I did not send them, nor did I command them or speak to them. They are prophesying to you a lying vision, worthless divination, and the deceit of their own minds.... By sword and famine those prophets shall be consumed."* (Jeremiah 14:14-15).

This is worse than just not going up to the battlements. It means falsely reporting what you see, white-washing over the problems. A false prophet would not care less about the breaches in the walls, because they could not see them! While judgement is coming they are proclaiming, "God loves us, there will be no attack."

False prophets build a false wall of security, when in fact the fury and judgement of the Lord may be coming, and a time of retribution at hand. These prophets falsely whitewash over the iniquity and preach a false "peace and prosperity" message so absolutely inappropriate to the day of battle.

Conclusion

I look forward to the time when local congregations can say, "We are in fear of nothing, for the Lord has appointed watchmen for our walls, and they provide good testimony of the coming of God and the movements of our enemies. We have sought the Lord together, we agree with the word and have acted on it. We are prepared." Leaders, servants, prophetic persons, and all the Body must work together in this effort if it is to succeed. To use Paul's analogy, we should pray that eye salve be bought, that we may restore sight to the blind, remove our hands from over the eyes, and prepare for the incoming reports!

References

Cain, Paul. "The Days Ahead." Audio Message, Kansas City Sept 17, 2001.
Socha, Aaron. Private conversation, September 2002
"Twister" Universal Pictures, 1996.

Chapter Twenty Eight
THE GIFT OF THE SEER

"God testified by all His prophets, yes by every seer."
(2 Kings 17:13).

There was a time in the history of Middle Eastern lands, when men who were inspired to speak for God were known as seers. They could see into the realm of the spirit; they could communicate with spirit beings; they heard from God, but they were generically referred to as seers. Then there came a kind of man who lived in the spirit realm; who had relationship with God, and they spoke for Him. These they called prophets.

A wonderful, parabolic picture of the seer is found in, "The Horse and His Boy," by C.S. Lewis (part of the classic Narnia series). Shasta the boy is running away from an oncoming army. His companion Aravis is injured and they flee to the safety of a hermit's hideaway. This hideaway is like a compound, with a house, stables, grassy open areas, and a large pool. They recoup their strength, and Aravis comes out to the yard to find the Hermit gazing into the pool. The Hermit could observe the outside world and all goings-on, at a great distance by seeing a reflection in the water's surface. Gazing – that's the core technology of a seer. Looking, at a distance; seeing with the spiritual eye.

Another good example, for J.R.R. Tolkien fans, comes halfway through the second chronicle of Middle Earth. In "The Two Towers," the band of travellers, called the fellowship of the Ring, are taking refuge in the forests of the elves. The Western Elf Princess invites Frodo, their leader, to gaze into the pool, and see what might be. He sees things which are, which might be, and the potential of his own heart.

THE SHIFT AT SAMUEL

At a certain point in human history the seer ceased to be the only "supplier" of revelation in the marketplace. A new player entered in, and they called him by another name. In Israel when a man went to inquire of God, he used to say, *"Come let us go to the seer; for he who is called a prophet now, was formerly called a seer."* (1 Samuel 9:9). The time at which this transition took place is pivotal to understanding the shift. This comment is made about Israel's first king (Saul), seeking the advice of a prophet (Samuel).

The time of Samuel necessitated a shift from seeing to prophesying, from seer to prophet. Until that time, Israel had judges and scribes whom the seer served. Now there were emerging priests, and their first king. This necessitated a prophet. There were men called prophets before this, (marginal references, hints and allegations). But Samuel – the prophet served Saul – the king.

The old "technology" went on, as it always does. Though, seers no longer stood alone as a gift; they became integrated into a wider range of ministry functions. Seeing became part of priestly, worship and prophetic functions alike. Before we examine those gift mixes, we must understand that there are two kinds of seers, and we must explore seeing technology a little. There were two Hebrew words for Seer.

– *Ro'eh (ro-ay')*: one who looks, a perceiver, an advisor, to approve or pass.

– *Chozeh (kho-zeh')*: a beholder, one who makes a compact, brings decision or agreement.

They both saw, but one saw so as to advise. The other saw so as to bring agreement. As we look at examples of the seer in operation, we will understand this difference more clearly.

In Scripture, the word seer is almost always used in connection with another role – that of prophet, priest, minstrel, scribe, or recorder. We only have one example of a man for whom both "seer" words are used: Hanani. Here is every reference in the Bible:

PERSON	SCRIPTURES	OFFICE/ GIFT
Samuel	1 Samuel 9:9-22 (prophet)/ 1 Chronicles 9:22 (seer)	Prophet/ ro'eh seer
Hanani	2 Chronicles 16:7 (ra'ah)/ 2 Chronicles 19:2 (chozeh)	Ro'eh seer/ chozeh seer
Gad	2 Samuel 24:11 (prophet)/ 1 Chronicles 21:9 (seer)	Prophet/ chozeh seer
Asaph	2 Kings 18:18 (recorder)/ 2 Chronicles 29:30 (seer)	Recorder/ chozeh seer
Jeduthan	1 Chronicles 15:19 (prophet)/ 2 Chronicles 35:15 (seer)	Minstrel/ chozeh seer
Heman	1 Chronicles 16:42 (minstrel)/ 1 Chronicles 25:5 (seer)	Minstrel/ chozeh seer
Iddo	2 Chronicles 13:22 (prophet) 2 Chronicles 9:29 (seer)	Prophet/ chozeh seer
Amos	Amos 7:14 (prophet)/ Amos 7:12 (seer)	Prophet/ chozeh seer

The role of seer is now subsidiary, ancillary to, or part of another role, and is most often harnessed to the call of a prophet. It makes up a part; it is a sub-unit of the prophetic equipment. However, not all prophets are seers; that much is clear from the swath of prophets who are never spoken of with either seer term.

DISTINGUISHING RO'EH AND CHOZEH SEERS

Both kinds of seers (obviously) see! They see visions of various kinds (refer chapter five), and they dream. They can see at a distance (more on that later). But why? What motivates them?

1. Ro'eh – advisor, to approve or pass

One of the core motivations of these seers is to share God's perspective on a situation. This may include bringing a perspective the leader has not thought of, preparing him for an encounter he is not ready for, or even announcing judgement if they do not "pass muster".

Samuel and Hanani are the only two *ro'eh* seers we find in Scripture. Personality type, communication style, and the portfolio of the prophet all have a bearing on the stories we read of both these men. Yet we can learn more of the seer from a couple of key interactions.

Let us examine two examples of Samuel acting under the seer gift. In 1 Samuel 9:19, Samuel ministers to Saul before his coronation. He advises him on the upcoming challenge and change as he joins the company of prophets. He helps Saul prepare for a supernatural encounter. And he tells Saul what kind of man he will become. Samuel stands at a geographic point in space and time, and sees down the road, and sees down Saul's life line.

In the second story, in 1 Chronicles 9:22, Samuel joins David in appointing men into their office as gatekeepers. Prophets were typically part of coronation, ordination and appointment ceremonies. Samuel, however, is mentioned as a seer in this context, presumably because he had a part in advising David on the selection of these men.

He understood their genealogy, had insight to their call, and commissioned them into their destiny. Hanani by contrast, did not have particularly good relationships with the leaders God sent him to help. In 2 Chronicles 16:7, Hanani brings a word of judgement to Asa, and gets thrown in jail. Asa did not pass God's "muster" (standard). Hanani stood at a juncture in time, looking back, estimating Asa's conduct from God's perspective, then speaking of his future sins.

2. Chozeh – pact maker, to bring decision or agreement

One of the core motivations of this seer is to help the leader make a decision, or bring him into agreement with heaven's opinion. As a secondary element, they write what they see, they journal and as a result they end up documenting, or writing down (observing) history. We have more examples of this gift in play, but for the sake of brevity let's look at just three: Gad, Iddo and Amos.

In 1 Chronicles 21:9, Gad the seer brought a word of choice judgement to David, who had numbered Israel. It fell to Gad to "see" the choices David had, and pick his judgement. He saw into the heavenlies, and discerned the angel standing over the threshing floor of Ornan, the Jebusite, ready for destruction.

Gad was also a recorder, who brought order to the house of God. He issued commands relating to orchestrating worship.[1] Gad and David together left commands about the order of worship and serving the Lord. As a seer, he served the worshipping leader, and together they made choices about the order things should be in.

---

1. 2 Chronicles 29:25

Iddo also did not have good relations with his kings (who can blame him, they were evil!). In 2 Chronicles 9:29, it is said that the visions of the seer Iddo were recorded, concerning Jeroboam. Iddo saw (foresaw) the actions of Jeroboam. These he recorded. He also foresaw the actions of Rehoboam,[2] and also Abijah.[3]

Jeroboam was a fairly hassled man. He had several prophets and seers on his case! Amos the seer prophesied against the reign of Jeroboam, and the priest, Amaziah reported it (Amos 7:12). Amos looked and saw the work of Jeroboam. He lived at the same time as Isaiah, and has seen expansion in the kingdom (through military aggression and control of the major trade routes). Religious fervour and obedience to God, though, was at an all time low! In Amos 7:16, he prophesied about the king's family and the nation, calling on Israel to make a decision to follow God.

The Gift Of Seeing

Some have called me a seer. Those who know me, understand a little of how this gift works in me. The seer does not walk around "seeing" all the time. They cannot peer into private rooms, or see things which the Lord wants hidden. However, walls and distance are no obstacle when God wants to reveal a matter. There have been numerous occasions when I have stood in the room of a house, seeing and hearing conversations in another house or room. The Lord opens up a window, or creates a connection, just like video, (though not always with sound), and you see.

This "ability" can be abused. One must not engage it, to peer, and see what is none of our business. It must either come unhidden (by the Holy Spirit) or it must be given in prayer to us. For us to use seeing technology, without reference to God, is witchcraft.

---

2. 2 Chronicles 12:15   3. 2 Chronicles 13:22

Perhaps a look at the Hebrew language will help the explaination. Underlying the role of seer is the gift of seeing. That is to say, beneath the surface of the man *Ro'eh* is the ability to *ra'ah (raw-aw')*; underlying the man *Chozeh* is the ability to *chazah (khaw-zaw)*.

The technology is used for both good and bad, righteous and evil "ministers". It is a gift that can be abused. This is the way people involved in the occult can "see" so clearly. Right sight, wrong source.

Ra'ah – to notice, perceive, see, understand an appearance

- In 2 Chronicles 18:22, Micaiah saw (*ra'ah*) the Lord lifted up;
- In 2 Kings 6:20 Gehazi saw (*ra'ah*) the angels in the city;
- In 1 Samuel 28:8 the witch in Endor saw (*ra'ah*) Samuel after death.

Chazah – behold, envision, gaze, look

- In Daniel 4:5, Daniel saw (*chazah*) in a dream;
- In Isaiah 30:10, the people asked the prophets to speak illusions (*chazah*);
- In Isaiah 47:13 astrologers divine (*chazah*) by the stars.

It would seem then, at this level, that the gift is available to all: saved and unsaved; sanctified and unsanctified. That is, we can all see, spiritually speaking, but we are not all seers. It is how we employ the gift, and what motivates us to look which matters. So God gave us a pair of binoculars, but what do we see and why are we looking? More to the point, what are **we** going to do with the information?

The New Testament

There is no place in the New Testament that we find mention of the Seer. However if we examine the Greek language closely we find mention of close relatives, roles described which relate to seeing. Three words spring up:

- *Theoros*: envoy, observer; [4]
- *Skeptomai*: watchman, watcher; [5]
- *Mantis*: diviner, seer. [6]

Underlying these roles are the functions, or abilities to see:

- *Theoreo*: to gaze, to look, to see; [7]
- *Skopeo*: keep your eyes fixed upon; [8]
- *Manteuomai*: to tell by fortune, seeing. [9]

Once again the ability to see in the New Testament is applied equally to both good and bad; righteous and evil practitioners of their gift. It is safe to assume that the gift of seeing is subsidiary to the role of prophet in the New Testament just as it is in the Old Testament.

One Day in Johanessburg

One day I was minding my own business at a café in Johanessburg, South Africa. I was with a friend, and we were talking about the gifts, particularly technology (technical use of a spiritual gift). Suddenly, we both became aware of a "watcher", a woman at the back of the café who was "peering" into our conversation. Given the noise, she could not naturally hear us, but we knew.

---

4. Luke 10:18, Revelation 11:11
6. Acts 16:16
8. 2 Corinthians 4:18

5. Phillipians 3:14
7. Acts 10:11
9. Acts 16:16

It turned out that this woman was a witch, full of control, intimidation, and manipulation. We observed her treatment of co-workers, the staff, and people nearby. It was ugly. We simply prayed, and stopped talking about "spiritual" issues, and waited for a chance to confront her. She promptly got up and left the café.

Another day, I was sitting at an airport in Dallas Fort-Worth, Texas praying about the upcoming meetings in Mobile, Alabama (a significant distance away). Just then, a scene opened up before me, it was sketchy, but I could see our host David White, how he was dressed, what he would say to us as he picked us up, and the decision he was making about where to host (house) us. I call this a "long range scanner". I shared this information with my team mates, and later, these things did indeed come to pass. It is not 100% accurate, but it is helpful to know what is about to happen to you.

On the way into Mobile, another thing happened. I was taken in the Spirit to a very particular house in Mobile. It was built before the civil war, double story, square posts, rails, white paint, topiary in the garden, and a fountain. When we got to the city, I asked our hosts to take us to the suburb where such houses might be found. The Lord had given me a very clear instruction, "Go to that house, and say to the owner such and such, and they will let you in."

We found the house in fairly short order, and I went to the front door. I said to the owner what I needed to, and they let me in! A complete stranger was granted access to a house in a strange city, and given a guided tour! The Lord used that experience to speak to me about the church I was invited to speak at, about the leadership and the decisions they had to make. It was a very helpful prophetic insight. It was the seer gift, turned to counselling. It was given by God, to help them make a decision. That's what this gift is for.

A FINAL NOTE

Though the word seer is never used in connection with Elisha, he found difficulty with the seeing technology. One day he was travelling from Mt Carmel. He was on the road with Gehazi, and the Shunnamite woman was coming to them from a distance. He sensed in his spirit that something was wrong, and asked Gehazi run and find out what was wrong. He confessed, *"She is in bitter distress; but the LORD has hidden it from me and has not told me."* (2 Kings 4:27).

Not all prophetic people can "see" like seers do. Elisha knew his limitations! We should each be satisfied with our role and calling in life, and learn to work with the other kinds of prophetic gifts in the Church. Jim Goll makes this excellent observation, "In the spiritual realm, the flow of the prophetic from heaven to earth resembles the Nile River. Just as the White Nile [from Lake Victoria] and the Blue Nile [from Lake Tana] join to create the greater river called the Egyptian Nile. So too, streams of prophetic anointing come together to feed the greater concourse of the mighty prophetic river of God on earth."[10] Amen.

REFERENCES

Goll, Jim. "The Seer." Destiny Image. 2004
Harfouche, Christian. "The Prophet – Today's Divine Seer" audio series. Global Revival Distribution, 2002.
Lewis, C.S. "The Chronicles of Narnia: The Horse and His Boy" Harper Collins, 2002.
Tolkien, J.R.R. "The Lord of the Rings: The Two Towers." Harper Collins, 1994.

---

10. "The Seer", Pg 17

Chapter Twenty Nine
THE OFFSPRING OF ISSACHAR

"Elisha said, "Listen to the word of the Lord... tomorrow about this time a measure of fine flour will be sold for a shekel and two measures of barley for a shekel at the gate of Samaria." (2 Kings 7:1).

Ben-Hadad had laid siege to the city of Samaria, and they were in a terrible state. Food and water were running out. Food had become so scarce that children could be bought for less than a meal, and they had started with cannibalism. Desperate times. The king of Samaria blamed Elisha, as though his mercy on the king of Aram a few months earlier had caused this defeat. He looked at the skies and an inner thought welled up inside him, "Heaven is not pleased." Elisha declared that in one day, the food would sell at normal prices at the city gates, (where the markets were held). This would mean a couple of things: firstly they would have to win a battle, secondly the siege would have to end, and thirdly there would have to be massive provision to bring prices back to normal. How could this possibly happen in 24 hours? It sounds impossible right, but with God...

It did happen, just as Elisha had predicted. God scared the entire army of Ben-Hadad, and they fled in the night. Some lepers were out begging for food and found the campsite deserted. They ran back to the city to tell everyone else and raised the alarm. The enemy's camp was deserted, they'd left behind food stores and all. Sure enough, the prices fell to normal, and the city rejoiced. Here was a man who knew what time it was, and when God would act. We call this skill – this gift, the anointing of Issachar.

Issachar and His Gift

Some generations before this story there were two sons of a wealthy and influential man. They were both skilled in battle and trained equally well in fighting. One of them led his men into victory time and again by the strength of his hand and the lessons he had learned on the battlefield. He drew experience from his victories, and from his defeats. His brother also won in war, by the strength of his wit. The second brother was widely travelled, had been through foreign lands, and stood in the counsel of kings – watching, listening. He saw when traders and fighters squabbled. He had stood for hours in the by-ways of the wise men, listening to their arguments.

The first brother was a warrior. The second brother added wisdom to his warfare. They each trained their men, and their sons in their learned arts. The first brother taught skills of war, the second brother taught the skills of observation. After two generations, the great king called all the families in their district to be counted. The first brother's children stood among the most numerous and seasoned warriors in the land. The second brother's children led in every tribe!

These men's children served king David. Zebulun and Issachar were two of the sons of Israel of the twelve tribes of Judah. Issachar and his sons – Tola, Puvah, Jashub, and Shimron [1] immigrated to Egypt with Jacob's family. [2] At the census of the new generation, [3] the children of the four sons of Issachar numbered 64,300, and the children of Zebulun numbered 65,500. It was an equal start in the promised land. Issachar's offspring later fought for Deborah and Barak [4] against Sisera. Their home territory was the scene of several key battles in ancient times including those of Gideon and Saul. [5]

---

1. Genesis 46: 13   2. Exodus 1: 3
3. Numbers 26: 23- 24   4. Judges 5:15
5. 1 Samuel 28

In the time of David, Issachar had the fewest chiefs (by number) in the chain of command in Israel: only 200, yet they were as valuable to David as an entire tribe. The armies were at their command because they were, *"Men who had understanding of the times, who knew what Israel should do."* (1 Chronicles 12: 32).

KNOWLEDGE OF THE TIMES

The children of Issachar had understanding of the times, knowing what Israel ought to do. We learn from Esther 1:13 that when it came to timing, it was the Babylonian king's procedure to consult those who were versed in law and custom. Today, those people are called secretariats or diplomats. Issachar had a virtual monopoly on this position in Israel. It was not for nothing that these men were called sages in the ancient world, for their knowledge of the timing of vital decisions was paramount.

Those who would counsel pastors and leaders, those who would serve the apostles, those who would serve businessmen and kings, must understand this gift. It relates to helping, counselling, and advising; there are three vital aspects:

- It must be the word of the Lord (not ours or the enemy's);
- It must be given to the right person (not just the one we think will need it);
- It must be given at the right time (not before and not after).

The Psalmist cried out, *"We do not see our signs: there is no longer any prophet, nor is there any among us who knows how long."* (Psalm 74:9). Jesus reiterated this lament saying, *"You know how to interpret the appearance of the sky, yet you can not interpret the signs of the times!"* (Mathew 24:1).

For all our zeal, we also do not understand the signs of the times! This is especially so with the judgements of the Lord. Jeremiah lamented, *"The stork in the heavens knows her appointed times, and the turtle-dove, swallow and crane observe their times of coming, yet my people do not know the judgements of the Lord."* (Jeremiah 8:7).

KNOWING THE TIMES

The current prophetic movement is full of conflicting voices, especially when interpreting the signs of the times. Consider:

- Y2K and the predictions of destruction that filled the Church;
- 9/11 and the response of US prophets saying "go to war," while other prophetic groups in the UK criticised the US invasion of Afghanistan.
- The Tsunami, with groups saying, "This is not judgement," and others clearly declaring it was;
- The second Gulf War in Iraq, again some prophetic voices supported, and others denounced it;
- The nation of Israel as it is today. Some supporting her, (tacitly approving of her actions), whilst others (including some Jewish philosophers) saying, "Another diaspora and another judgement is coming upon us."

Recently, a well known African prophet in America declared on TV that, "Osama Bin Laden will be captured within 30 days" of the broadcast. This was to be a sign of God's blessing upon the nation over a period of time, and of God's endorsement of a certain political leader. Osama was never captured. This kind of thing brings disrepute upon the prophetic integrity, especially when no apology is offered. This same prophet later accurately prophecied about a series of natural disasters to befall a certain state in the US.

Shortly before Calvary, Jesus taught about what we would see in the end times. Then, He proceeded to say, *"Consider the parable of the fig tree."* (Mathew. 24:32). The point He made, was that when a fig tree puts forth its tender shoots, you know summer is near. So too, when you see "these things" you know He is near. His coming is at hand. Yet how many of us can truly say, "We can read and understand the signs of the times?" Jesus has given us the ability to know the times we live in.

How powerful it is, to be able to read the front-page news, and go to work – able to explain these things to those around you, which may be full of fear. To be able to understand the times we live in will bring them hope about the future.

KNOWING THE TIME, WHAT TIME?

To understand the anointing of Issachar in the modern day, it is helpful for us to understand the concept of time. For knowing the times, knowing the seasons (*kairos*) is a gift. No one can know the hour of the return of Christ, but we are told to look for the sign of His coming, and told to seek to understand the season of the end. There are seven words for time used in common Greek:

Chronos is the most easily understood time – a space of time, moment-to-moment time, hands of the clock time. Acts 20:18 is a good example, *"I have lived among you the entire time, since I came on the first day."*

Mechri means a point in time, a terminus, an end or a completion moment. It is a defined moment in history, the end of an era. Harvest time is like this – when the hours have passed, the rain has fallen, the sun has had its fill – then it is time to harvest.[6]

---

6. Mathew 13:30

Ede means "by this time", or when the fullness has come. When circumstances are complete – when all is ready as when Lazarus' time had come to be raised. [7] All things must come to pass before your *ede*.

Popote means 'ever yet' or 'at any time'. No one has ever seen God, [8] no one has ever heard Him, [9] but having seen Christ we have now seen Him. It is close to "God" time that is…

Aion from which we get our word Aeon. It is an age, an era, a period of infinite duration – eternity. It means to be without time! Christ is a priest forever [10] and we will have eternal life, [11] or life without end.

Hora means an instant in season, high time, about time, or your time has come. It is "the hour of visitation" such as in Romans 13:11, It is high time for your salvation. The moment has arrived. Jesus said, no man could know the hour of His second coming. [12]

Kairos is a season of time, due time. For example, it is 'time for rain' or 'spring time'. 1 Thessalonians 5:1 speaks of, "times and seasons" and understanding them. Jesus lamented for Israel because they did not recognise the time of their visitation. [13] We are supposed to understand the times we live in!

THE COURT PROPHETS

The ones who will lead the army of God in the battles ahead will be like the offspring of Issachar– ones who know the seasons of the Lord, who know without a shadow of doubt what to do.

---

7. John 11:39
9. John 5:37
11. John 17:3
13. Luke 19:44
8. 1 John 4:12
10. Hebrews 5:6
12. Mathew 25:13

As God restores the ministry of the prophet to the body of Christ, He is also re-establishing the position of the court prophet. Nathan served David, Samuel served Solomon, and Micaiah served Ahab in this position. These men and women stand in a place of influence to the rulers of their nation.

It is not just national leaders who need counsel. In the previous chapters on Marketplace ministry we pointed out how General Managers can profit from consistent prophetic counsel. So too can the Church! The Lord is restoring prophetic counsel to the leaders. They will stand among the elders and deacons, no longer sitting on the sidelines to be trotted out for the occasonal annual conference.

It is my dream, my vision that the prophetic will no longer sit in isolation, 'handing in' their words to elders. The Church needs those who are raised in the line of Issachar, to bring wise counsel to the Church on what it should do. Only unwise leaders will rejects this kind of counsel. God is restoring a position of weekly counsel, guidance in prayer meetings, and prophetic persons to be on staff of local churches.

THE KIND OF LEADER CHRIST IS AFTER

One of the great strengths of Issachar's offspring was that they set their hearts on being servants to the leaders. They were swept to prominence by virtue of their wisdom. Scripture indicates that at one time they would become slaves, bearing the burdens of others. They were not to strive to be leaders but knew how to follow and serve. They were known as princes [14] yet they carried the burdens of the others. This is the nature of Jacob's prophetic blessing of Issachar and his offspring, *"Issachar is a strong donkey, lying down between the sheepfolds; he saw that a resting place was good,*

---

14. Judges 5: 15

and that the land was pleasant; so he bowed his shoulder to the burden, and became a slave at forced labor." (Genesis 49: 14- 15). The sons of Issachar will at times be misunderstood, and treated with contempt, but in the eyes of the Lord, they are princes.

Christ teaches us that to lead in the Church today, we must be servant of all, and any who would set their hearts on the high place, must first sit in the lowest place at the table. [15] James reminds us that God will exalt only the humble, and He will destroy the proud. [16] To be an apostle or a prophet means to be at the bottom of the ladder, not the top. They serve all, they do not Lord it over others. Do not be deceived, if we set our hearts on selfish gain, we will not be trusted with the ministry of a prophet!

WISE COUNSEL IS A BLESSING

In the land that Issachar inherited was the town of Abel. At one time, king Joab had besieged it, and was about to destroy it. A wise lady in this city came forward to declare this wonderful account of this city – *"They used to say in the old days, 'Let them inquire at Abel; and so they would settle a matter. I am one of those who are peaceable and faithful in Israel; you seek to destroy a city that is a mother in Israel; why will you swallow up the heritage of the Lord?'. "* (2 Samuel 20:14- 22 especially vs. 18).

The entire city had a spirit of reconciliation, wisdom, and maturity that had become a mother to Israel. People would resolve their differences, and unity could grow because of the ministry that liberated the city. The people would inquire of the wise children of Issachar about a matter.

---

15. Luke 14:9   16. James 4:6

This is this kind of ministry the Lord is raising – not striving to lead, but wisely counselling. I believe in the days to come we will see this kind of anointing return to certain cities. Because of the position of the church, because of their embrace of the prophetic, because of the pursuit of the anointing of Issachar, the entire city will be like Abel.

Moses also blessed Issachar saying, *"Rejoice Zebulun, in your going out, and Issachar, in your tents. They call peoples to the mountain; there they offer right sacrifices."* (Deuteronomy 33:18-19). The blessing of Issachar also brings the children back to offer right sacrifice to the Lord.

This is one of the great blessings of the prophetic movement to the Church. It brings believers close to God, where they can know that their sacrifices – of praise and whatever else – are not only acceptable, but are a joy to the One who received them. What genuine church would deliberately rob their people of that?

REFERENCES

Clement, Kim. Interview, TBN Florida. 2004.
Denten, Kerry. "The Sons of Issachar." Greentree Ministries, 1998.
White, David. "The Sons of Zebulun." Storm Harvest Journal. Vol 1, Iss 2.

IN THE FOOTSTEPS OF ELISHA

Chapter Thirty
PROPHETS SERVING AN APOSTOLIC CHURCH

"Now Elisha was sitting in his house, and the elders were sitting with him. And the king sent a man from his presence."
(2 Kings 6:32).

In every location, in every situation, Elisha appeared to have access to those in leadership. He served them faithfully and made himself available to be of assistance to them. In this passage, the elders of a city under-siege, consulted the prophet, in his home. He could say to the widow, "Do you want me to get you a session with the king, or the general?" He could invite them around for a meal. The king would send envoys to him, and he would send his servant to the temple or the palace to take a message from the Lord.

The kind of partnership displayed by Elisha does not have to be everyone's ambition – rubbing shoulders with the top brass! In fact it needs to start at the most earthy level – in the home. There needs to be a partnership between a prophetic person and their spouse. There needs to be teamwork built within the family. It would be hypocritical for us to desire to speak to kings, if we had not first taught our own sons and daughters to hear His voice. The team dynamic needs to be found in the local church, before it is ever found in the hallowed halls of power.

As we saw in the chapter on the Kingdom of God, it will work out into the business and political spheres eventually! This outward flow of the prophetic is also well described in the New Testament.

As we consider those partnerships, we must consider what role New Testament prophets have. To do this, we should look at John, the cousin of Christ. He had the first, and had perhaps most difficult job of any New Testament prophet. He lived in what theologians call the "inter-testamental" period. The Old was not fully over, the New was not fully here. Even as Elisha offers us a good view of how prophets relate to kings, John offers us an excellent view of the conduct of a New Testament prophet, as he related to Jesus, the Christ – our Chief Apostle and the High Priest of our confession. This naturally flowed outward to affect the rulers of his age. [1]

JOHN THE BAPTIST

According to Jesus, *"John the Baptist was the greatest prophet ever born."* (Luke 7:28). Yet he never appeared on TBN, never wrote a book, or started an international ministry. There was no www.john-the-baptist.com, he did not heal the sick, did not travel far, and gave no words of knowledge. The 700 Club did not have his mailing address.

Yet John radically impacted his family, his region, his religion, and his nation by bringing a powerful and anointed message of repentance. He prepared the way for Jesus, the Christ. He partnered with Jesus in eight specific ways.

1. He prepared the way

John made way for Jesus. Fundamental to his calling was to prepare the way of the Lord. [2] Prophets of the New Testament make way for the apostolic Church to emerge. *"He must increase, and I must decrease."* (Luke 3:30). They work before, and introduce the apostolic, then they come in to support and quietly undergird.

---

1. Mark 6:18   2. Isaiah 40:3

2. He edified the congregation

John prepared the hearts of the people for Jesus.[3] He edified them with exhortations to holiness (not pampering them with soft words). Prophets of the New Testament edify and build up the people of God,[4] moving them away from sin. They exhort the people and point them to Christ and His way of life.

3. He yielded to apostolic leadership

John was yielded and submitted to Jesus.[5] He affirmed the worthiness of Jesus. Prophets of the New Testament know their place is second, after apostolic leaders.[6] They work on the foundations with the apostle,[7] and they sit in the circle of elders.[8]

4. He launched other ministries

John baptised Jesus, preparing Him for the work of ministry and fulfilling all righteousness.[9] Prophets of the New Testament work with teachers to launch apostolic ministry from their midst,[10] and may travel with them to resolve disputes,[11] just as Paul and Silas did.

5. He had team ministry

The work of John (repentance and water baptism) worked seamlessly with the work of Christ (baptism by fire and the Spirit).[12] Prophets of the New Testament do not work alone, but partner with apostles, in laying the foundation of Christ in the Church.

6. He was free to release, and did not gather

John did not insist that his disciples stayed with him — when they wanted to follow Jesus he let them go![13] Prophets of the New Testament are leaders in the Church, but in the larger context of teachers and apostles.

---

3. Luke 3:18
4. Acts 15:32
5. Mark 1:7
6. 1 Corinthians 12:28
7. Ephesians 2:20
8. Acts 15
9. Mathew 3:13
10. Acts 13:1
11. Acts 15:40
12. Mathew 3:11
13. Luke 7:18

They know that those who become their disciples will, in turn, need to be released. The aim of a New Testament prophet is to build the church – not their ministry.

7. He shared in the sufferings

John was not exempt from the sufferings of Christ. He was beheaded.[14] Prophets of the New Testament are promised suffering and persecution,[15] next to their apostolic team mates. They will also share in the localised sufferings of the congregation. They must not be removed from the local church community or the burdens of the pastors.

8. He restored sons to fathers

John demonstrated the spirit of Elijah, restoring sons to the fathers.[16] Prophets of the New Testament move in the spirit of Elijah, bringing people back to the fathering nature of the apostolic Church.[17]

MY LESSONS IN TEAM

God leads us step by step into the fullness of His plan. After I had grown in the 1 Corinthians 12 and Romans 12 gifts, I was asked to lead worship at St Mark's Anglican Church, one of the first Churches in Sydney, Australia at which the "Toronto Blessing" broke out. We had enormous opportunity for ministry, working with 12,000 people in a 15 month period. Many came to receive from God, to be touched by Him – we saw lives changed. The senior minister, John Davies, oversaw the renewal at St Marks, and I had the privilege of working with him during this time, learning to work with a number of ministries within the church as part of a team.

---

14. Mathew 14:10
16. Mathew 11:14
15. Mathew 23:34
17. Malachi 4:5,6

In 1995, we moved to the Telopea Church of Christ, then overseen by Rick Lewis. We needed a time of rest, after a prolonged time of ministry. It was not long before worship and the prophetic were calling again. By now I was travelling, speaking at conferences, and publishing a prophetic magazine. (I was still learning and making many mistakes!) The best thing about Telopea was the diversity of ministry expressions found there, and the strong emphasis on teaching and evangelism. After some of my prophetic words had come to pass, Rick and his successor David Wilson, decided they wanted to explore working with the prophetic in leadership. Several prayer meetings, pastoral meetings and a planning meeting took place at my home. I learned a lot about their passions and the way a teacher thought. I also learned how to work with local eldership and a stronger city-wide emphasis.

In 1998, we relocated to Cootamundra NSW and started a small house church, mainly for single mothers and people who had unsaved partners. I pastored it for two years, and then quickly found friends to co-labour with me in taking care of the flock. We worked hard to develop a team environment. By now, my heart was yearning for more. I knew the Church had more to it than prophets and pastors, but no-one seemed to present as an apostle. I knew they existed, and I knew people in America thought that way, but there was reticence to use the term in Australia. Through to this present time I have worked with, restored, or encouraged apostolic ministries in Australia, Canada, Ghana, India, New Zealand, Nigeria, Philippines, Singapore, South Africa, United Kingdom, USA and Zambia.

In Australia this has particularly included Ray McMartin in Sydney, Brian Medway at Grace Christian Fellowship in Canberra, and John Alley in Rockhampton. I have worked in partnership with them in three very different ways. Ray and I got to know each other through a common friend, Kerry Denten. Although Ray has access to other prophets, I have enjoyed serving Ray in his home church environment. We bring speakers into his church, and participate in their regular citywide prayer meetings. I have at times also been trusted to minister to his extended network of Family Life Churches.

In Canberra, Brian and I have come to know and trust each other closely over the years. Initially, it was a psuedo-professional relationship. I would come and teach in their school, do weekend workshops, and encourage their local prophetic teams. In time we started to pray together, share our heart for nation-wide networking, and see how we might serve the greater Kingdom purpose together. Now, I am involved in many of the aspects of local church and citywide work Brian does. Once again, he has access to other prophets, but I have enjoyed working with an apostle of his calibre.

FINDING A FATHER

It was at a conference in Adelaide in 2001 that I met John Alley. He and I were slated to speak at the same event, and we immediately connected. He had a prophet with him on team, Phillip Walters, but nevertheless, I felt drawn into relationship with him. John had a burden too, and was indeed reaching the nation with the Apostolic Revelation, and I was ministering nationally in the prophetic. The connection seemed natural. Within a very short space of time I realised that God had something more for us. I had actually found a spiritual father. In the intervening years, I have come to know, love, and trust John as a son would. I am sure there are exciting realms left to explore, but we can minister as apostle and prophet, father and son, co-labourers in the gospel, and achieve so much more than ministering alone.

CHAPTER THIRTY-ONE
APOSTOLIC/ PROPHETIC PARTNERSHIPS

"They said to [Elisha], 'See now, we have fifty strong men among your servants; please let them go and seek your master [Elijah]; it may be that the spirit of the LORD has caught him up and thrown him down on some mountain or into some valley.' He responded, 'No, do not send them.' But when they urged him until he was ashamed, he said, 'Send them.' So they sent fifty men who searched for three days but did not find him. When they came back to him (he had remained at Jericho), he said to them, 'Did I not say to you, do not go?'." (2 Kings 2:16-18).

The leader of the company of prophets in Jericho wanted to search for the body of Elijah. They had seen Elisha go over with Elijah, but their master did not come back! Here comes Elisha, across the river with the master's mantle. Elisha testified, "He has been taken up," and the local prophets had also twice predicted, "Do you not know your master will be taken from you today?"

The local leader questioned the integrity of Elisha. He did not partner with knowledge; he did not receive revelation – Elijah is gone, the Spirit of God has caught him up. He believed the body of Elijah could be found by searching for it. There was doubt and fear. They hassled Elisha until he was ashamed. Hardly a relationship of mutual respect! There was no recognition, no appreciation of Elisha.

I believe that the local leader was acting like a shepherd, a pastor of the local flock. The community of prophets in Jericho had a pastoral oversight, who came into conflict with the new prophetic leader, Elisha.

What to do with Broken Prophets

As I pointed out in the introduction, we had a wave of prophetic "fireworks" in the 1980's, followed closely by dramatic failure, character flaws, and devastation in the Church. Into this vacuum, a range of ministries tried to stand prophetically, and after that, apostles began to rise.

In many cases the apostle has followed the same path – rising, shining, burning out, disappearing. So what do we do now? Who restores who? How do teams develop? Some authors erroneously assume that because the pastor reigns supreme in the structured and organised Church of today, they are the "gatekeepers" of the Church. They assume authority rests with the pastor, and any prophet or apostle must submit into this structure.

Frankly, I think this logic is flawed. It assumes that what we have is Biblical, and God's best for the Church. This is wrong on both counts. For the most part, the modern day Church bears little resemblance to the Church of the New Testament, or to the plans laid out by God in Scripture. The Church of today is surely not a glorious and spotless bride (yet)!

No, it is the apostle that must come first, calling on the prophet to come forth. It is Jesus who called Nathaniel from under the tree, and on Simon to leave his zealotry. The prophets (and pastors too) must come forth and be healed from:

- Their fear: fear of man, fear of failure, fear of rejection;
- Their woundedness: holding hurt and grudges against one another from times past;
- Their rejection: backsliding in heart, and walking away from their call;
- Their anger: the boiling emotion from injustice and powerlessness.

It is the apostle who will help them through this transitional time.

AN OVERVIEW OF THESE TWO GIFTS

To understand a prophetic contribution we must first contrast these two gifts, the apostle and prophet, so we better understand them:

The prophet is a skybreaker – rending the heavens;
The apostle is a ground breaker – rending the hearts.

The prophet is a sower – sowing the word of God;
The apostle is a waterer – nourishing the seed.

The prophet brings insight – revelation knowledge;
The apostle brings oversight – applied wisdom.

The prophet is the draftsman – with the vision of the work;
The apostle is the architect – with management skills.

The prophet is the dynamic force – cutting edge, motivation;
The apostle is the static force – the grounding, resourcing father.

The prophet gives the diagnosis – the consulting G.P.;
The apostle does the operation – the surgeon.

The prophet is the change agent – agitating the stationary;
The apostle is the pioneer – agitating new fields and frontiers.

Looking Back to Look Forward

How then should leaders work together? How does a leader test the revelation without bringing shame on the prophetic person? How are the apostle and prophet to work together? What realms do they share? What role does the prophet play, and what specific things do we see the prophet adding?

To answer these questions, new as they seem in the 21st century, I think we must actually look back through the pages of Scripture. The true model is in Christ. The solid object of Christ and His Church stands in eternal present, casting a shadow back into Church history. That shadow, that type, that image, can be seen cast across the pages of the Old Testament relationship between prophet and king and in the New Testament relationship between apostle and prophet.

There are 38 separate relationships between a king and a prophet in the Old Testament, and 5 relationships between an apostle and a prophet in the New Testament. More than half of these were based on a personal relationship, and less than half were on a professional (ministerial) basis. So we must accept that both professional and personal relationships are acceptable in this partnership.

There are 72 interactions between a prophet and a king in the Old Testament (62 if we don't count Moses going back 10 times with the same message to the same king). From these interactions we discover that two thirds of the time the prophet went to the king, and one third of the time the king sought out the prophet. It is perfectly acceptable for a leader to seek specific prophetic counsel from a prophet. It is also acceptable for a prophet to bring a message unbidden to the leader.

From these interactions we can deduce fifteen specific things that prophetic ministry gives or brings to an apostolic/ kingly leadership team.

1. Leadership aspects
The prophet leads by fathering, serving, and commissioning others.

A prophet provides fathering to other prophets and to kings:
- The King of Israel viewed Elisha as his father;[1]
- Prophets and teachers birthed apostolic ministry.[2]

A prophet provides leadership:
- Samuel was a leader over military personnel;[3]
- Silas and Judas were leading men among the brethren.[4]

A prophet can commission and anoint other leaders:
- Nathan anointed Solomon as king;[5]
- John baptised Jesus, preparing Him for ministry.[6]

2. Team aspects
The prophet is a companion, consultant and accountability partner.

A prophet is a companion to the apostle:
- The prophets were with leaders, helping them build the temple;[7]
- Paul chose Silas as his travelling partner.[8]

A prophet is one of the king's consultants:
- Elisha sat and consulted with the elders;[9]
- Micaiah was called upon to consult the kings.[10]

---

1. 2 Kings 6:21   2. Acts 13:1
3. 1 Samuel 19:20   4. Acts 15:22
5. 1 Kings 1:34   6. Mathew 3:13
7. Ezra 5:2   8. Acts 15:40
9. 2 Kings 6:32   10. 1 Kings 22:15

A prophet goes as an ambassador for the team:
- Jehoshaphat sent the prophets to teach the law; [11]
- Silas and Judas were sent as messengers by the apostle. [12]

A prophet assists with personal accountability in leadership:
- Nathan helped David see his own sin; [13]
- John the Baptist addressed Herod's adultery. [14]

3. Revelatory aspects

The prophet knows seasons, strategy, has foreknowledge and prophetic insight that is not otherwise available to the team.

A prophet brings knowledge of the times and seasons:
- The Sons of Issachar knew what Israel should do; [15]
- Agabus predicted the event and extent of a drought. [16]

A prophet provides strategic information, and overall guidance:
- Jahaziel helped Jehoshaphat in battle strategy; [17]
- Elisha helped the king of Israel avoid snares and traps. [18]

A prophet can provide secret knowledge, specific insight:
- God reveals His secrets to His servants the prophets; [19]
- Prophets are the key of knowledge. [20]

A prophet can bring foreknowledge of specific events:
- Elisha predicted the end of a famine, [21]
- Agabus told Paul information about his future in Rome. [22]

---

11. 2 Chronicles 17:7,8
12. Acts 15:32
13. 2 Samuel 12:1
14. Mathew 14:4
15. 1 Chronicles 12:32
16. Acts 11:28,29
17. 2 Chronicles 20:14-19
18. 2 Kings 6:8-10
19. Amos 3:7
20. Luke 11:52
21. 2 Kings 6:32
22. Acts 21:10

4. The presence of a prophet
The prophet brings blessing, prosperity, encouragement and healing.

A prophet's words and presence bless and prosper the team:
- Ezra obeyed the prophets and prospered;[23]
- Jehoshaphat prospered by believing the prophets.[24]

A prophet's words and presence can be of great encouragement:
- Haggai prophesied and strengthened the people;[25]
- Paul said that prophecy edifies, exhorts, and comforts.[26]

A prophet's words and presence can bring judgement to the team:
- The unnamed prophet withered the hand of the king;[27]
- Elijah brought fire to bear on the captains.[28]

A prophet can bring healing to leaders:
- Naaman was healed by Elijah's word;[29]
- Hezekiah's life was extended by Isaiah's word.[30]

Admittedly fathering, leadership, anointing, companionship, strategy, blessing, encouragement, prosperity, and healing are not the exclusive domain of the prophetic ministry. The members of a local team might bring these elements, in the absence of a prophet. But prophets can effectively express them in the Church too.

THE NEED FOR APOSTLES

It is not the pastor who leads the church. It is the apostle who leads; he is the one who chooses. Jesus chose the twelve. Paul chose Silas (the prophet). Their work is based on relationship and trust,

---

23. Ezra 6:13-15
24. 2 Chronicles 20:20
25. Haggai 2:1-4
26. 1 Corinthians 14:3
27. 1 Kings 13:1-7
28. 1 Kings 1:3-20
29. 2 Kings 5:1-20
30. 2 Kings 20:1-7

love and respect, not on position, rank, or organisational skill. Paul and Silas went through everything together, (jail, shipwreck, stoning, riots, escape). When Paul had to depart – he left Silas in charge of Timothy,[31] not in charge of local pastoral elders. In fact he told his spiritual son Titus to appoint elders[32] not the other way around.

Elders and apostles then work together in a city (e.g. Jerusalem), and groups of prophets travel together to encourage the local teams (e.g. the prophets from Jerusalem). We see in Antioch a collection of prophets and teachers working in a city to birth new outreach, and a pair of prophets staying behind to encourage the brethren in that city.

What we do not find anywhere in the New Testament is the concept of a pastor controlling the Church. There is only one brief and hyphenated mention in Ephesians 4:11 of this gift (it is connected to teacher in the Greek). Not one person is actually labeled "pastor" in the New Testament. This is why the Church is in for such a major earthquake – because at the moment, pastoral leadership holds the reigns of the Church. In many cases they are in sharp conflict with rising prophetic and apostolic leadership. They have largely failed to reform the church and desperately need to humble themselves to apostolic and prophetic leadership.

As we move forward, it is the apostle, particularly expressing the father heart of God, who will restore wounded or timid prophets. It is the grace, love, acceptance, and forgiveness that will call on the prophets to come forth. For our part, we must choose to trust again.

REFERENCES

Wagner, C Peter. "Pastors and Prophets." Regal Books, 2003.

---

31. Acts 17:15   32. (Titus 1:5)

CHAPTER THIRTY-TWO
THE SONS OF THE PROPHETS

"Elisha the prophet called one of the sons of the prophets and said to him, 'Gird up your loins and take this flask of oil in your hand and go to Ramoth-gilead. When you arrive there, search out Jehu the son of Jehoshaphat the son of Nimshi.' " (2 Kings 9:1,2).

We read here a story of amazing trust. Elijah was told in the cave, *"Go, anoint Jehu... anoint Hazael... anoint Elisha."* (1 Kings 19:15,16). Here is Elisha, the spiritual son of Elijah, choosing and anointing "one of the sons" to go and perform a heavy duty. Search for Jehu, and anoint him as king. The principle of mentoring, discipling, or training takes us just so far. We need the fathering dynamic.

How do you get to a place where, like Paul, you can say, *"Receive Timothy as you would receive me,"* (Phillipians 2:22,23) or as Peter could say, *"My son Mark sends you greetings."* (1 Peter 5:13). Titus was put in charge of the churches in Crete, *"As a loyal son in the faith."* (Titus 1:4). The promises, legacies, prophecies, and inheritances pass on to the sons.

We stand at a juncture in history, where the Church is undergoing tremendous change. We are moving from religion to relationship. We are moving from structure and format to organic growth and freedom. We are moving from a focus on giftedness to one of connectedness. The Church is being given many opportunities to rise up and meet need in the community. Before she can go and answer world problems, she must move into a new paradigm herself. She must move into sonship.

SONS OF JESUS

Moses prophetically declared that Israel would one day have, *"A prophet like me from among your own people; you shall heed such a prophet."* (Deuteronomy 18:15). In Acts 3:22 the apostles of the New Testament declared that Jesus Christ was this prophet.

Jesus chose twelve men, and travelled through Jericho, Jerusalem, Bethel, Shiloh, and other parts with them. These men, these apostles who followed Him, came to understand that, *"All the prophets, as many as have spoken, from Samuel and those after him, predicted these days."* (Acts 3:24) and then they made this profound statement:

"You are the sons of the prophets and of the covenant which God made with our fathers." (Acts 3:25). You – the audience, the gathered peoples, from many nations, hearing this address – are the sons of the prophets. What on earth are they talking about? They were speaking from their heart, they were speaking from their experience. They were not just disciples, they were sons. They were not just sons, but they were sons of the prophets.

We need to understand the meaning of this phrase – so well known to those listening to Peter but lost to us today. As we examine the lives "of all the prophets from Samuel" we find several patterns, or ways in which their anointing affected those with them, and those who followed them.

The first kind are prophets who raised their own physical sons into the ministry. The second kind are those prophets who raised partners, associates, and other ministries. The third kind are those prophets who raised students or disciples in a school or large setting.

1. The literal sons of prophets

Azariah defined himself as, *"son of Obed the prophet."* (2 Chronicles 15:8). Azariah operated as a prophet, and brought a word to Asa the king.

Jonah defined himself as, *"son of Amittai the prophet."* (2 Kings 14:25). Jonah operated as a prophet and brought a word about boundaries to the city/state of Ninevah.

Zechariah defined himself as, *"grandson of Idalo the prophet,"* (Zecheriah 1:1) and one can assume his father Berekiah was therefore also a prophet in the lineage.

Jehu was known as, *"the son of Hanani the seer."* (2 Chronicles 19:2). He ministered to king Jehoshaphat, even as his father had.

Isaiah was married to a prophetess. That must have been an amazing home.[2] We do not know if their son Maher-shalal-hash-baz went on into ministry as a prophet, but he certainly would have suffered the persecution and rejection of one (for his name meant "Damascus and Samaria will be spoiled")!

In this case a clear bloodline can be established. I don't know of any study done in this area, but it may be that spiritual gifts are passed on in the same way eye colour, nose shape, and vocal quality are. There may be some credence to the idiom that, "The apple does not fall far from the tree." Great tennis and cricket players have in-built genetic capacity to play tennis. They inherit eye hand co-ordination, muscular frame, and other qualities. Certainly by the time of Amos it was common to say, *"I am so-and-so, the son of a prophet."* (Also refer to Amos 7:14 where Amos says he is neither).

2. The prophetic sons in partnership

Elijah co-laboured with, and raised Elisha up as a son in the ministry.

Jeremiah co-laboured in ministry with Baruch. Whenever Jeremiah was in trouble, in prison, or unable to minister, Baruch would scribe his prophecy, and read it out in the courtyards and houses.[1]

In the case of a partner, or spiritual son, there is no clear bloodline, but a relational line through which the gift functions. There was a corporateness in which the gift could flow through both of them. Who was Elisha without Elijah; who was Baruch without Jeremiah? It would seem that if you took the primary person away, the other one would also be without a ministry.

3. Students turned sons

Lastly there were students and disciples who attended the schools of the prophets. Invariably they were given the title "sons of the prophets". We know of several communities established by several prophets in this manner (Bethel, Jericho & Gilgal for example).

Samuel, a father to Saul and David in their kingly role, itinerated from Ramah to Shiloh, Mizpah to Bethlehem, and Gibeah to Gilgal.[2] We do not know of any "schools" he established, but we have evidence of men gathering to David at Naioth in Ramah (near Gibeah), *"with Samuel standing over them,"* as a father figure.[3] The influence of the prophetic in their midst was enough to cause Saul and his spies to fall down under the anointing of the prophets and prophesy. So it was said, "Is Saul also among the prophets?"

---

1. Jeremiah 36:10
2. 1 Samuel 7:16
3. 1 Samuel 19:20

indicating that these men were known as prophets, or that this gathering also attracted other prophets besides Samuel. An unnamed "man of God", influenced by Samuel's ministry in Bethlehem, came from David's base in Adullam, from "Judah" to Bethel to condemn Jeroboam.[4]

It is from here that the first mention of the "sons of the prophets" occurs. Ahab is soundly condemned by one of the sons of the prophets[5] – a man no doubt connected with, the ministry of Elijah. Elijah had at least four schools, with at least 50 men in each, which were taken over by Elisha. These were located in Bethel,[6] Jericho/ Jordan,[7] Gilgal,[8] and Dothan.[9]

Elisha visited these communities, assisting them in practical ways (like healing their water, retrieving their axe heads, assisting their widows with oil, and raising their sons from the dead!). The sons of the prophets related to him long after Elijah had gone.

SO WHO ARE THE APOSTLES REFERRING TO?

Let's go back to the book of Acts. Peter is addressing the crowd gathered after the revival outpouring of the Holy Spirit. He says to them, *"You are the sons of the prophets and of the covenant which God made with our fathers."* (Acts 3:25). You – the audience, are the sons of the prophets; you are sons of the promise; you are sons of the fathers; you are sons of the covenant.

He is clearly not speaking biologically. His audience was not born to a vast number of modern day prophets. He is not speaking

---

4. 1 Kings 13:1
5. 1 Kings 20:35
6. 2 Kings 2:3
7. 2 Kings 2:5-7
8. 2 Kings 4:38
9. 2 Kings 6:1-13

about partners in ministry. His audience are not all in ministry with prophets. His audience are surely not all students in the school of Christ either! So why did he call them, and by inference us, sons of the prophets?

These people are the recipients of the promises given to Abraham, Isaac, Jacob/ Israel, Moses, and all the fathers. They are the sons of Jeremiah, Isaiah, David, Jonah, Joseph, Daniel and all the prophets. Why? Because of Christ. Every line of law, every word of the Old Testament, every man or woman born into Israel, every utterance of the prophets, was given for one thing – to speak of Him. *"The righteousness of God has been disclosed, and is attested by the law and the prophets, the righteousness of God through faith in Jesus Christ for all who believe."* (Romans 3:21,22).

Any person who calls upon Christ can be saved. [10] All who believe, through faith in Christ become sons of Abraham. [11] The finished work of the cross was for all mankind, for all time. We are able to become sons and heirs by partaking of the promises in Christ. [12]

Now we are in Christ; we are part of His family, His line, His nation. We come into our inheritance, and the laws of inheritance are retrospective. It goes all the way back – all the promises of Abraham and all the utterances of the prophets now apply to us. Every prophet exists to speak for God, and his instrumental message, his eternal purpose, was to reveal Christ. In Him, they (and we) have become sons of the prophets. This is perhaps the best way to understand that misunderstood verse:

---

10. Romans 10:12
11. Galatians 3:7
12. Ephesians 3:6

"God, who at various times and in various ways spoke in time past to the fathers by the prophets, has in these days spoken to us by His Son, whom He has appointed Heir of all things." (Hebrews 1:1,2). All who are in relationship with Jesus are in relationship with the fathers, to the promises, to the covenant, and to the prophets.

REFERENCES

Sandford, John Loren. "Elijah Among Us." Chosen Books, 2002
Scheidler, Bill & Iverson, Dick. "Apostles, the Fathering Servant". City Bible Publishing, 2001.

Chapter Thirty-Three
LOOKING TOWARD THE FUTURE

"As they were burying a man, suddenly they spied a band of raiders; and they put the man in the tomb of Elisha; and when the man was let down and touched the bones of Elisha, he revived and stood on his feet." (2 Kings 13:21).

The first question that came to my mind as I first read this passage was, "What is the anointing doing there?" It's resident in the bones of Elisha; it's sitting in the grave under the ground! What on earth is it still doing there? Elisha had any number of people he could have anointed, any number of students, any number of sons of the prophets he could have raised up. He had a string of servants, the most notable of whom was Gehazi.

Here we find Elisha's weakness, his Achilles heel as it were. He was able to relate to those in power, but he did not sire a son. He could heal the sick, but he could not give of himself personally. Here perhaps is his most significant departure from prefiguring the life of Christ. It explains why Scripture equates fathering with Elijah and not with Elisha.

Jesus only used one example from Elisha's life, and it is found in Luke 4:27. There were many lepers in Israel, and Elisha healed none of them – only Naaman and he was Syrian. He had little compassion upon his own. In fact, when presented with the taunting of the young people in Bethel (who called him baldy), he cursed them "in the name of the Lord."

Two raging she-bears came out of the woods mauling forty-two of them.[1] Very compassionate I'm sure.

WHERE ARE THE FATHERS?

In 1988, it was the Australian bicentennial. It was also the heyday of the prophets, with John White, Paul Cain, Bob Jones, and others making a splash. There were conferences and tapes, books and seminars beginning to come out and I fed on them all! It was an exciting time. Prophetic conferences were just starting to be held. The Vineyard Movement with John Wimber was making a way forward, and the renewal was strong.

I was attending an Anglican Life Center (Pentecostal Episcopal) church in Canberra, overseen by Dr. Rev. Chris Simon. He had all sorts of speakers come and speak to the youth. One especially stood out for me – Kerry Medway from Port Macquarie. He taught us on the 1 Corinthians 12 gifts, and took a special interest in me. I appreciated his warmth and openness.

In 1993, I married my lovely wife Kellie, and we moved to Sydney. As I mentioned earlier, we joined another Anglican Church – St. Marks in Northbridge, and I was hungry for the prophetic. I went to John, my pastor, and we drafted a list of every prophetic person we knew of in Australia: big or small, famous or infamous. I wrote 12 letters asking for help, opportunity to learn, time for a coffee, anything. Three men responded. Steve Penny invited me to his conference and gave me a copy of his book.[2] I spoke with Terry Appel on the phone and read a copy of an article he had written. Terry and I were later to connect strongly in 2004.

---

1. 2 Kings 2:24,25
2. "Look Out! The Prophets are Coming." Prophetic People Int. 1993.

Fergus McIntyre, from Christian City Church had been in the game for quite some time. We did breakfast, we did lunch and we travelled to Melbourne together. I learned from his teaching, but more from his conduct. He took the time to read a draft manuscript of a book I had written (which never saw the light of day), but he and I grew busy with our schedules, and lost touch… it made me hunger for more.

I drew up another list, raising my sights I boldly wrote to "famous" ministries seeking help. I wrote 12 letters, and this time obtained 4 responses. John Paul Jackson took some interest – he was visiting Australia each year at the time, but planned dinners and lunches just never eventuated. His schedule was always packed to overflowing with needy pastors and hungry admirers. Paul Cain responded openly, and I was given access to visit him any time I was in the United States. Given his amazing schedule at the time, and his profile, we only met on three occasions. He was warm and personable, but not good at long distance communication.

To my thankful surprise, John Sandford replied also. On his next visit to Australia he took the time to share a meal, then gave me his fax number. I listened to his tapes, bought his books and we corresponded for several months. We went over my "portfolio" and the things I needed to pursue for balanced ministry. In fact his book, "The Elijah Task" was my very first Christian book, solid reading for anyone seeking to grow in the prophetic. Later John and Paula graciously accepted an invitation to come and minister at our conference in 2004 in Sydney, and we were able to reconnect.

Lastly, though I did not get through to Rick Joyner, his then personal assistant, David White, took an interest. We built a stronger connection, and he and I have corresponded ever since. He worked with me on articles written for magazines. He reviewed material I had prepared, and on two occasions I was able to go over and minister in his church in Mobile, Alabama.

Why tell you all this? Because I exhausted the range of options available to me, and still never found a father in the prophetic. I gained access to some of the "luminaries" – people most of us would never dream of writing to, and still did not make much headway. What does that tell you about the state of the prophetic movement worldwide? It is an indictment. It bears more resemblance to the ministry of Elisha, and less to Elijah than it should. There are ten thousand mentors, and not many fathers!

One eminent minister, a man considered a father and founder of the prophetic movement, confided to me, "I wish we had not coined the phrase 'Prophetic Movement'. I wish it had never been started, at least not the way it has come to be known." When pressed further he admitted, "It's so full of division, so full of strife and striving, so full of competition. I don't claim to be a father of anything, most certainly not this." He lamented the lack of heart, the lack of relationship, the lack of teamwork evident in the US expression of the prophetic movement.

WE NEED A REVIVAL

The bones are in the ground – not many sons have been raised up. The giants are passing away, and I wonder how many of them are taking their anointing to the grave? Oh sure, they laid hands on thousands of us, and prayed over the Television too. But did they impart their lives? Did they share their heart? Were they accessible? Could you reach them, or were they trapped above an impenetrable glass ceiling? Our "star" oriented culture has given rise to luminaries in the Church, "the chosen ones" are out of reach. I don't believe this is the way it should be.

Paul said (to the church he founded and loved as a father), *"Our heart is wide open to you. There is no restriction in our affections, but only in yours. In return, I speak as to children, open wide your hearts also."* (2 Corinthians 6:11b-13 NRSV). Again, to the Thessalonian church he said, *"So deeply do we care for you that we are determined to share with you not only the gospel of God but also our own selves, because you have become very dear to us."* (1 Thessalonians 2:8). This is not a man who hid his affections for the Church, or restricted his heart toward those he begat in the gospel! Oh that it would be so in the Church today, in the prophetic movement today.

We need to be thrown down there into Elisha's grave along with the soldier, and see a massive revival of the prophetic in our day. We need to obtain the things our forefathers took for granted! We need to learn from the past, from the mistakes, and make sure we do not repeat it.

Another eminent minister in the prophetic admitted recently at a conference, "I have been known as many things, a man of the word, a man of the Spirit, even a man of power. There is one thing I am not known as though, and one thing that matters more than all of these things. I should be known as a man of love, but I am not. I make it my intention, my commitment in the years ahead, to grow in this one thing – in love." Stunning admission; stirring goal. Let us learn from him, and pursue it also.

WANTED... PROPHETS

I travel 150 - 200,000km a year on ministry. Each year it is not uncommon for me to be in eight or ten nations. I find myself in wealthy living rooms and filthy fields; in staterooms and smoky city squares; among the tens and among the thousands; with political leaders and with prisoners; with housewives and apostolic pioneers. One thing stands out to me in all these settings, there is a dearth of prophets today.

We have prophetic dance, prophetic song, prophetic worship, prophetic intercession, prophetic art, prophetic preaching, prophetic seminars and conferences and workshops... but a real, wholesome, holy prophet who can find? This is in every setting imaginable, in every sphere of life.

Let me use politics as an example. An influential politician in the House of Representatives of Australia lamented to a pastor in Canberra one day, "It occurs to me that we are the kings of this land, we rule and reign instead of Her Majesty. We listen to the kings of commerce, the businessmen. We hear from the priests, the pastors and the ministers of the Church. Yes we know what the sectarian Church thinks. But where are the prophets?" Fair question. His remarks were reminiscent of those made by David Ben Gurion to the British Parliament.

Shimon Peres, his protégé and two time president of Israel, said of him, "Ben-Gurion believed that what was unique about Jewish life was that in addition to the historical side, we had the kings, the priests, and we had the prophets. The prophets represented the moral side of the story. The Bible gives the history, the prophets give the vision."

It is no different in business. The shifting sands of management theory overwhelm many business leaders. In the last 20 years we have seen purchasing then outsourcing; leasing then buying; downsizing then rightsizing; centralisation then decentralisation all in an attempt to fix the bottom line. It profits management consultants, but the company is left reeling. All the acclaimed savings supposed to be made by computerisation simply never materialised, and the advancement of the Internet gave us more information to consume in less time. What the boardroom needs is a word from the Lord!

It is no different in the Church. Recently a key citywide leader in Canberra was taking a team in to see our Governor General. He was seeking a balanced team, one that represented the Church. Eventually he chose twelve – men and women, black and white, pastoral and intercessory, radical and conservative. The assumption? This would be representative of the Church, and therefore it would be apostolic and prophetic. The truth? There was not a single prophet among them!

RIGHT DIRECTION, WRONG CONCLUSION

Perhaps this is where city-wide unity efforts have come off the rails. I am a big fan of renewal, revival, and across the board Church unity. I believe in one city, one Church, one set of elders for the Church. I also believe in intercession and prayer efforts. But if prayer and unity alone could have carried us over the line, we would have had full-blown revival by now. We do not have revival, and nor do we have true unity. Why not?

I believe it is because we don't have a Biblical basis for our prayer and unity. Apostles and prophets are the foundation of the Church, not pray-ers and pastors. No movement, however well intended, that is led by pastors and intercessors is going to bring home the bacon. God appointed, *"First apostles, second prophets, third teachers then..."* (1 Corinthians 12:28). Perhaps this is why efforts in Fiji and the Solomon Islands have worked so phenomenally, because national leaders have instigated the repentance[1]. Many of them are recognised apostolically.

---

1. "Let the Seas Resound", DVD. It was the Great Council of Chiefs, the Prime Minister and denominational heads who brought this issue to a head in Fiji.

Only when right order is established, right foundations built, will pastoral unity and intercession carry the church over the line and into revival.

LOOKING BACK, LOOKING AHEAD

At the beginning of this chapter we discussed the eighties and nineties. Those years are dear to my heart. There was such a buzz in the Church about discovering our gifts, serving the Lord, holiness, and the prophetic. Many schools were being run, many people being raised up. But looking back, it seems that the prophetic movement derailed itself too. On the one hand, we were not satisfied with being purely prophetic, so prophetic people extended the reach of their ministry into other "departments." They began to skew the direction of the prophetic ministry, as prophets became apostles; apostles became bishops, and so it went!

In Australia, dozens of overseas speakers were brought in, each one "bigger and better" than the last. It got so bad, that one year a prophet from America came and his central Friday night address was about, "The spiritual gift of translocation"! He told stories about being translocated, quoted the only two Scriptures which deal with the subject, and by the end of it, had the room split up for prayer to impart the "gift"! Our need for the notable and the marginal has really come to a ridiculous level. Like a drug addict, who needs larger and larger quantities of heroin, the "phenomena" addicted Church needs a stronger and stronger dose of "signs and wonders".

On the other hand, we were so consumed with giftedness and skill that we overlooked character. Many of the famous ministries have since derailed themselves. Closed due to moral failure, ransacked by financial distress, broken marriages, broken promises, and broken trust in the prophetic. No wonder the pastors of today's churches are sceptical, stand-offish and careful. They have a right to be. "Are there still sharks in the water?" they quietly wonder.

It is right that pastors and leaders demand higher levels of character, integrity, and honesty. It is right we raise the banner of purity, holiness, and trustworthy behaviour. That is where this book began, and this is where we will end. There's a poster on the wall in my office. It's a photo of an iceberg, above and beneath the water line. The caption reads,

> *"It is not what appears*
> *on the surface that counts,*
> *but the depth of character*
> *supporting it beneath."*

REFERENCES

Feiler, Bruce. "Walking the Bible." Pg 329, 330, 340.
Jackson, John Paul. "The Spiritual Gift of Translocation." Audio message. Dayspring, 2000.
Joyner, Rick. "Opening Statements." Audio message. Colorado Springs Conference, 2002.
Sandford, John and Paula. "The Elijah Task." Elijah House, 1984.
Sentinel Group, the. "Let the Seas Resound." DVD, 2004.

Appendix One: An Example Prophetic Policy

This policy governs anyone who wishes to bring a prophetic word of any kind, whether belonging to this congregation or visiting. It covers all areas of life in the church, internally and externally. It reaches beyond the services and properties of the church, extending to the conduct of its members in the broader community.

Internal Environment
- We value accountability (a valid or appropriate witness and/or a record or transcript of prophetic words).
- The recipient has the right to weigh, test, judge, accept/refuse and act on the prophecy.
- Your delivery should be gracious and demonstrate godly love and integrity.
- You should be sensitive to the privacy of the issues, and be careful not to broadcast personal matters.
- Simple prophecy must be confined to exhortation, edification and comfort. That means no mates (marriage), dates (date setting) or babies to be prophesied unless prior permission is granted.

External Environment
- No 'Carpark' prophecy (no private/personal one-on-one Prophecy), which includes no bullying using prophetic words.
- Unless the prophetic minister is recognised and trusted then it is given that all other prophecy will be regarded as simple prophecy.
- All other prophecy must be approved by a leader in the church before it is delivered.
- Recognised and trusted individuals will be given liberty to speak at will, based on relationship.
- Prophetic words must be clarified in terms of revelation, interpretation and application.

STORM HARVEST INC.

Additional copies of this book and other book titles by other authors are available from Storm Harvest.

For a complete list of titles, visit us at:
www.storm-harvest.asn.au

Send a request for a catalogue and price list to:
Storm Harvest Inc.
PO BOX 600
Cootamundra NSW 2590, Australia.
www.storm-harvest.asn.au

COOTAMUNDRA, N.S.W. AUSTRALIA
CAPE GIRARDEAU, MISSOURI, U.S.A.
JOHANESSBURG, GAUTENG, SOUTH AFRICA
GUNTUR, ANDRAPRADESH, INDIA
CAGAYAN DE ORO, MINDANAO, PHILIPPINES

In The Footsteps Of Elisha